# Basic Magazine Writing

# BASIC
# Magazine
# Writing

## -Barbara Kevles-

Cincinnati, Ohio

**Basic Magazine Writing.** Copyright © 1986 by Barbara L. Kevles. Printed and bound in the United States of America. All rights reserved. No part of this book may be reproduced in any form or by any electronic or mechanical means including information storage and retrieval systems without permission in writing from the publisher, except by a reviewer, who may quote brief passages in a review. Published by Writer's Digest Books, 9933 Alliance Road, Cincinnati, Ohio 45242. First edition.

Library of Congress Cataloging-in-Publication Data

Kevles, Barbara L.
  Basic magazine writing.

  Includes index.
  1. Authorship.  I. Title.
PN147.K48   1986      808'.02      86-15928
ISBN 0-89879-077-8

*Design by Charleen Catt Lyon*

To Gerald Dickler

*who once said*

*"A writer is one who stays in and writes."*

# Acknowledgments

I want to thank Writer's Digest Books Editor-in-Chief Carol Cartaino, who commissioned this book. I also want to express my great appreciation to Writer's Digest Books Managing Editor Howard I. Wells III for his efforts and steadfast commitment during this five-year project.

My thanks to text editor Darrell Husted for his judicious pruning. I appreciate the financial assistance Penelope Loeb lent in the project's last stage. Finally, my gratitude to typist Mary Klein for accurate and enthusiastic work with a complex text.

# Contents

# Basic Magazine Writing

# I How to Become a Magazine Writer

How can I break into magazines? How can I get my articles published? These questions drive poets, newspaper editors, public relations consultants, advertising executives, editorial assistants at national magazines, or veteran magazine editors to my writing classes. But my classes attract another type, my favorite kind of beginner. An anecdote illustrates my preferences and reasons. Recently, an administrator at the West Side YMCA Writer's Voice Program, where I have just started teaching, wouldn't permit a student to register for my course because, she said, the instructor required sample writings for admission. After I learned of the incident, I informed the administrator my entrance requirements differed from those of other teachers in the program. "I don't want any writing samples submitted," I told her. "I prefer students who've never written anything. These beginners have no bad writing habits, no ingrained market restrictions or editorial limitations that I have to reprogram. I feel I can help them the most."

This textbook is tuned to the beginner writer of basic forms of magazine articles. Everybody mentioned above fits this category, and probably you, my reader, do too. Either you are in transition from poetry to nonfiction, from the "who-what-where" of newspaper journalism to magazine writing, from public relations hyperboles to reporting, from writing magazine fillers to longer pieces, or, as published magazine writers, you want to expand your markets and vocabulary of forms.

## MAKE THE COMMITMENT

For all of you new to a writing genre, print medium or different article form from the one you know by rote, I have the same advice as for the novice. You have to identify as a freelance magazine writer in your mind first and then work to earn this professional identification if you want magazine editors and readers to recognize you as one. By free-lance, I mean you are not employed full-time as a writer, so you have to search for assignments from editors just like a salesman prospects for orders. In successive chapters, I will assist you in finding article ideas, targeting compatible magazine markets, soliciting assignments, then researching, and writing your commissions for publication. To give you the versatility to handle different types of articles, I will introduce you to seven basic article forms and teach you the professional skills necessary to execute them. As long as you attempt to research article ideas, secure commissions, and complete them for submission, you can consider yourself a magazine writer. Your first published piece confers the right to call yourself a professional.

## TEST YOUR TALENT

Among my beginning students, some have been so determined to achieve this first milestone they drove through pelting rain or went out in bone-chilling cold for interviews. Former student Michael Siconolfi waded through four feet of water for his first by-line in a neighborhood New York City paper, the *Queens Tribune*. When I recently contacted Mr. Siconolfi to resurrect the details, the night work number given by his family turned out, to my amazement, to be *The Wall Street Journal*.

Now a *Journal* commodities reporter, Michael Siconolfi wryly recalled his foray inspired by my class four years past. He intended to play football that particular Friday afternoon, but because of the downpour, he went to the offices of the *Queens Tribune* to see about work. "There might be an opening for a reporter," the editor told him. "Tell you what," and he threw the twenty-three-year-old Queens College graduate this challenge: "Go find me a weather story." So Mr. Siconolfi trudged the streets asking strangers if they had or knew of a flooded garage. "People must have thought I was out of my mind," he laughed. Then he decided to go to the police precinct where he introduced himself as a "Trib reporter" wanting information on any "major street flooding." The on-duty sergeant knew of one.

When Mr. Siconolfi arrived, the Environmental Protection Agency officials refused him entry into the filthy muddy water. "But I'm a reporter," Mr. Siconolfi protested. So they reluctantly gave in. "The muck," he said, "came up to my waist."

People on porches waved him over. "They had lost all they had in their basements and first floors," reported my former student. One family whose teenager was on a respirator had gotten her a battery-run one, "So she could breathe," he said. "There was no electricity."

His "weather story" got first page play in the *Trib* and that led to a position as full-time reporter and, eventually, N.Y.U. Graduate School of Journalism and *The Wall Street Journal*. Yet that first reporting experience was the pivotal one. As Mr. Siconolfi recalled, "Later, after I trashed my clothes, I went out on a date. But I cut it short with an apology and returned to the flooded street. I wanted to find out what had happened. And I realized, 'If I'm going to cut a good time short to do this, then this must be what I want to do professionally—be a reporter.' "

As Mr. Siconolfi discovered, you find out if you have the talent to be a free-lance writer by the test of doing the work of a free-lancer. If you have the determination to endure difficult hunts for assignments, demeaning fee bargaining, exhausting research, the solitude of writing, article rejections, and editorial compromises, and the discipline and perseverance to repeat these hurdles, you'll be rewarded with your by-line in print, varying sums of money and, sometimes, public influence.

## OVERCOME YOUR FEARS

If you've never tried to free-lance, you're probably afraid to for a number of reasons. One student, Mindy Schanback, now a local theatre/movie reviewer, got her start only after a class discussion unraveled her fear of calling up editors cold. During one session, she asked for advice about whether she should try to secure a famous playwright's cooperation for a profile before approaching an editor or get the commission first. She later explained, "I wasn't sure whether I wanted to embarrass myself by asking a newspaper to assign something I then couldn't deliver, or suffer the embarrassment of asking a famous playwright for an interview and then not be able to publish it." Finally, she did nothing. As she said, "I decided no embarrassment is best."

In a couple of days, she changed her mind. As she later said, "A decision to take no action is a decision. If you don't call any editors up, they'll never publish you. And the worst they can do is reject you." So, she began phoning local papers. She asked every editor she reached for the opportunity to write a review. The first half dozen said no, but the next asked her to do one, and bring it in, and he'd decide on the basis of her work. She now publishes reviews in two weeklies.

This story of my student's angst illuminates a dominant anxiety in the beginner writer's psyche. New entrants or even veterans hoping to free-lance for unfamiliar publications often have this fear of rejection. That fear can stymie a call or letter to the choice editor. It may be the only obstacle to your published by-line.

Like many of you, I was terrified at the start of my career as a magazine journalist. I was so fearful of admitting my ambitions, I could only whisper them—and I mean, whisper—"I want to be a magazine writer," across the dinner table to a close friend, Barbara Connell. In two days, this Oscar-nominee filmmaker was leaving for Vietnam to coproduce her first documentary for the Public Broadcasting System (P.B.S.). Yet that night she took the time to tell me how she became a success in her field to encourage me at the start of mine. Somehow, she understood I could only whisper what I wanted to be because I was so terrified of failing. By voicing my goal even *sotto voce*, I was acknowledging the possibility I might not achieve it.

The facts prove the contrary. In my first years of free-lance writing, I broke into numerous national magazines like *The Atlantic, Redbook,* and *Mademoiselle,* and *Good Housekeeping* carried my first cover story. If your pulse quivers when you imagine entering the competitive field of magazine writing, the fear you are experiencing could be your greatest asset to drive you to success. You only fear failing at the things you care about deeply. So, in the attempt to achieve them, you try harder because the success means so much to you.

## SET REALISTIC GOALS

During your first months as a free-lance magazine writer, your goals should be realistic. If you expect articles in *Esquire, McCall's,* or some other well-paying national magazine immediately, your aims are unrealistic and will defeat your success. These grand expectations will channel your efforts solely toward keenly competitive markets where beginners are more likely to receive a rejection of a query than a commission.

An unpublished writer needs quantities of clippings far more than just one well-placed published article. Numerous published works will prove to a new editor that you deliver assignments. Also, work for smaller publications builds professional confidence, so when a major magazine gives you a commission, by drawing on these past experiences, you will be able to come through on deadline. If your article ideas warrant, try for work from large-circulation national magazines, but don't rule out publications with smaller readership and skeleton staffs ready to publish untried writers. As a beginner free-lance writer, aim to build a resume of published articles, so that, on your record, you can gain more assignments at the same or different publications.

Clippings not only help secure future work, but may aid advancement at your nine-to-five job. Such was the experience of New York University School of Continuing Education writing student, Jeannette Sanderson. At the start of the course, Ms. Sanderson was working in the business department of the Periodicals Group at Children's Television Workshop. For class, this twenty-six-year-old wrote and rewrote a profile of Judy Leak, 25, the black star of the workshop's four-time Emmy-winning production, "3-2-1 Contact." Between drafts, she phoned the editor of the *Daily Challenge,* the only black daily in Brooklyn, to see if the editor wanted this famous Brooklyn resident profiled. He did.

Publication of her first nonfiction effort in the small Brooklyn daily garnered not only praise from family and Children's Television Workshop staff members, but Ms. Sanderson reports, "It boosted my confidence." For some time, she had known the editor of C.T.W. *Sesame St. Magazine* needed help. The shower of attention from the profile's publication strengthened the writer's resolve, " 'Well, this is what I want. And if I have to volunteer to get from the business into the editorial end of the workshop publications, then that's what I'll do.' "

Your first publication credits may intensify your efforts to gain entree to the editorial ranks of your current employer, or your article research for small circulation outlets may give you materials for major pieces for prestigious publications. You can never predict. So, initially, you have to locate the magazines, weeklies, or dailies willing to give you the opportunity to write the articles you want published.

Despite over a hundred published articles, I still identify myself as a beginner magazine writer. When I work for a new publication, even ones with a small circulation of 30,000 or 111,000, I still try to write my best. I have the perennial beginner writer's fear that my sources of assignments will dry up unless this piece, like each preceding, is an exemplary professional credit. Though personally wearing, that desire to excel with each work separates me from the hack who churns out every article by some tired formula. So I suggest you make every assignment a model demonstration of your talents, so that its publication adds powerful persuasion to securing your next commission and insures your longevity as a free-lance writer.

When you have filled one or two manila envelopes with published clippings, then you may wish to reevaluate your goals. If your clippings demonstrate your expertise in one subject area and several saleable magazine forms, you have the proven skills and connections to try for assignments for "the money," "the exposure" in a leading publication, or "your say" on a significant timely person or issue. I subdivide these aims for the experienced free-lance writer because rarely do you achieve all three in one published article. So, please don't take these aims as anything but flexible guidelines.

Few writers can control with certainty where even a commissioned work will appear. Once, when a *Mademoiselle* editor rejected an assigned first-person on my development into a thirties-plus competitive distance runner, I tried to sell the piece to many different women's magazines and sports publications without success. Desperate to get the work published, I finally gave it to the Road Runners Club of America tabloid, *Footnotes*, gratis. Given a choice between publication or not, I'd rather have an article published. It's my experience that editors whom I want to know about publication of an article outside the mainstream magazines eventually hear about the work. If not, I can always send them the clipping.

Sometimes, I report something for an obscure publication that, in another version, makes its way into print in a very famous one. I'll give an example. Once Fred Lebow, President of the New York Road Runners Club, asked me to write on a controversy surrounding the New York City Marathon, of which he is the founder and director, for the club magazine, *New York Running News*. In fairness to the parties in conflict, the complexity of the issue, and its history, I wrote about a 5,000-word article for the agreed fee of $250. When a N.Y.R.R.C. lawyer, who reviewed the piece for possible charges of libel, suggested *The New York Times* might be interested in the topic, I called the paper's sports desk without knowing a single editor's name. The *Sports Monday* editor switched me to the man filling in for vacationing Arthur Pincus, in charge of the Sunday *Sports* section. I had to await the return of the Assistant Sports Editor who, to my amazement, commissioned an article on the controversy with updated information. Under the banner headline, "Dispute on Wheelchair Athletes Stirs New

York City Marathon," my article covered nearly two-thirds of a *Times Sports* page in the Sunday edition published two weeks before the 1979 New York City Marathon.

A few days prior to publication, I came to the *Times* office to proof my copy and lunch with Arthur Pincus. As we walked to the restaurant, I asked why he had commissioned the article in hope of hearing words of praise. He said the editors were looking for "something offbeat" about the marathon, which, of course, deflated my ego. Months later as we negotiated another Sunday *Sports* "Viewpoint," for even lower pay than the first, Pincus asked me, "How many assignments did you get from publication in *The Times?*" "None," I shot back. No editor had called with a commission because of my *Times* debut. But the publication credit paid off in professional power of another sort. When rattling off my resume to editors for whom I wanted to work, for a time I liked mentioning my publication in *The New York Times*. The *Times* credit did not give me *quid pro quo* financial reward, but that unexpected assignment for a local sports club publication, revised and updated for *The Times*, had enhanced my professional pride in my writing achievements and added to my prestige with other editors.

To the beginner and professional alike, I give this advice: do any assignment that piques your interest that you can afford the time and fee to complete. As free-lance writers, we all like to perform the tasks of our craft that in their execution reaffirm our professional identity. If necessary, keep your writing muscles flexed and strong by short training pieces and middle distance ones, so you're ready with your best for the longer, more taxing articles when you find the right editor to assign one.

So far, I've urged you to make the commitment to become a professional free-lance magazine writer, test your journalistic talents despite your fears, set realistic marketing goals and do any decent assignment to maintain your skills in top condition. Now I'll explain the best methods to obtain business as a free-lance writer.

# II The Query: How to Get Assignments

The misinformed speak of "selling articles." Such people, I believe, have backgrounds in fiction, criticism, or some other genre. You place short stories, poems, or critical essays by mailing them in completed polished form to editors, but you send an unsolicited finished article only as a last resort. Free-lance magazine writers use a different approach to selling their work. You forward marketable ideas for articles to magazine editors who, if they want the pieces, will commission them. A commission means the editor guarantees you a fee for the accepted assignment or a kill fee should your article be rejected. (I'll say more about negotiating commissions later.) But I repeat, never research, write, and mail uncommissioned manuscripts to editors. Editors usually will tailor an article idea to the taste of the publication in initial discussions, so it's often counterproductive to research and write the article without consulting the editor first. Excise that phrase, "selling articles," from your vocabulary.

## TYPES

Query editors of local papers, regional publications, or national ones by three methods—a letter, phone call, or appointment. A query is a proposal of an idea for an article you'd like assigned. Letter queries should not be dry business communications. Style them on winning principles of salesmanship—controlled enthusiasm for your topic's worth to persuade any skeptic; honest reporting of the facts; and just enough knowledge to impress and inspire trust in your command of the proposed topic. In addition, your upbeat, confident, authoritative presentation should cover certain essentials germane to any query form. I'll state these basic points briefly and explain them later in this chapter. Your query should stress your idea's uniqueness, its timeliness, your approach, its suitability for the special publication, and your qualifications to write it.

### Letter Query

A query has three distinct advantages: first, it saves a free-lance writer money. It prevents you from wasting effort on unsaleable articles and it protects you against distraction from potentially bankable projects. Yet, because of your inexperience in drafting queries, you may squander money-making time in too much investigation. One beginner spent an expense-free month "taking the waters" at a spa to get the facts for her query. For a one-page letter proposal, that month should have been, at most, a day at the spa or, total, an hour phone call to its owner. Don't substitute the collection of facts for the harder act of writing a query. Don't let a query's research feed the illusion that you are a professional magazine writer when you have not sold the idea for the article that would give you the opportunity to develop into one.

Second, a written query serves as a better entree to an editor for an unpublished beginner. If you have no clippings to demonstrate your writing abilities, an editor can judge what you can do by your written proposal. A well-written query is a convincing argument that you can deliver a publishable piece.

Finally, a letter query may better cushion the beginner's frail ego against the hurt of rejection. A well-written query may elicit a fuller explanation for a no from a sympathetic but harried editor than the few words he or she has time to give an unknown over the phone.

Some students are afraid to trust a strange editor with their article ideas. They think an editor might steal ideas from an unknown. Indeed some do, from better-known writers as well as from novices. But not often. As protection, some neophytes mail a registered copy of the query to themselves as evidence of their ownership, in case a magazine publishes an article based on their query idea.

That is a useless gesture. Your registered letter is no legal copyright on your idea. Only articles—published or unpublished—can be copyrighted, not ideas for articles. So don't mail your query registered to yourself; this meaningless act cannot guard your idea against cooptation.

There are better options to preserve title to your queried article ideas. Forward them to magazines with a greater need for free-lance material. Editors for such publications will be more respectful of custom-tailored queries from prospective steady contributors. Or, try to develop interest in your query by alerting the editor's assistant of its contents and date of posting. Then in a week or so, call to see if your envelope made it through the mails to that office. You may gain editorial attention with these personal calls that, without published credentials, you might not otherwise receive. Eventually, if you develop a professional relationship, the editor will treat your ideas with greater respect for your ownership. An editor who depends on a writer regularly for article ideas is less likely to reassign that writer's proposals and risk jeopardizing a mutually sustaining professional partnership. Finally, temper your paranoia with sportsmanship.

Some of my students are so eager to publish, they want to forward the same query to several magazines at once. I oppose simultaneous submission of the same query idea to different magazines at the same time. While this practice is sometimes used for submission of book proposals, I deem simultaneous submission unethical for magazine queries and possibly counterproductive. If two editors both want to commission you, your acceptance of the assignment from one can alienate the other.

However, one of my students sent one idea to a total of fourteen publications, but she assured me, "Only three had it at one time." She justified the simultaneous queries by arguing, "I sent them to select publications in only three different markets at one time that didn't overlap subscribers—the women's magazines, physical fitness magazines, and newspapers." Out of the fourteen queried, one newspaper evinced interest and later bought the article. Still, I am not convinced that the end sale justified the means employed to achieve it.

## Telephone Query

Use a phone query to place an idea with a short time fuse. When you are privy to an insider's tip or have convenient access to a celebrity scheduled for a short-lived local appearance, reach for the phone. You need an editor's quick response, because if the editor believes your timely topic to be inappropriate for the publication, you'll have to try elsewhere immediately. For example, as soon as I learned from a Washington source that Sargent Shriver would announce as a Democratic hopeful for the party's 1976 presidential nomination, I dialed a top editor at *Ladies' Home Journal* for the assignment to profile Shriver's wife, Eunice Kennedy Shriver. When my students confide that they know someone who knows someone starring in a film soon to open in New York or someone about to have a one-man gallery exhibition, I always advise them to call the dailies or Sunday arts section the next day. In phoning queries, plan to make the oncoming event or entree to the celebrity part of your pitch. Probably, though, you will have to argue with the editor's assistants for an editor's time, so reserve phone queries for urgent ideas about to happen the next instant, a scoop, or special entree to a famous name involved in a brief newsworthy event.

I warn you, though, every writer faces greater risks of losing a sale with a receiver in hand. Particularly a beginner. Without the clout of publishings in good places to run past an editor's ear, you have to work harder for the yes that awards you space in a publication where it is at a premium. By phone, you can misinterpret polite silence as hostility and lose your enthus..asm to a stifling case of self-doubt. Or, your idea can be stolen "over-the-wire . former student, then a *Sports Illustrated* researcher, picked up the phone ana after rapping with a *People* editor about an idea, heard, "That's a good profile idea. I'll give it to a staff person."

When a magazine editor wants to reassign your article idea "in house," you have two options. Request a finder's fee, which can range from $100 to as low as $25. If the editor refuses, never approach that staff member again with future queries in any form. Some students prefer to accept cooptation in silence. But if you don't protest the theft, will you trust that editor again with another query? Wiser to argue diplomatically, "A writer's ideas are her bread and butter. Can't you afford a small finder's fee?" Most editors will accede to a reasonable polite demand.

Though I've warned you against phone queries, I confess at the start of my career, I used this method often. In fact, one editor later told me he thought I wrote "with the phone in one hand." Perhaps I was tougher-skinned, more foolhardy, or just desperate. I needed to find out how editors might receive my queries even before I wrote them, even queries about not-so-urgent subjects. Initially, I lived wholly on monies I made as a free-lance writer. So, I had a pressing financial need to know as quickly as possible where I might successfully place an article idea that could bring me next month's rent. I used to say I had just sold an article idea whose check I needed the day before yesterday.

Besides the pressures of living so close to the bone, I was impelled to phone query—more likely than not—because of a strong competitive drive. If a magazine intended to print something on an idea of great interest to me, I wanted to be the free-lance writer assigned to write it. So when I felt fired by a prescient insight about what a celebrity's life represented in terms of emerging feminist issues or current trends, I would phone a magazine editor without a single thought of caution or self-protection. When I reached the editor, my enthusiasm for my idea usually generated a cascade of eloquent perceptions for the listening editor whose interest I hoped to forge into a commission. But though an editor may have liked the idea and my approach, I rarely hung up the phone with an assignment, as I often do now. I still had to write a query letter.

As Benita Feurey, Metro Editor for the New York section of *Good Housekeeping,* explains, "A great talker may not be a good writer. I like queries to see how well someone can write. When I see a published clipping, I never know if the editor rewrote it for the writer or not. With queries, you can get a real sense of what a writer can do." Query letters are important for another reason, as Ms. Feurey adds, "Rarely does any editor have final complete say on an idea. An editor needs a written query to circulate among her editors for their consent. I have to pass mine on to John Mack Carter, Editor-in-Chief of *Good Housekeeping,* for his final approval." So, I take notes of what I say during a phone query, and I advise you to do the same. I am extremely articulate when trying to convince an editor. I like to jot down those precise phrases my heightened enthusiasm elicits or those responses I never thought of before that empathetic editor drew them out of me. That day or the next, I put these jottings together into a draft, which I polish before typing the query to send out for editorial authorization.

Sometimes phone queries can be very wearing, especially if you're dealing with a hard-to-reach editor. In the late 1970's, I was confronted with just that problem. I was trying to sell an expose to an editor in charge of sports at *The Village Voice.* Because of the pressures of weekly deadlines, he was inaccessible most days but one. On that day, I could sometimes reach him around 11:30 in the morning. Or, if he hadn't shown for work by then, I had to pysche myself up and phone this editor around 4 in the afternoon. If he wasn't at an editorial meeting, he had a line of callers holding. Finally, the receptionist would say, "Yours is next." When finally this editor picked up, I had to repeat my credentials and my ideas almost verbatim from the previous call a week before. Invariably, this editor would get excited again as he remembered my purpose and apologize for not getting back to me with a definite response from his editors. And softly, I would repeat that I couldn't do the piece without a commission. And he would invite me to call back the next week when he hoped to have "a definite answer." This routine was repeated four weeks in a row till I got my commission.

The controversial piece, "Selling Out the Big Run," nearly got first-page play. It exposed under-the-table fees famous runners received for appearances or for placing in the New York City Marathon and sponsors' exploitation of runners entered in their road races. This *Voice* exposé was well read because of timing and luck. It was published in an issue on sale at newsstands just four days preceding the Sunday, 1978 New York City Marathon. By good fortune, New York City was in the midst of a newspaper blackout; the dailies weren't being printed. So no other major paper was available in the city but the *Voice*. Copies were so scarce, I saw runners at the New York City Marathon expo borrowing copies to read my piece. As I called the editor back week after week reciting the same "spiel," who could have forecast this kudo and attention? So if the sought-after editor is nearly impossible to reach by phone, keep trying.

For both the newcomer and oldtimer, I want to recapitulate the pros and cons of the different forms of the query we've just reviewed. Again, all queries are an economic time-saver. The letter query is a good entree for the unpublished writer and a cushion against a refusal. Save phone queries for urgent ideas that must be placed right away. Risks of loss due to theft have to be weighed against the strong advantage of a rapid editorial decision. Your enthusiastic advocacy could find the right editor for your idea days before a letter arrives.

## Editorial Meetings

Meetings with editors, which I discuss next, build a personal rapport with an approachable editor already familiar with your work. Meetings offer greater possibilities for assignments because they give you time to argue your ideas. If you can get an appointment with an editor, take it. You stand to gain an assignment from a meeting because an editor is ready to give you one on the basis of your forwarded clippings and resume. Defer conferences about future assignments till you finish current ones. Don't break stride or mental momentum on a present project by meeting for new work. Upon return to your work desk, you'll only have to spend a lot of energy retrieving the mental drive you lost by the interruption. So exercise your option and make the date when you'll be clear of present obligations.

Before a privileged conference, make sure to read the magazine's newsstand issue so you can present your ideas with references to its current format. Moreover, editors are more well-disposed to writers who read their magazines. If, during such encounters, the editor turns down all your proposals, then ask, "What type article do you need?," and you can mentally flip through other possibilities filed to find one that meshes with the magazine's editorial perspective.

To such meetings bring ideas you believe deserve publication, even if previous attempts to market them elsewhere have received a cold reception. If you never persist, you'll never get a cherished idea into print. I remember how, for a year, I'd taken one article idea on women's sports injuries due to previous limited athletic participation to various magazine editors, without obtaining a "go ahead." Then one afternoon during an appointment with an editor I'd never met, I volunteered it again. This particular one brightened at my conception and, picking up a huge sheath of papers, came around her desk to my chair, saying, "Read this." She thrust into my hands the editor-in-chief's blocks of topics—meted out page by page—to be covered in the forthcoming May issue. Within one block was handwritten a synopsis of the exact idea of the article I craved to write. It was an uncanny collision of circumstances—an identical editorial view and my unswerving persistence with a prized idea. That is the true story about how I broke into *Harper's Bazaar's* May, 1980, sports issue with my first piece commissioned by the magazine, "Choose The Sport That's Right For You."

All right. You've learned three ways you can contact editors. You can query editors by letter, phone, or prearranged meetings. Most often, you'll use the query letter, so let's give some thought now to the written query form and points to cover in the presentation of an idea.

## Form of Letter Query

First, a word about appearance. Type your query letters. Handwritten ones look very unprofessional. I always enjoin students who lack typewriters, "Don't you know a single secretary who would allow the use of his or her typewriter during a lunch hour?" You can't expect a magazine editor under a deadline or just emerging from one to have the time to decipher your scrawl. So type your query to make a good impression and receive a fairer evaluation of your article idea.

In written queries, follow the format of the simple business letter. In the upper right hand corner, place your address either at home or at business, and beneath, the date. Choose single or double spacing, whatever you prefer, but be consistent. Several spaces down, by the left margin, put the editor's name (correctly spelled), title, the magazine's name, address, and zip code This same information should appear on your envelope. If you don't possess the correct spelling of the editor's name or the publication's zip code, call the magazine's switchboard and ask. Or, if you can't figure out from the masthead which editor handles what subject area, then ask the operator, "Who handles free-lance writers?", or, "Which editor should I query about. . . .?," and name your topic. Don't forget to include the editor's title in your inside mailing address. A few spaces below, type your salutation: "Dear. . . .," using the editor's last name preceded by "Mr." or "Ms." Then proceed with your query.

Close with a "Sincerely yours" or, as I do, "Very best wishes," and your name typed with your written signature above. If relevant, insert beside the left margin below your name the abbreviation, "enc.:" (for the word "enclosed") and the words, "resume, four clippings," or the number you're sending. These are just tips to draft a professional-looking query.

## INFORMATION REQUIRED FOR ANY QUERY

Now you are ready to learn the information an editor needs to decide about an assignment. Think of them as criteria for a persuasive proposal. Some former students call them "standards." I am very uncomfortable with the word "standards," which conjures up something beyond human reach. I'm not talking about idealized, inflexible standards beyond your grasp here or anywhere in this book. I'm simply passing on proven suggestions for the contents of any query which, in most proposals, will apply. However, decide case by case which requirements best pitch your sale.

I'll explore these information requirements by narrowing in on the specifics for profiles published in national weeklies like *People* and *US*. Queries for a short profile should touch on the same concrete points you should cover in any article proposal. So if you succinctly write a query for a profile, you can draft a winning one on almost anything.

I mentioned these requirements before, but now I'll define such terms as "your subject's uniqueness," "timeliness," "your slant," "suitability for the special publication," and "your qualifications." Your "fillers" for these requirements can help persuade that your idea merits a commission.

### Uniqueness

At the start, explain quickly why the proposed subject is unique. In queries for profiles, you can answer this requirement by pinpointing the subject's outstanding achievement. For example, in the late seventies I got an assignment from *People* because my proposal subject, Phyllis Keitlen, had helped launch the T-shirt as a staple of fashion in America. At the time I suggested Keitlen, this thirty-year-old was manufacturing her T-shirt designs through her firm, Tric-Trac, Inc., in a multimillion dollar business annually. If your query concerns an unusual product or service or person of outstanding accomplishment, stress that distinction.

### Timeliness

Your topic has commercial value if it's timely. Always emphasize the timeliness of the idea in your proposal. Fall, 1975, *Ladies' Home Journal* commissioned my full-length profile of Eunice Kennedy Shriver because her husband,

Sargent Shriver, a declared Democratic nominee hopeful in the 1976 presidential race, was involved in a timely national political event. Too, the *Journal*'s editors may have been influenced by the "times" and the feminist movement's spotlight on women's achievements and, in particular, the significant contribution to government legislation and policy on the retarded made by Eunice Shriver. The editors captured their editorial viewpoint in the title of my profile, "The Kennedy who could be president (if she weren't a woman)." So the newsworthy facet or trendiness of a profile subject, new restaurant, or emerging social issue can add important sales appeal to your query.

### Slant

Next, include your slant. Often in profile queries, your attitude is mirrored in your outline of selected achievements. For instance, when, at thirty-three, the famous marathoner, Katherine Switzer, became one of the country's youngest corporate directors, I would have attempted to place a profile on her from this approach: How did this former winner of the New York City Marathon make the successful transition from her sport to public relations and the corporate echelons at Avon? Are her qualities as a star athlete the same ones propelling her forward as a succcessful business woman? From this example you can decipher one oft-repeated profile theme: Is the proposed subject an outstanding achiever in two fields? Another enduring profile slant is this: Is the subject a "comer" who's just beginning to command national media attention? Is the subject a paradox? One published *People* profile analyzed for class portrayed a professional wrestling teacher who, while he taught a seemingly violent contact sport, was personally a pacifist and vegetarian. So think for a moment—what is your slant? Is your subject a contradiction, peaking professionally, twice successful? That attitude or slant should emerge in the query. Otherwise, your query will sound as factual as an encyclopedia or department store catalogue. Your personal viewpoint should show in your one-page query, so that the editor will assign the subject to you rather than to a staffer.

### Suitability for the Publication

Then ask yourself what appeal your query has to the magazine's readership. What's its special attraction, say, to the low-income, married-woman reader of *Redbook?* To the well-heeled, not necessarily intellectual guy who buys *G.Q.?* Include that attraction for the publication's subscribers or newsstand buyers. For instance, *People* capitalizes on stories composed of photos with text. In my initial presentation, I always noted the photo possibilities of the half a dozen profiles I published there. For example, when I suggested Marcy Blum, twenty-three-year-old food consultant, whose menus grossed over $30,000 weekly for a new Manhattan restaurant, I also recommended a photo modeled after a musical number in *Hello Dolly!*. In the Broadway musical, Carol Channing descended a staircase lined by dancers with welcoming arms outstretched. In my query, I suggested this young food consultant be surrounded by sitting, kneeling, standing waiters and waitresses with outstretched arms holding trays of her food creations. The assigned photographer took this photo that accompanied my text from atop a restaurant bar, as I, perched precariously behind, watched what his 180-degree lens might capture. I included the photo possibilities for the *People* story on Marcy Blum in my query to interest my editor of this magazine with a special format style. So if your proposed subject strikes a resonant chord with the publication's visual format or readership interest, don't forget to note that clearly in your query.

To summarize, the first couple of paragraphs of a query usually skim through your topic's uniqueness, timeliness, your slant, and the idea's compatibilities with that magazine, in any arrangement of these points natural for your presentation. The last paragraphs—most times, but not in every case—list your qualifications for the assignment like a lawyer's final argument.

### Qualifications

Your qualifications can be special connections, work experience, volunteer jobs, or—the best—published articles in the same style or similar in subject to the article proposed.

State your qualifications without embellishment. Beginners lacking published work shouldn't despair. Novices can argue for assignments by other means. For instance, entree. A recent NYU/SCE student devised his own connection to Woody Allen's film composer by several visits to the jazz club where the composer regularly performed sets as a musician. Your improvised connections or that of friends to a proposed subject—particularly, a celebrity known to be inaccessible—are excellent persuasions, no matter how little you've written. Or, your professional employment may be relevant. One student, querying on the uses and fees of commercials in cable TV, was advised to mention her current position as Commercial Coordinator for ABC-TV network to suggest both expertise and access for her research. Besides professional employment, volunteer work or hobbies may give your proposal an edge over any similar one proposed. When an older Queens College graduate wanted to approach a neighborhood weekly about a piece on new burglary-proof apartment devices, I suggested her job as president of her building's Tenants Association could argue for her practical evaluation of these devices and entree to local police.

Naturally, if you have published, list as credentials appropriate clippings, or note your main magazine outlet and area of expertise in your query. State the number of clips enclosed after the word, "enc:", and attach them. One of my students had few articles published. *Woman's Day* had bought three, but only one had appeared. I advised her to say in her query, "*Woman's Day* has purchased the following articles," and to name each by title and publication date. For the two that had not yet reached publication, I suggested the word, "unscheduled," following their titles.

Another student had a different listing problem for her qualifications. Her piece about a new Manhattan diet gourmet shop had been accepted by a local weekly, but before its publication, the shop went out of business. In such cases, refer to the piece by title, publisher, and the words, "accepted, but unpublished."

In the case of unsolicited work, don't list as "unscheduled" any unsolicited magazine article you voluntarily mailed to a publisher that has not yet been returned. Such a statement would misrepresent the facts and your credentials.

The well-published writer who is on staff or free-lances can choose to demonstrate qualifications by articles relevant to the proposal's subject or the queried magazine's editorial style. Note these clips in the letter, at its end, and attach them. After three months of by-lines in the *Queens Tribune,* one student could select from his portfolio samples of stories on such subjects as tenant-landlord disputes, crime, gentrification, or grass roots political issues. Besides exhibition of published work, veterans should always send a resume of their publication credits. And in their query, mention, "I am also including a resume to document my extensive publication record," or some such notation, in addition to placing the word, "resume," after the symbol, "enc." Clips are helpful persuasion for assignments, but resumes add greater force.

What do I do to show my qualifications as an established free-lance writer? When I feel confident enough to call an unfamiliar magazine and seek advice from the editorial assistant answering about whom I should talk to, I give my credentials by phone to that editor with a suitable query or request for meeting. Then I usually have to write a letter stating my qualifications similar to ones I've been advising for you. In such letters that I either bring to an editorial conference or forward with a written proposal, I state my area of specialty, masthead credit, and related recent track record and enclose sample work compatible with the magazine's format or on the subject I am proposing.

In a letter of credentials written in the fall of 1984 to *Working Woman*'s Articles Editor Julia Kagan, preliminary to our meeting just before Christmas, I said:

> *By way of introduction, I [mention] I have become a nationally recognized writer with a specialty in sports medicine. Currently, I am a Contributing Editor to* American Health, *where in the last six months I've published six articles. In addition, as the enclosed resume documents, my cover line articles have appeared in* Esquire, Harper's Bazaar, *and many leading magazines. As samples of my work, I include the following:*
>
> *"Sporty Underpants,"* American Health, *Nov., '84.*
> *"Stilting Runner's Tilt,"* American Health, *Nov., '84.*
> *"Endurable Eating,"* Sportswise, *Jan./Feb., '84.*

"*Sports Clinic: The Chiropractor*," Esquire, *April, '84.*
"*The Pregnant Problems of Working Out*," Sportstyle, *Aug., '83.*

*Please return my resume and sample clippings from the four publications at your convenience.*

*I look forward to bringing my ideas to you.*

*Very best wishes,*

*Barbara Kevles*

*enc: resume, 4 clippings*

Two *Working Woman* editors—independently of each other—photocopied my clips and resume and sent them back to me. I sent my proposals after my meeting with Julia Kagan, now the magazine's Executive Editor.

But whether you query in person, by phone, or letter, your proposal still must cover the essential points with which an editor can decide to make the commission or not. To help you draft masterful queries to secure coveted commissions, I'll repeat these essentials with the succeeding questions. Your answers can design a proposal that beyond doubt proves the merits of your article idea and capabilities for the proposed assignment. Ask yourself,

"Why is the subject special?"
"Why should it be reported now?"
"How do I view it?"
"Why should this magazine cover it?"
"Why should I be assigned the article?"

## SAMPLE QUERY LETTER

I learn best when someone shows me what I'm to do, and so may you. To demonstrate how these essentials combine in an effective query letter, I want to show you one of mine and several excerpts with common flaws by former students. By studying the strengths and weaknesses of these samples, you'll be better prepared to write and rewrite your own.

To allay charges of one-upmanship, I've dug from a dusty file carton my first flawed query for a *People* profile. It answers the questions a query must, but its writing certainly could be improved. In my defense, I offer that the query is a first draft—and the only one—hastily fashioned under unusual circumstances. After an introductory meeting over lunch, *People* Senior Editor Cranston Jones

invited me back to the magazine's offices in the Time Life building to write up
my suggested profile idea. I interpreted the invitation as a test to see how well I
could perform, like any regular staff writer, under deadline. The editor quartered me in an airless cubicle across from his office, usually occupied by the magazine's fact checkers. I wrote, propped on telephone books to reach an old man-
ual typewriter, half the size of my torso. No erasure paper was in sight. The following query is truly my work on the spur of the moment.

*Mr. Cran Jones*
*Senior Editor*
People *Magazine*
*29th Floor*
*Time Life Building*
*Rockefeller Center*
*New York, N.Y. 10019*

*Dear Cran,*

*Thank you for a gourmet lunch and a . . . probing exchange at Le Berry—a
new Gallic haunt to add to my list of select restaurants.*

*I want to outline the story proposed on James De Priest—nephew of Marian
Anderson and recently appointed musical director of L'Orchestra Symphoni-
que de Quebec. De Priest is the first American to assume supervision of any
Canadian symphony orchestra. In this current heyday of French nationalism,
this appointment has stirred and will stir controversy among Canadians.*

*Besides, Jim's personal story adds a bit of piquant—a latecomer to music, a
victim of polio the same month he discovered his talents for conducting, assistant to Leonard Bernstein after winning the Dimitri Mitropoulos Contest
(1964), and no critical recognition until a Dutch concert in 1969. Following
four years of free-lancing in Europe, Antal Dorati, a former Mitropoulos
competition judge, invited Jim to be principal guest conductor of the Washington Symphony at the Kennedy Arts Center. Jim reached the pinnacle of artistic and financial security afforded by his Quebec directorship only after a
road of seemingly insurmountable obstacles and detours. Despite leg braces
and the necessity to conduct from a chair, Jim possesses little obvious self-
pity. He told me recently, "It's not what happens to you, but how you take it."*

*Jim will conduct concerts with the Quebec Symphony October fourteenth
and twenty-eighth. He will feature Quebec's concertmaster Suzuki and Wal-
ter Klien as his star soloists. Only your approval is needed to proceed with the
story on De Priest as a latecomer overcoming more handicaps and obstacles*

*than most conductors for his success.*

*Again, thank you for an incredible lunch for which the food was the hors d'oeuvres and the conversation, the entree. I hope we will have time in the future for more of the same.*

*Very Best Wishes,*

*Barbara Kevles*

*enc: photocopy of De Priest's recent record album*

## Analysis

I'm going to dissect my first *People* query so you'll understand how it handles the points essential to the query form  Its second paragraph mentions the uniqueness of my story—De Priest as the first American to head a major Canadian orchestra. But that feature is subordinate to the profile's political timeliness—the new appointment to a prominent organization headquartered in the seat of the current nationalist movement.

My third paragraph contains my approach. De Priest, a latecomer to his calling and polio victim, has overcome difficult obstacles to achieve the professional success symbolized by his Quebec appointment. The story fits the magazine implicitly; photo possibilities of a conductor of a symphony orchestra were unlimited. As proof of my capabilities to deliver a publishable manuscript, I could cite published profiles in *Good Housekeeping, Show,* and *New York.*

So despite long Jamesian sentences in the third paragraph and heavy-handed repetitions in the same and next, the query obtained my first commission from *People* and an expense-paid trip to Quebec during De Priest's debut concert season. The resulting *People* profile of James De Priest appeared November 25, 1975.

## CRITIQUES OF STUDENT LETTER QUERIES

Now I'll review some queries written by former students who were all beginner magazine writers. I'm not going to correct their writing, but flaws in conception of their ideas. Poor writing is a result of poor thinking. Beginner magazine writers produce ineffective queries, often because they don't know what facts will best put their idea over. Out of indecision, they write vaguely, or with too much detail, repetition, or disorganization. So I'm not going to critique their errors of style, but their poor conception. I'm going to focus on their choice of profile topic, whether they queried at the right time in their subject's life, and the omission of their attitude toward their topic—their slant. "Just fill in the blocks, and you'll write well," I tell my students. So since I've defined some of the required blocks for the query form as uniqueness, timeliness, and your approach, I'll be judging how well these beginners filled them to measure the effectiveness of their queries. And when you become efficient in conveying the information block by block that a query needs, you'll become a better writer, like a runner who naturally develops efficiency with practice.

At the start, beginners fail to get profile assignments because they may select their subjects for the wrong reasons. For instance, one student wanted to profile Messrs. Joel Dean and Georgio DeLuca, founders of New York and East Hampton specialty food stores bearing their names because of

> the far-reaching impact these two men have had on various aspects of food in America . . . including their introduction of new display techniques which have changed the look of food shops all over the world, their . . . efforts to . . . upgrade American awareness in foods (and) new food items they are importing . . . likely to be the next "in" gourmet foods.

This student purportedly wants to do a portrait of two men, but what truly interests her is their achievement as gourmet food merchants at the moment they were launching national distribution of their exclusive specialty items. You can't focus your query wholly on a profile subject's work and expect to stimulate editorial excitement in an intriguing personality readers would want to know more about.

Beginners figuratively shoot themselves in the foot when they propose profile subjects whose ideas captivate them more than their personalities. One student suggested a profile of local deejay Les Davis of WRVR-FM, which, he wrote, "recently changed its format from jazz to country—a drastic move considering that RVR had been the only all-jazz station in New York. . . . The piece will stress the choice between artistic and commercial demands in radio, especially in the coverage of jazz." This reporter is obviously captivated by the issues other than the deejay's personality. Again, beware of proposing as a profile someone whose work you admire more than what the work mirrors about the person who achieved it.

One last example to illustrate this short-sighted perception of a proposed profile subject. One former student, whose work was published in *People* and *Sports Illustrated,* proposed

> Ms. Lois Alexander, a long time Harlem resident . . . curator of the Black Fashion Museum . . . [who] has collected pieces from the 1800's to the present that reveal new insights into the way clothing was made before the onset of new technology, and has thrown back the covers to reveal a rich black past in the world of fashion.

This writer was fascinated by Ms. Alexander's "fountain of knowledge as far as clothing is concerned," and we might be too, but not as a subject of a profile. Again, expertise, controversial views, or professional influence may make a person unique. But unusual work alone cannot package a person as a profile for publication without qualities of timeliness or an approach that can move a reader further.

If students don't sabotage their profile query by choosing a subject lacking personality appeal, they choose someone at the wrong time. One student, for instance, suggested an aspiring opera singer, veteran of ten local productions, about to start a two-month contract with the Michigan Opera Company. I told the student she would be writing a publicity release by profiling this singer so prematurely before his career warranted such attention. So would another student who queried about profile possibilities for Bobbi Fisher, publisher of the one-month-old paper, *The Staten Island Black Press*. Unless the profile were done after the paper had proven success, it would be misconstrued as a promotion for it and its publisher.

Besides choosing the wrong subject to profile or the wrong time, beginner magazine writers may forget to say why their timely, unique profile subject interests them. The following query exhibits the glaring omission of a personal viewpoint:

> I would like to propose a story on Ms. Jean Doumanian. Having spent the past four years as the associate producer of the popular television show, "Saturday Night Live," Ms. Doumanian has recently been promoted to the show's producer and is now preparing for her first show, which will air November 15 [a month away].

The student had insider's knowledge of a timely event in the life of a recently promoted network television executive, but she neglected to offer her personal "behind-the-scenes" view of the person.

By contrast, another student, who wrote a query on a unique and timely achiever, fulfilled this prerequisite for an assignment marvelously. She proposed Michael Klauber, twenty-four, who, in a joint venture with Ziff Davis Publishers and his own company, has just leased the Astoria Movie Studio for future film production with this focus:

> Michael Klauber is about to be named Vice-President of this studio.
> I would like to write this story focusing on the pressures and problems a young person would have being thrown so unexpectedly into such a powerful position.

Rosebud! This student's insight into what this achievement may mean to the achiever gives her query a powerful approach that is saleable to an editor.

Lest you think my students never submit queries that fulfill all the requirements of the form, I mean to dispel that presumption. I include the following by
Jerri Senior. In her query on computers operation manager, Mary Bennett, the
first paragraph contains Ms. Bennett's achievement and timeliness as a profile
subject; the second, an insightful slant about why Ms. Bennett went "for the
money"; the third, Ms. Bennett's appeal to the queried publication's readership;
and the fourth, Ms. Senior's work and educational qualifications for the assignment.

*Home address*
*City, State, ZIP*
*October 8, 1980*

*Editor's Name*
*Essence Magazine*
*Street Address*
*New York, N.Y. ZIP*

*Dear Ms.:*

*I would like to submit the article, "What Makes Mary Run" for publication in
"The Essence Woman" column of* Essence *magazine. While the majority of female white collar workers frazzle in corporate typing pools or rerun Hollywood's overworked, underpaid, "Girl Friday" theme in their secular lives,
Mary Bennett, a young black mother of three, has been climbing the corporate ladder at American Telephone and Telegraph Co. (AT&T). Shortly after
her husband died, Ms. Bennett joined AT&T as a general clerk. Eleven years
and nine promotions later, she is manager of computer operations at the New
Jersey plant and winner of AT&T's 1980 Greatest Achievement Award.*

*The scenario was typical: young widow, three children, burial insurance, no
savings, and no obvious marketable skills. Even the dreams were typical. The
children would have what their workingclass parents had missed, a college
education. What is not typical is what Ms. Bennett did about it. She says,
"When Floyd died I was determined not to let our dream die with him. I had no
alternative. I had to go for the money."*

*Mary Bennett's successful simultaneous management of a fast-track career
and single parenthood makes her the classic "Essence Woman." Please contact me at your earliest convenience regarding your interest in the proposed
story.*

*I am a free-lance writer and an educational administrator. I have recently
completed a study on black women in managerial/administrative positions in
cooperation with Bank Street College of Education.*

*Respectfully,*
*Jerri Senior*

The past pages summarize the common errors in concept beginners make in using the query form. They stumble either because of choice of topic, its timing, or lack of a personal attitude about their subject. And some, at the start, get everything right in their first query. But those who understand uniqueness, timeliness, and slant immediately, and can apply those requirements to query letters are rare.

## RESUME

I've not said anything yet about students' errors in citing their qualifications. Mainly, they usually fill this requirement properly. Why? Because it's the easiest part of query writing. You likely have something appropriate for this slot like a work credit, hobbies, entree or some pertinent fact.

So I'd like to suggest three resume formats for now or the future when you have clips to list in a resume to send with a query letter. The following early resume by Michael Siconolfi contains an introductory statement to his work on different topics for one publication, good subdivisions, and suitable headings.

MICHAEL SICONOLFI
Home Address
City, State, ZIP
Phone: (home)

RESUME

Since the fall of last year, I have written numerous news feature pieces for the *Queens Tribune*. These published articles cover the following topics:

Tenant/landlord disputes—"Complaints Abound at Alley Pond Apartments Rally," Jan. 8, 1981; "Tenant Leader Facing Eviction Is Still Fighting," February 5, 1981; "Bayside Auburndale Problems Widespread," February 12, 1981.

The murder of a Queens policeman—"Local 'One in a Million' Cop Becomes No. 10," December 31, 1980; "Second Suspect Nabbed," January 8, 1981.

Building restoration—"Poppenhusen Has Heat but the Future Is Dim," December 18, 1980; "Pop: The Fight Continues," January 15, 1981.

General interest stories about Flushing—"Maple Avenue Montage," January 22, 1981; "Downpour Leaves Queens Under Water," December 4, 1980.

Political profiles—"Q&A Interview of Queens Borough President Donald Manes," expected date February 26, 1981; future profile of Queens D.A. John Santucci.

A frequent contributor to *Billboard,* Robert J. Riedinger submitted this resume of his work to class. A quick reading of the chronology of his work will reveal what's wrong with this structure.

ROBERT J. RIEDINGER
Home Address
City, State, ZIP
Telephone (office)
Telephone (home)

RESUME

Freelance reporter, reviewer, and feature writer.
*Billboard* 1978-1980

3/2/80 Review: UFO p. 40
2/16/80 Article: "Kiddie Clubs Seeing No Letdown" p. 54
2/2/80 R: Aerosmith p. 29
1/12/80 A: "Long Island Deejays Probe Public Tastes" p. 37
11/10/79 A: "Clubs Swing To Beat Of Varied Jazz Styles" p. 34
11/10/79 R: Kenny Loggins p. 38
10/20/79 R: Robert Palmer p. 40
10/13/79 R: Fabulous Thunderbirds p. 48
9/29/79 R: Dire Straits p. 45
9/22/79 A: "20,000 See 'Woodstock Reunion' Gig In N.Y." p. 47
9/29/79 R: Grateful Dead p. 50
9/1/79 A: "Revue Mixes Rock, New Wave, Disco" p. 37
8/11/79 R: Kinks p. 36
7/21/79 R: Newport Jazz Festival pp. 44, 53, 63
6/30/79 R: Yes p. 42
6/23/79 R: Tom Robinson Band p. 39
5/26/79 R: Art Farmer Quartet p. 42
5/12/79 A: "Fans Dance Night Away On New L.I. Strip" p. 37
5/12/79 R: John McLaughlin p. 29
5/5/79 R: Joe Ely p. 40
4/28/79 A: "WABC Turns To Disco" (with Doug Hall) p. 1
4/28/79 R: Harry Chapin p. 48
4/21/79 R: Nazareth p. 36
4/14/79 A: "Gino Soccio: Unsuccessful As A Rock Artist, He Clicks In Disco" p. 54
3/31/79 R: Eddie Money p. 79
3/31/79 A: "Terpers Earn Two Corvettes" p. 129

3/24/79 A: "Nuts, Bolts Of Franchises" p. 43
3/24/79 A: "Owners Cover Every Base" p. 50
3/24/79 A: "Even The Beer Brewers Get In On The Scene" p. 53
3/24/79 R: Disco Forum p. 52
3/3/79 A: "Franchised Clubs Like Burger Kings Soon?" p. 46
3/3/79 A: "Moppet Market Is New, Open And Available" p. 86
2/17/79 R: Flight p. 55
1/27/79 R: Alessi Brothers p. 52
12/16/78 R: 10cc p. 46
12/9/78 R: Doobie Brothers p. 48
12/2/78 A: "Clubs Help Combat Multiple Sclerosis" p. 72
11/25/78 R: Marshall Tucker Band p. 62
11/18/79 R: Janis Ian p. 42
11/11/78 R: Billy Cobham p. 60
11/4/78 R: Kenny Loggins p. 38
10/7/78 R: Engelbert Humperdinck
9/23/78 A: "Light-Up Clothing Flashing In N.Y." p. 73
9/16/78 R: Woody Shaw p. 29
7/29/78 A: "Long Island Clubs Seek To Diversify" p. 61
   (Two parts, concluded 8/5/78, p. 60)
7/22/78 A: "Say 12-Inch Singles Cry For Uniformity" p. 61
7/15/78 R: Newport Jazz Festival pp. 40, 64, 82
5/13/78 A: "Community Relations Vital To 14th Uncle Sam's Club" p. 54

Although, like Mr. Siconolfi, Mr. Riedinger had published in only one place, he had produced a variety of work. He had written on trends in disco music, disco clubs, their programs, profiles of disco artists, reviews of live performances and records. No editor on the basis of this chronology could truly assess Mr. Riedinger's strengths and scope as a reporter on the music entertainment industry. If the resume of published articles were reorganized by subject groups, it could be improved and serve as a better demonstration of the writer's proven credentials.

I include my own professional resume for your criticism because it shows how to subdivide works published in many national magazines. At the start of my career, I grouped my publications by form—profiles, interviews, and other type articles. When I wrote in two forms primarily for two publications—*Working Woman* and *People*—I used the two magazines as main categories. In recent years, as I've specialized in articles on fitness, sports controversies, and sports medicine, I've tended to arrange my work in chronological sequence under these subject headings, while mentioning other areas in passing.

BARBARA KEVLES
Street Address
City, State ZIP

*RESUME*

I worked full-time as a free-lance writer from 1968 until 1971, when I began research on a book. During this brief period, I wrote a prolific amount of profiles, interviews and articles for both mass and literary magazines.

I profiled "Through Bedlam's Door With Anne Sexton," (LOOK, Dec., 1968);
"An Intimate Portrait of Joan Kennedy," my first cover story (GOOD HOUSE-
KEEPING, Sept., 1969); "Althea Gibson: 'I Don't Want Any Sympathy,' "
(SPORT, Nov., 1970); and "Shirley Temple Black at the U.N.," (THE SATURDAY
EVENING POST, Summer, 1972).

I interviewed "Jerzy Kosinski: The Guest Who Didn't Arrive At The Sharon Tate
Murder and Lived," (LADIES' HOME JOURNAL, bought and unpublished);
"The Electric Tom Wolfe," (a two-part series, CHARLIE, Dec., 1968, Jan., 1969);
Judy Collins speaking on "I've Looked At Both Sides Now!" (REDBOOK, Oct.,
1969); Kathleen Kennedy: "Everything That Happens Has To Change You,"
(SEVENTEEN, Sept., 1970); Anne Sexton on "Anne Sexton: The Art of Poetry
XV," (THE PARIS REVIEW, Summer, 1971); Joan Baez, Eleanor Holmes Norton,
Sharon Rockefeller, Shirley Temple Black, Colleen Corby on "When I Was 17,"
(SEVENTEEN, 1971); "Melinda Muskie, Mary McGovern, John McCloskey:
'Why My Dad Should Be President,' " (SEVENTEEN, Feb., 1972).

In new journalism style, I chronicled "A Documentary of Birth and Death," by
filmmaker Arthur Barron (NEW YORK, Dec., 1968); and "Looking for Karen
Sperling," (SHOW, June, 1970); and "In Search of Nan Page," (THE ATLANTIC,
July, 1970). In addition, I wrote survey pieces on "Make Love Not War In Your
Own Life," (EYE, Dec., 1968), and "Women in TV," (MADEMOISELLE, March,
1969).

From the summer of 1972 until early 1975, I worked on a reportage about a radical feminist cadre during the height of the second feminist wave. Because of my
work on this non-fiction book, I curtailed my free-lance assignments to the following publications: "Raising My Fist For Feminism: I Discovered The Movement In
Jail," (The Literary Guild's WORKS IN PROGRESS, Issue #5, 1972); "The Ex-
amined Life From a Feminist Viewpoint," (BRYN MAWR ALUMNAE BULLE-
TIN, 1973); "Feminism & Sexuality & My Changes," (NEW TIMES, bought and
unpublished, 1974).

In 1975, I returned to free-lance writing with the following articles—"chasing the
lonelies," (SEVENTEEN, August, 1975); an interview with Jerzy Kosinski, "A
Loner Meets the Insurers," (EAST APPLE, Oct. 21, 1975), a profile of Marian Anderson's nephew, conductor James De Preist, (PEOPLE, Nov. 24, 1975), a profile
on PEN President, poet, translator, biographer "Muriel Rukeyser: After the Revolution," (THE VILLAGE VOICE, bought and unpublished), Pulitzer poet "Max-
ine Kumin: The Art of Poetry," (THE PARIS REVIEW, bought and unpublished);

and a major profile of Eunice Kennedy Shriver: "The Kennedy who could be president (if she weren't a woman)," (LADIES' HOME JOURNAL, March, 1976). During this period, my lead book reviews appeared in NEWSDAY and WEST SIDE LITERARY REVIEW in addition to occasional reviews in HARPER'S BOOKLETTER.

In 1976, I wrote for THE VILLAGE VOICE—"The Dying of a Poet," (Anne Sexton), April 5, '76 and "Gordon Parks: 'I Don't Make Black Exploitation Films,' " May 10, 1976. In addition, I published a number of profiles in PEOPLE—Paula Hughes (Wall St. broker), April 26, 1976; Phyllis Keitlen (innovator of t-shirt as fashion), May 24, 1976; Lally Weymouth (historian), July 5, 1976; Sandra Brown (venture capitalist), August 9, 1976; Marcy Blum (food consultant), Dec. 13, 1976; Barbara Pearlman (exercise consultant), March 28, 1977; Naomi Sims (world famous model and wig manufacturer), Lead Profile, Aug. 22, 1977. My profiles of celebrated women have also appeared in US—Sharon Rockefeller (public television consultant), Aug. 9, 1977; Laure Conolly (horse trainer), Aug. 9, 1977; and Lynnie Greene and Bess Armstrong (stars of CBS-TV situation comedy "On Our Own"), Jan. 10, 1978.

During 1976 and 1977, I published an interview series in WORKING WOMAN as a contributing editor. My interviews with women of achievement included actress Liv Ullmann (Nov., 1976—the charter issue); television comedy writer, Gail Parent (Dec., 1976); film costume designer, Edith Head (Jan., 1977); book editor Gene Parks (April, 1977); actress-film director Jeanne Moreau (cover picture, March, 1977). Also I contributed topic interviews to PEOPLE on teenage pregnancy (March 15, 1976); child abuse (November 22, 1976); moral education (June 13, 1977); diet therapy (April 25, 1977), as well as a job interview to COSMOPOLITAN's December, 1978 issue ("Notes of a West Point Woman").

My health and fitness articles and writing on the politics of running have appeared in the "Official Program: New York City Marathon," published by NEW TIMES, Oct., 1977 ("Women: Going the Distance, Closing the Gap"); in SPORTSWISE's "Official Program: Mini Marathon," June, 1978 ("The Pied Piper of Central Park"—profile of national running coach, Bob Glover): THE VILLAGE VOICE's Oct. 23, 1978 issue ("Selling Out the Big Run"), in RUNNING REVIEW's Dec./Jan., 1979 issue ("Women Marathon Runners: The New Breed Sportswoman"); in RUNNING REVIEW's Feb., 1979 issue ("Running Clothes—Designed For Women by Women"); NEW YORK RUNNING NEWS' Spring, 1979 issue ("Should Wheelchair Racers Run?"); DANCE SCOPE's Spring, 1979 issue ("Jog or Jette?" An Interview with consulting orthopedist to the NYC Ballet, Dr. William Hamilton); MADEMOISELLE's April, 1979 issue ("Women's Sports Injuries"); THE NEW YORK TIMES, Sunday, Oct. 7, 1979 ("Dispute on Wheelchair Athletes Stirs New York City Marathon"); FOOTNOTES' Winter, 1979 issue ("Fritz Mueller: Running Master"); HARPER'S BAZAAR's May, 1980 issue ("Choose The Sport That's Right For You"); THE NEW YORK TIMES, Sunday, May 18, 1980 ("Olympic Marathon Is More Than A Physical Struggle for Women"); FOOTNOTES' Summer, 1980 issue ("Why I Pump Asphalt").

As a specialist in sports medicine, I wrote the following national magazine articles: HARPER'S BAZAAR, coverline story, May, 1981 ("How To Run A Marathon");

ESQUIRE, coverline story, August, 1982 ("Where To Marathon"); HARPER'S BAZAAR, coverline story, May, 1982 ("How To Finish A Marathon"); AMERICAN HEALTH, May-June, 1983 ("Varsity By A Hair"); AMERICAN HEALTH, July-August, 1983 ("Do You Catch Like a Four Year Old?"), SPORTSTYLE, August, 1983 ("Bodysense: The Pregnant Problems Of Working Out"); AMERICAN HEALTH, July-August, 1983 ("Shoe Inserts—Need 'em?"—coverline story); AMERICAN HEALTH, November-December, 1983 ("Run, Mom, Run, But Not Too Hard"); NEW YORK RUNNING NEWS, December-January, 1984 (New York City Marathon, 1983 "Medical Report," "Course Report"—Edited and supervised ten adult magazine writing students from NYU & The New School in their reportage of 1983 NYCM); GOOD HOUSEKEEPING, February, 1984 ("Way To Go: Fairway"); SPORTSWISE, January-February, 1984 ("Nutrition: Endurable Eating"); ESQUIRE, April, 1984 (Sports Clinic: "The Chiropractor: The Long Misunderstood Profession Is Making a Comeback"); AMERICAN HEALTH, March-April, 1984 ("Five Minute Run Tells Enough"); AMERICAN HEALTH, July-August, 1984, ("Back Again To Cartilage," "Stretching Out"); AMERICAN HEALTH, September-October, 1984 ("Happy Feet"); FOOTNOTES, Summer, 1984 ("Keeping Athletes In The Fast Lane"); NEW YORK RUNNING NEWS, August-September, 1984 ("Pregnancy: The Forty Week Workout"), AMERICAN HEALTH, Nov., 1984 ("Sporty Underpants," "Uneven Legs"); Dec., 1984 ("To Straighten Kids' Feet"); FOOTNOTES, Winter, 1985 ("Why Train?"); AMERICAN HEALTH, April, 1985 ("Vanquishing yeast infections . . . and preventing them"); THE RUNNER, April, 1985 ("Innovations: Shoe-ins"); AMERICAN HEALTH, May, 1985 ("Chest Pains: Twinges of the Heart"); THE RUNNER, May, 1985 ("The Runner Talks To: Diane Dixon"); AMERICAN HEALTH, June, 1985 ("Anal Sex: Of Sperm and Immunity"); OUR TOWN, May 26, 1985 ("Precautions to take to reduce heat risks") THE RUNNER, July, 1985 ("Training: Hot Tracks"); THE RUNNER, July, 1985 ("Swimming: A Fat Advantage?"); THE RUNNER, January, 1986 ("Body: Running Flats"); THE RUNNER, February, 1986 ("Beating the Clock").

In addition, I have written articles on atraditional education, interracial marriage and music for CHANGE MAGAZINE's January, 1980 issue ("Democratizing the Curriculum," co-authored with James W. Hall, President, Empire State College, S.U.N.Y.); GLAMOUR's January, 1980 issue ("What's It Like to Be the Child of an Interracial Marriage?"), and ROUTE's March, 1980 issue ("Maitre Jimmy of L'OSQ").

I contributed the introductory essay, "Occupation: Writer," to the *1981 Writer's Market* and co-edited the essay collection on atraditional college curriculum theories and practices, *In Opposition To Core Curriculum,* published by Greenwood Press (1982).

## FOLLOW-UP

If you've not heard from an editor of a monthly after, say, three weeks (two in the case of a weekly), then call. Ask the editorial assistant or secretary whether your envelope arrived and whether the editor has had the chance to review your query. As a free-lance writer, periodically remind editors about your queries, lying somewhere on their desks, and your need for a decision. After all, your assignment may be a primary source for your basic living expenses. In the interests of your survival, you have to try to get your queries read and assigned or retrieve them to send to other possible purchasers.

If your phone reminders reach an editor in a crunch of deadlines, be considerate. Put a note in your calendar for another call when the editor will be less preoccupied. After a reasonable wait, if you don't personally speak with the editor or the assistant, or the assistant can't plead your case for attention successfully, you have the right to try the idea at another publication. Should you find the next editor more receptive and forthcoming with a commission, let the first know by note your idea is no longer available for consideration.

## REJECTION LETTERS

Should your prized query elicit nothing more than a routine rejection letter, you may, on reading that dehumanized phrase, "We regret to say . . . ," feel a sting of wetness in your eyes, a craving to snack, or desire to hide the offending letter under your dictionary. You have reasonable cause for disappointment, but not despair. No refused assignment is a final judgment on the merits of your idea, your talents as a writer, or worth as a person. There may be valid reasons that pertain to circumstances beyond your control. Your article idea may duplicate one already "in the works" or even published. Or, the magazine's inventory may be so overloaded that the editor may not need or have the money to make current assignments. Or, the editor may not like the idea, despite your well-written proposal. Or superiors may have overruled the editor on the commission.

Whatever the cause of your rejection, which may not reflect unfavorably on you at all, a rejection hurts. No matter how many published credits you have. To bandage the wound, try calling a friend to distract you from the pain. Or confront the rejected query, retype it in the same or revised format, and mail it to another editor at a different publication. If an article idea is sent aloft again, like a bird in flight, it becomes a moving target that is harder to shoot down.

Though I published so many articles during my first years, one of my strongest drives for assignments was an editor's rejection of a query. That rejection of my idea made me more determined to place it. Rather than weaken me, the pain of editorial rejection stiffened my backbone and will to succeed as a free-lance magazine writer.

These first chapters have explored your dreams, fears, aspirations, and hopes of becoming a free-lance magazine writer, and the best methods to make that goal a reality. The next chapters help you find assignment ideas and teach you to write the easiest form to cast—the profile.

# III Where to Find Saleable Article Ideas: Your Best Sources

In the last chapter, you learned the essential elements of effective queries and methods to submit them to editors. You were advised to query about timely, unusual article ideas you're especially qualified to write, from a vantage appealing to the publication. Now you may ask, "Where do I find saleable article ideas that fit these requirements?"

## FIRSTHAND RESOURCES

I don't recommend articles already published as sources for queries. A subject previously reported has much less commercial appeal. Prospective editors seek new topics or new information that will distinguish their pages from competitors'. A query about a subject in print even presented with a fresh viewpoint can still strike an editor as stale. Secondly, I don't suggest the use of other writers' works, because to succeed in free-lance writing, you have to originate article ideas. If you want to break into magazines that employ staff writers, the submitted proposals have to center on developments unknown to the staff to justify a commission from an outsider. It's possible, however, to win entree to heavily staff-written magazines like *Vogue, People,* and similar publications if you learn to produce article ideas from your immediate personal resources.

To develop an instinct for commercial subjects, a feeling for what's timely, and connections for privileged information for queries, plumb such firsthand resources as your experience, interests, gut feelings, interviews, and your editors. These private caches will give you the best ideas for name-making articles.

### Your Experience

Ideas derived from your experience are easiest to peddle because usually they are not frayed, worn topics, which have been exhaustively covered in magazines. These query ideas can be generated by a chance conversation, work routine, a traumatic incident or any number of possibilities. For example, one hot spring morning while running six miles in Manhattan's Central Park, I teamed with another runner doing my pace who, after a couple of miles, announced that he was boycotting the Bloomingdale's-Perrier race that day. I questioned his reasons. He said entrants had to pick up registrations blanks in Bloomingdale's running gear shop. He protested the unethical exploitation of the racers for the sponsor's commercial gain. That chance meeting on the run was the motivation for my article, "Selling Out the Big Run," published in *The Village Voice.* With further interviews, it evolved into an exposé about not only race sponsors who took commercial advantage of race entrants, but also about how race promoters, at that time, paid rank finishers "so-called" under-the-table fees in this "amateur" sport.

Chance encounters can provoke ideas for articles, but so can mundane routines. My student, H. D. R. Campbell, got one of these nuggets from her days as a waitress in the theater district. Ms. Campbell recalls the seminal experience: "The staff ate dinner at eight every night because everyone had left for the theater." Her article with the banner, "DINNER AT EIGHT," and the subtitle, "Where to get last-minute dinner reservations? At these popular restaurants on 46th Street—left almost empty every night from 8 to 10 p.m. as theatergoers temporarily desert them," graced a recent *Good Housekeeping* New York Metro section. In her introduction to twenty listings on Restaurant Row, between Eighth and Ninth Avenues, the former waitress wryly observed, "While this is not the chicest of New York neighborhoods, knowing how to secure a table at the last minute may prompt your friends to think of you as a trend setter!"

Besides the unpredictable or ordinary routine, personal traumas are another source for national magazine articles. Paradoxically, a private, intense experience can spawn a magazine article of interest to millions. In the Fall of 1983, when I finished a 400 m. at the North American Council Masters Track & Field Championships with a personal record, I threw myself on the field at the finish, besieged by wrenching chest pains, unable to catch my breath. I thought I was having a heart attack. Later I found out I was only hyperventilating. Air had been shuttling between my windpipe and nasal passages but had not been reaching my lungs. I had no concrete focus for an article utilizing my race trauma for about two years. Then Jim Fixx, author of one of the first signature books of the fitness boom, died during a run. So I called Steve Kiesling, a senior editor at *American Health,* and pitched a piece to ward off the Fixx "fixation" of fear of death from exercise. The piece would differentiate between symptoms, causes, and treatment of chest discomfort from exercise as in hyperventilation and a heart attack. My editor wanted to know more about symptoms and types of heart disease. So I interviewed cardiologist Dr. Nino Marino, Physician in Charge of the Echocardiography Laboratory, Lenox Hill Hospital, and relayed my interview to my editor. I got the assignment.

The published piece, "Chest Pains: Twinges Of The Heart/When not to Worry/Heart Pains: When to Worry," had such wide appeal that it was syndicated by the *Washington Post.*

## Your Interests

Scrutinize not only the special event, accident, or ordinariness of your daily life, but also your personal interests for possible articles. If you enthusiastically follow the latest fashions, top forty on the radio, or neighborhood politics, you may have leads about a social trend, changing life-styles, or an emerging political movement.

When folk protest-song singers captured the vogue in the sixties, I used to buy their latest albums. Bob Dylan's tough bitter lyrics, Joan Baez's ethereal bird-song tones, Judy Collins' daring "say it like it is" songs expressed much of how I felt about private and public events. After one painful break-up, a friend sent me the solace of Judy Collins' first million-copies-sold record, "Fifth Album." Its gold-record success spurred me to query *Redbook* about a profile on Collins because the readership, I thought, would identify with the singer, then a single parent trying to manage a skyrocketing career while at the same time raising a son. The published interview took its title from the album cut, " 'I've Looked At Both Sides Now!'."

If you review the concerns you keep constantly updating, you may discover a gold mine for back-to-back assignments. Under pressure of a class deadline, one of my students, Virginia Maida, B.A. in journalism from the College of White Plains and a former columnist for *The Brooklyn Paper*, decided to turn her penchant for high fashion at bargain prices into an article. She reported on the eastside thrift shop where, she claims, "I buy about a third of my wardrobe." The class' enthusiasm for the piece prompted the writer to call and drop off a copy at a local paper, *Our Town*. Upon return from a weekend business trip, Ms. Maida found her first by-line in print in Manhattan. Some excerpts from "Shopping for Charity . . . Irvington House," tell why:

> Nothing is as exciting as buying a new spring outfit for $25 . . . especially if it was broken in by Claudette Colbert or Candice Bergen.
> They are among the 25,000 donors, famous and unknown, who contribute "experienced" clothing, furniture, and other goods to Irvington House Thrift Shop, at 80th St. and Second Ave. Celebrities are not only donors but shoppers as well . . . Apparently the rich like a bargain as well as anyone else.

This student rightly perceived her interest in budget tips for fashion buying to be a concern many share.

Your interests may spawn an article because others may be galvanized by the same things you are. Once I told this to a class, and a young married student countered, "If I'm interested in something, I think nobody else is." Yet with probing, she confided that during her first pregnancy, she wondered whether the photocopying she did at work could harm her unborn child. Her classmates wanted her to pursue the subject for a possible article on health risks during pregnancy in the office. If hesitant about the worth of your concerns for possible ideas for articles, let a friend act as your sounding board.

The chance to tell a friend ideas stemming from your interests may be all you need to appreciate their merits for assignments. Once after a Broadway show, I waited at a bus stop with a friend, Denise Fortino, who is Health Editor at *Harper's Bazaar*, to shepherd her on to her ride home. To pass time, I told her about a recent visit to a chiropractor for a running injury—achilles tendonitis. I quipped that I was so green about chiropractors I thought they were one and the same as "chiropodists," which I remembered was the name my grandmother used for her foot doctor. Denise was intrigued that chiropractors treated not only problems of the back, but athletic injuries to the limbs as well. Her enthusiasm inspired me to draft an article proposal right there as the east-bound bus arrived at the 57th Street and Fifth Avenue stop. A high-fashion fantasy magazine like *Harper's Bazaar* turned the article down, but Denise's endorsement of the proposal as a sound one encouraged me to persevere and contact several more publications till a savvy, sympathetic *Esquire* editor commissioned the piece "The Chiropractor: The long-misunderstood profession is making a comeback," for the *Sports Clinic*.

My interest in ideas for sports medicine articles usually occurs after the fact. Something will happen to me as an amateur in a race or in training and then an article idea will emerge out of my desire to analyze why it happened or, more likely, how I can prevent its recurrence. Your interests before the fact can make you vulnerable to ethical infringements in your researches, and you should be aware of the grey areas to prevent damage to your professional reputation.

I caution: Don't initiate article ideas from motives to gain a social entree or product for nothing. You may accept gratis a product or service to try it out and report honestly its advantages or disadvantages; this is an acceptable practice as long as your motivating impulse is a desire for knowledge rather than a desire for the product or service for free.

By contrast, the following illustrates an improper journalistic motive arising from misuse of a personal interest for research. A graduate of a famous Ivy-League college with an M.B.A. confessed in class she intended to profile millionaires in order to meet and marry one. I explained her motive was not a valid one for an article. If she purposely thought up article ideas in order to meet men, she would be using her interest in an assignment for a personal advantage rather than the advantage of reporting the assignment. So guard against conceiving an article for personal benefits that exceed the article's professional purpose.

## Your Intuitions

Besides direct experience and common concerns, intuitions can turn up valuable article ideas. For instance, hunches about the influences of childhood on celebrities' lives may prompt insightful original pieces. Once, reading a newspaper interview with famed actress Liv Ullmann, I discovered her father had died when she was at the pivotal age of eleven. A couple of weeks later, I had a story conference with Beatrice Buckler, the editor-in-chief and founder of the then new *Working Woman* during the publisher's snatched morning at a posh hair salon. Despite the noisy distractions of dryers, sinks, and chitchat, I left with a commission to interview Liv Ullmann for the magazine's premiere issue. On nothing more than my intuition, the assigned interview with Ullmann was to explore her romanticizing of men as idealized father figures for the real father she had lost in her preteen years and her disillusionment when her illusion shattered.

The "Interview: Face to Face with Liv Ullmann," confirmed my hunch about the film actress' view of men and its source. Describing the years spent living in isolation with film director Ingmar Bergman, on an island in the Baltic Sea, she responded to my question, "Didn't you limit each other?"

"Yes . . . by expectations of what the other represented, by closing a circle around our love. But on the other hand, I also grew. The last years, I knew the pillar—the image of the man being the father, the strong one who would protect me—was falling. As long as the child thinks the parent is without flaws she accepts his demands as part of his wisdom. But when she knows they're part of his egotism, she rebels. That was true for Ingmar and me. I had mistaken his need to dominate me for strength."

So, as I suspected, Ullmann candidly confessed to idealizations of men as surrogate fathers and a healthy outgrowing of this need. When you scan newspaper or magazine profiles about oft-reported celebrities, your instincts can guide you to new perspectives about these media subjects. Trust those gut feelings to develop your most commercial quality—a point of view. If you see things differently from other writers, your original perspective can transmute the hackneyed article idea into a truly remarkable one.

## SECONDHAND RESOURCES

### Your Research Sources

After an article is accepted, feel free to ask persons you interviewed for contacts or sources for other articles. After one of my students, Richard Pokorny, published a profile of an advertising executive who, as a sideline, cared for cats on their home turf, I suggested Pokorny ask "the cat lady" to suggest other subjects for profiles. She mirrored something of his life. Just before Pokorny took my course, he had quit a well-paying advertising job at N.W. Ayer Advertising Agency to seek more meaningful employment. Like him, his profile subject had left a career in high school teaching for one in advertising. So I recommended he ask her for names of similar people who had successfully switched careers, which represented what he was trying to do.

One subject will lead to the next. Research for one article will often point toward your next published credit. When I received the galleys of an *American Health* piece about a new cause and treatment for chronic monilia, I called my source, immunologist Dr. Steven Witkin, Research Associate Professor, Cornell University Medical College, to verify its medical accuracy. After we completed the galley check, I asked him for names of other researchers whose publishings in peer group review journals might be of practical interest to *American Health* readers in future articles. He suggested he had another vein of research that might serve the purpose. As a result, my initial article, which took up the entire first editorial page of the April, 1985, *American Health*, precipitated another in the magazine's "Medical News" two months later.

## Your Editors

Even as you scan your daily life, concerns, hunches, recent interviews for smidgens of articles, don't neglect your editors as possible sources. Editors sometimes will give away an article they are too busy to handle, or simply think should be done. During a call to confirm expedition of a payment, the Editor of *The Runner's* "WarmUps," Linda Villarosa, asked me to review the just-released videos for runners. She said she just didn't have time to track them down and screen them. After many phone calls one long morning and part of another, I had workout tapes by Jim Fixx, Frank Shorter, and Bill Rodgers being messengered or mailed U.P.S., and a friend at RCA standing by to lend a corporate screening room to help me research the piece, later published as "Training: Hot Tracks."

Another time, a nonwriting editor assigned me something because she simply wanted a writer to do it. Once when newly appointed *Glamour* Features Editor, Wenda Marrone, had just K.O.'d all my prepared article suggestions and I eagerly asked, "For what articles do you need writers?", the editor related this incident. At a recent suburban gathering, the mother of an interracial child confided she couldn't advise her daughter which parent's race to choose as her own. From that perception emerged the published *Glamour* feature, "What's It Like To Be The Child of An Interracial Marriage."

Editors sometimes will take a chance on unknown writers and assign them features because time pressures permit them no other choice. One former New York A.P. editor, Cole Mobley, broke into a Manhattan hotel giveaway publication, *Broadway Bill of Fare,* in such an emergency. Mobley, who had sung in off-Broadway choruses, learned a fellow chorus line member had landed a minor part in the Broadway revival of *The King and I,* starring Yul Brynner. When Mobley phoned the profile idea to the editor of *Broadway Bill of Fare,* he discovered the magazine already had planned a feature on the show's leading lady. But the regular reviewer didn't like the production and had refused to do the assignment. So Mobley was asked to fill in. Remembering the commission, he compared his lucky break to that of an "offstage understudy who suddenly, when the star breaks his leg, hears someone say, 'You're on.' " His surprise pinch-hit performance won him not only his first cover story, but a column about goings-on on Manhattan's west side and more features.

Among the sources of article ideas mentioned so far, you'll notice there are no recommended texts to read, no lists of supplementary reading for reference. There is no source book to tell you the best materials for articles, because you are the best resource you own. You have within you the powers to recognize the ideas worth space in some magazine. Learn to trust your intuition to identify what unreported trends are just edging into public consciousness. An astute sense of timeliness can earn your query an editor's attention before staff obligations. Get used to transforming your experiences, pastimes, insights, or suggestions from interviews into queries, with confidence.

Free-lance writers should try to think up article ideas of interest to them and then search out the best markets for those interests. Don't first decide in what markets you would like to publish and then try to find ideas that fit those magazines. Such a method would hobble your success from the start. If you never seek within yourself and from immediate, secondhand sources the ideas that excite you, you'll never find your area of expertise that will insure your survival as a free-lance writer.

## Your Specialty

As you publish more articles, define your area of specialization. In-depth knowledge of one subject will enable you to free-lance repeatedly in that specialty for one or a number of magazines. When I started, I noticed that Gloria Steinem wrote about political personalities, Tom Wolfe specialized in sociological trends capsuled in famous pacesetters and events, and Jimmy Breslin concocted marvelous personal reportage that mirrored the thoughts of everyday people. These star journalists were known for their special type of articles and wrote on subjects in the area of their expertise in many places. In imitation, I have had different specializations at different times of my career.

In general outlines, the subject of my current specialty has always reflected my personal search for identity. In the late sixties, I broke into print writing about women artists—filmmakers, folksingers, writers. This period culminated in the twice-authorized interview for *The Paris Review* with Pulitzer poet Anne Sexton, who was the poet I wanted to be.

From profiles of creative women, I turned in the early seventies to chronicling the battle for a woman's right to self-definition on her own—not on the arm of a man. The keystone piece, "Raising My Fist for Feminism: I Discovered the Movement in Jail," was published in The Literary Guild's magazine, *Works In Progress.* It was an excerpt from an aborted book about my discovery of my right to a professional identity during researches for a profile of a radical feminist and her cadre.

In 1975, I ran out of funds for the book and returned to free-lance work with feminist-slanted profiles and interviews with outstanding women achievers for *People* and *Working Woman,* which listed my name on the masthead as a charter Contributing Editor. I wrote about women professionals who'd gained financial independence through their work because they were models for what I aspired to be.

In the late seventies, my magazine journalism began focusing on women runners. My kick-off piece, "Women: Going the Distance, Closing the Gap," appeared in the premiere issue of *The Runner* published in the *"Official Program: New York City Marathon,"* October, 1977. I was fascinated by amateur women athletes because they contradicted the personal image of the dependent woman I was brought up to be. In races, they were assertive, rather than passive, physically strong rather than weak, competitive rather than self-effacing. The self-reliant woman athlete was a logical extension of my redefining my identity through the women I profiled as creative artists, reported on in the social struggle for women's right to selfhood, and interviewed as successful financially independent professionals. Finally, my interest in the new feminist frontiers of the woman athlete, combined with my experiences as a competitive amateur, have led to a strong specialization in writing about new developments in the field of sports medicine and health.

An area of specialization helps insure your durability as a free-lance writer for these reasons. With expertise in a subject, you more quickly recognize valid ideas for assignments, while, at the same time, editors begin calling you to write articles in your special subject area. So, specialization assures you both a constant flow of query ideas and the chance to make a name as a writer.

# IV The One Interview/ Biographical Profile Form: How to Profile a Newsworthy Subject

Your introduction to basic forms of magazine articles starts with the short profile. The one interview/biographical profile is six hundred words about the life and work of a person of distinct and timely achievement. To meet the form's requirements, think of someone timely and noteworthy to whom you have access. If you don't know anyone, ask friends for help.

Don't turn to your neighborhood library. A library is your least effective source for casting this form of journalism. The subject of a library book may be dead, famous for an achievement of another era, or live beyond reach of your connections or affordable phone bill. So drop the well-known name in a library book for a lesser luminary, perhaps, living nearby, of unique timely achievement, whom you know you can interview.

The short profile form is first because it compels you to use the basic research tool for free-lance articles, the interview. This is the preferred research technique because it offers you the most propitious opportunity to secure fresh material that can guarantee an article's sale and publication.

To study the short profile form, read samples of one-interview profiles in weeklies like *People* and *US*. Sections like "Jock," "In Style," "On the Move," and "To the Top" are slots where free-lance writers gain entree and national exposure.

One of my students, newly graduated from Brown, was reluctant to buy a copy of *People*. He felt he was condescending to buy the magazine because the articles about things like a high-diving dog or pacifist-wrestling teacher were so banal. "That's the point," I explained. "You won't be interested in the content, so you'll be better able to see the form."

As a free-lance writer, you need to know not just the short profile, but several article forms to maintain constant assignments. If you come across a good idea, you can't be stymied from a sale because you lack familiarity with the form that it best fits. That's why I'm teaching you the basic magazine forms, to make your career as a free-lance writer easier than it was for me at the start of mine. In the beginning, I didn't care where I published as long as I got my ideas into print. When I got an assignment from a new magazine, I had to study its back issues to learn the form in which the editor expected me to write the assigned article. So I used to analyze similar pieces published to discover their construction and what questions readers of that magazine form wanted the writer to answer.

You should learn the short profile form often used by *People* and *US* because it requires you to obtain from your interview all the types of information a written profile of any length, form, or complexity should give. And even if you can't get honest replies to all your questions, or don't want to use all the material you're given, you should get accustomed to blitz interviewing to understand the distinctive way your profile subject emerged into the limelight and the personal way he or she sees the world. Overresearch gives you in-depth knowledge of your subject.

The following sections explain the kind of information that goes into the short profile, so you can use your interview time efficiently to secure the facts the form requires.

## THE "OPENER"

From the start, be on the lookout for your "opener." At some point, invite your subject to tell you precisely how his or her work is timely and unique. Is it because of a new direction in a professional field? An age group distinction? Pioneer technique? Excerpts from my published *People* profiles demonstrate possible methods to communicate to the reader your subject's timeliness and uniqueness. I use my works not as paragons of fine writing in the profile form, but as examples of free-lance articles bought by the largely staff-written publication. In researching an opener for a profile of the late Paula Hughes, the following statistics expressed her unusual stature on Wall Street.

> Howard may no longer be around, but a new Hughes is shaking up Wall Street—Paula Hughes, one time Avon lady who now manages investments worth more than $25 million for individuals and is an adviser for another $300 million in institutional funds. She handles more transactions for private investors than any of the other 1,400 brokers on the staff of the New York Stock Exchange's fifth largest member firm, Thomson & McKinnon Auchincloss, Kohlmeyer, Inc. The achievement makes Hughes the only woman among the top 10 brokers on the Street.

Bullets of fact support my opening claim about Hughes as "the only woman among the top 10 brokers on the Street." You can prove timeliness and uniqueness of your subject, as I did with Hughes, by statistics on the financial power of your subject. Or, if relevant, other accoutrements of success will suffice, like names of famous clients, prizes, books published, or simply gross company sales.

Often, you can explain your subject's distinction with a contrast of accepted myth and your subject's views. A paradox begins my *People* portrait of Barbara Pearlman, doyenne of exercise for clients like actress Dyan Cannon, Mrs. Robert Culp, and *Vogue* editor-in-chief, Grace Mirabella.

> It's not tote that barge or lift that bale, or anything that really works up a sweat. Barbara Pearlman of New York is an advocate of getting into shape with modest "exercises you can do anywhere"—at home, in the office, even on planes.

So, during the interview be on guard for statistics, accoutrements of success, or an arresting paradox as ways to tell your reader why your subject is relevant at the start of your opener.

Vivid quotes of endorsements by someone of stature in your subject's profession or an allied one can also serve. My lead profile on Naomi Sims, the former black fashion model who broke the color barrier on the cover of *The New York Times Magazine* and other national publications, began with this type of "back-up" quote, which described her uniqueness:

> "People couldn't take their eyes off her," recalls designer Halston of the svelte black model, with her exotic proportions, 5'10" height, perfect oval face and lizard grace. Adds model agency head Wilhelmina Cooper: "She could make any garment—even a sackcloth—look like sensational haute couture."

During your interview, solicit from your subject a name and phone number of a leader in his or her field, or a related one, who can put his or her achievement in perspective. Praise of your subject's work by a third party who is neither you nor your subject gives the writing an extra dimension. Also, the insight from a prestigious insider enhances the credibility of your article.

Endure any genuflecting humiliation to get a back-up quote for your opener. During research for a profile of T-shirt fashion designer Phyllis Keitlen, she suggested I try to obtain a quote from Frances Stein, *Vogue's* Fashion Director. In response to my telephone request, Stein's secretary instructed me to call back the following Tuesday between 12:20 and 12:25 p.m. When I phoned precisely at the appointment time I was able to extend my five-minute interview with enthusiastic responses like, "Oh, that's so interesting. Can you elaborate?" Or, "Can you explain what you mean?" A Keitlen friend and partisan, Ms. Stein allowed me triple her time limit, but I needed it. From her informed vantage, I gained a true appreciation of Keitlen's trend-setting influence in transforming the former costume of the street hood into high fashion by varying sleeve lengths, hems, colors, and design.

Once you've understood your subject's timely distinction and elicited a well-known professional's name for endorsement, you'll have to delve into the chronology of events and your subject's reactions to them that tell how he or she achieved distinction. In your opener, you will use these recent events to support the claims you make for your subject's importance. In the profile, "From Cover Girl To Cover Up: Naomi Sims Turns Wigs Into Millions," the opening paragraphs traced her development from high fashion model into millionaire wig manufacturer:

> The times were right for Naomi Sims. When she made her debut as an 18-year-old in 1967, it was the peak of the civil rights movement. The chant of "black is beauti-

ful" was in the air, and Naomi became the first woman of her race to arrive in the world of high fashion. "She was the great ambassador for all black people," Halston recalls. "She broke down all the social barriers."

Yet when she was only twenty-four, Naomi quit to go into business for herself, despite fees of up to $1,000 a day. "Modeling was never my ultimate goal," she explains. Her new career was the manufacture of wigs for black women, who account for 40 percent of the market. A risky, highly competitive profession? Yes, but last year the Naomi Sims Collection grossed $5 million, making her one of the nation's top black businesswomen.

So initially try to unravel the materials to tell the reader in any sequential order why your subject is timely and unusual, his or her road to that achievement, and an endorsement. Then turn to your subject's living style. Elicit facts about daily habits, work or travel schedules, office or apartment decor, fashion preference, food favorites, exercise choice, pastimes, marital status.

Millionaire wig manufacturer Naomi Sims gave me an excellent description of her life-style in an interview by phone. I never knew what the famous former fashion model looked like till I saw the photos accompanying the published text. The interview was conducted the morning after a New York City electrical blackout. My phone rang with a call from her representative just as my apartment lights lit, the fridge started and my air conditioner went on simultaneously. Her representative announced that rather than do the interview in Ms. Sims' air-conditioned limousine, she preferred the phone. I asked for a fifteen-minute reprieve to clear the melted ice from my fridge. And then the interview came. Here is a condensed version of Ms. Sims' answers about her living style, given in a darkened west side co-op, which still lacked electricity.

> At 28, Naomi enjoys all the perks of a millionaire female executive—chauffeured limousine, Tiffany jewelry, designer clothes, a Manhattan co-op, a Connecticut summer home with houseboy and cook. She also has an Ecuadorian nanny to look after 2½ year-old John Phillip, nicknamed, "Pip," the product of her four-year marriage to British-born art dealer Michael Findlay, 32.

If you can discover your subject's distinction, the recent events leading to it, quote an outstanding professional to confirm it, and your profile's current lifestyle, you'll have the right information for the 150-200-word lead for your *People*-styled profile. This research will give you the facts to satisfy the short profile's structural requirements of A-B-A-C (present, past, present, future) which is the standard formula construction for this profile form.

## THE BODY

Before I show you a whole opener from one profile to illustrate the entire formula lead, I'll list the type of research to secure for the body of your profile, explain a principle for its structure, and the format for typed manuscript for all submissions.

For the profile's body, research such data as your subject's birthplace, each parent's occupation, seminal influences, and experiences during school years that helped formulate his or her professional choice. Pry with further questions to decipher what motivated that person to achieve distinction in his or her field. Focus these questions on the early landmarks in the career, later setbacks or advances and the person's reactions to these turning points that led to the present success.

Try to cover all this biographical terrain. If you get revelations in only a few suggested lines of thought, be content. You only have to fill a maximum six hundred words.

After the interview, review your material and decide on a theme. Will you, in imitation of a profile of a former Olympic coach who is now a television sports commentator, explore your subject's drive and the tolls and rewards of trying to "be the best." Or, your subject may reveal what propelled a woman into a profession previously thought for men only, as did one published on a twenty-three-year-old champion woman bowler. Whatever your chosen theme, use it to select and organize the profile materials. Each fact or anecdote should illuminate some facet of your theme.

The unifying theme will help structure your profile. Once, *People* Senior Editor, Cranston Jones, said, "This is the only advice I can offer you:" he compared the profile's construction to a slalom course, where each paragraph turned on a quote or thought demonstrating its unifying theme. According to Jones' theory, the body of the profile should move from one emotionally telling fact or event to the next in a chronicle of the subject's childhood to the present. Each paragraph concludes on some formulative element that illuminates the subject's primary motivation for achievement. The slalom flag at the end propels the reader onto the succeeding paragraph, which builds to another curve and revelation on the unifying theme. With this approach, the reader skis the article's course, weaving around, at each paragraph's end, a flagged pole that signals another thematic point that progressively unveils the subject's driving force. This survey of formulative influences concludes with the subject's personal or professional goals for the future.

You may not realize this effect every time. Yet this structural concept may help you shape the interview into a form that cogently and logically explains your profile's professional evolution.

## MANUSCRIPT FORMAT

In typing final copy for your profile submissions, follow these directions for page heading, margins, and line space for a professional look. At the top left margin, type with appropriate capitalization, single spaced: the magazine's name. Next line, immediately under the first, put your last name and a slash followed by your assigning editor's last name. On the third line, place the working title of your profile; then, on the last below, the page number. Use this four-line heading, with changing page numbers, on each succeeding page, to identify your work.

Set your text margins at 19 and 54. The same is true for pica, elite, executive IBM or whatever typeface you use. These margins mirror the column width in magazines like *People* and *US*. They allow 36 characters across or an average six words per typed line. With triple spacing, you'll probably get twenty lines per page. If you multiply twenty lines at six words a piece, you will total roughly 120 words per page. Five pages of this regimented typing style gives you 600 words, or the maximum word count of a short biographical profile. This typing procedure allows you to keep track of the word count of accumulated pages for any assigned article as you write it on your typewriter.

## SAMPLE ONE INTERVIEW/BIOGRAPHICAL PROFILE

Now we'll move on to a sample of the short profile form. The following submitted manuscript appeared in *People*'s "In Style" under the title, "Phyllis Keitlen brings Moroccan chic to the T-shirt craze." The catalytic encounter that led to the Keitlen profile demonstrates a journalism truism: one story leads to another.

During research for a feature on Shirley Temple Black, then a U.S. Representative to the United Nations, for *The Saturday Evening Post,* I hitched home from a reception with the new Iranian U.N. diplomat, Fereydoun Hoveyda, critic for the influential *Cahiers du Cinema* and a renowned avante-garde novelist. Eventually, I became friends with this accomplished diplomat and his wife, Gisela. Despite their station, both were extremely unpretentious, so I could call and bike over in jeans and no make-up without apology to their home, the official Iranian residence, located on Fifth Avenue catercorner to the Metropolitan Museum. One day, I propped my Peugeot in the marbled, mirrored foyer and found Gisela in the dining room with a young companion. They were seated on one side of the long dining table (that easily sat twenty-four for diplomatic dinners), stuffing envelopes for a charity function.

In the couse of the morning, Gisela turned to me and said, "Why don't you write about Phyllis?"

So I politely turned toward the jeaned volunteer wearing a ponytail and asked, "What do you do?"

She said she designed and manufactured T-shirts. The badge of the local hood was just beginning to turn up in prominent Manhattan department stores like Bloomingdale's, Bendel's, and others.

"How much do you gross annually?" I expected to hear a figure in the hundreds of thousands.

"Two or three million," Phyllis Keitlen said. Then coolly added, "Next year, maybe five." Phyllis was thirty.

That's how a ride home during the research of one story led by an unlikely route to the subject of the following *People* profile. As you read it, watch for my statement about her timeliness and uniqueness, the formula opener detailing her rise in the ranks of fashion, the back-up quote, the unifying theme in the body of the profile, and the seminal areas of biographical fact. The written material derived from a nonstop five-hour interview.

### IN STYLE
### PHYLLIS KEITLEN: ROOM AT THE TOP
#### by Barbara Kevles

Nowadays, every designer makes a version of the traditional, cotton-knit t-shirt. The tomboy top, formerly the costume of the motorcyclist, suburbanite, or working girl, has been coopted. In part, that fashion theft has been abetted by Phyllis Keitlen, thirty year old President of the million dollar plus bonanza, Tric Trac, Ltd. In 1973, Keitlen discovered the "caftan t-shirt," which put Tric Trac on the map, in a Moroccan "souk" (market place). "I was warned I couldn't do business as a woman in the Arab world, but the challenge made me more determined." She contracted a local Moroccan manufacturer to mass produce t-shirts exclusively for her and within a month of her return to the States had $100,000 worth of orders from American stores.

Today, Tric Trac's consistently attractive t-shirts are often featured simultaneously in the boutique pages of *Glamour, Harper's Bazaar, The New York Times,* and *Women's Wear Daily. Vogue's* Fashion Director, Francis Stein, credits Keitlen as "one of the first to take the conventional t-shirt and, by projecting, hiking or shaving its sleeves, neck or hemline, create infinite variations. And from there, extend it into a dress, a bikini, a jumpsuit. Other people have done that, but Phyllis was among the first to conceive a successful business around an entire collection made of t-shirts."

By chance, Keitlen launched her inexpensive tops when a recession economy made their practical comfort most appealing. But that timing has been a part of her all her life. The daughter of a Massachusetts obstetrician, Keitlen dropped out of college and went abroad just as London with the Beatles and mod hemlines became the jetsetter's mecca. "Europe gave me my first taste of fashion."

When her mother, temporarily blinded by corneal dystrophy, called her home to demonstrate her restored sight, Keitlen utilized her mother's "never-give-up" perseverance to badger a job interview at New York's famed mod fashion center, Paraphernalia. "It was natural for me to apply for a job there because I knew mod clothes, I understood them, and I had worn them." The owner offered her $115 a week, but she wanted more "or I can't live," she told him. After bulldozing her way into the company, Keitlen phoned a friend at *Harper's Bazaar* to ask advice on how to organize her first fashion show as Paraphernalia's new Publicity Director.

From there, Keitlen continued her on-the-job training as professional publicist for several Coty award designers until, a few free-lance assignments later, she took a glamorous position with the New York-based Consul General of Morocco "to rest and reevaluate my life. Aggressive women aren't happy working for others." Keitlen confessed, "I know I wanted to set up my own business, but publicity was such a pushy field, I didn't feel that was the real me." In the midst of this identity crisis, Keitlen got her lucky break. A girlfriend visited with Moroccan caftans which Keitlen envisioned as "great for beachwear." She immediately bought a ticket for Casablanca, but before leaving New York, shrewdly established a company with her attorney "on the chance something might work." Though she easily found the manufacturer of the "caftan t-shirt," she had to harangue him for hours until he would agree to give her a chance and do business with an American. Asked whether she used her womanly charms to gain the accord, she replied, "I used my normal charms, but no man even got too close."

However, the energy and time necessary to start a new business absorbed her private life. "I was too tired to be social my first year." Now Keitlen claims a better "balance." When designing a collection in Morocco, she water skis during long summer lunches or frequents the hamman, the primitive Arab bath for a full-scale scrubbing and the special "rassoul"—a mud shampoo. In New York, she drives herself to sell and distribute her Moroccan manufactured tops, but "no matter how busy, I can always take time for a phone call from a man. It's just as important as the office."

If, in her twenties, she longed to lead the leisurely, carefree life of a rich man's wife, like Christina Ford, now Keitlen prides herself, "I can work long hours, return to my apartment, bathe and dress looking like a woman who's been relaxing at home all day. I'm a business woman," she admits, "but I'm still a romantic."

## Analysis

I will analyze this sample of the one interview/biographical profile form to point out examples of the form's demands.

The beginning lines explain Keitlen's relevancy to contemporary fashion. The piece opens by citing a current social trend: fashion designers are coopting the badge of the working class. Then the piece names Keitlen—identifying her by age, name of her company, its annual gross—as a leader of this trend.

To document this achievement, the piece shifts from Keitlen's present success to the past—the source of her business, the resistance to her enterprise, the first big order. The opening concludes with a positioning back-up quote by *Vogue* Fashion Director, Frances Stein. Without counting widows (half-lines), the whole beginning which follows the formula A (present), B (past), A (present) takes 45 lines in typed manuscript format.

The piece introduces the theme of Keitlen's incredible aggressivity with a quote about her reaction to Arab hostility to a businesswoman. Each new anecdote forces the story forward and, at the same time, accentuates another pivotal "slalom flag" in the profile's development. Keitlen's drive gives her "chutzpah" to talk her way into a boutique job with no experience, makes her ambivalent about working for others, precipitates her identity crisis and finally propels her through Arab red tape and macho hostility to establish her business.

The body of the profile answers questions about formulative childhood, educational, and professional influences, work entree, and the circumstances that pushed Keitlen into business for herself.

The profile ends with Keitlen's current life-style—business trips, pastimes, social life, and romantic view of her ambitions and men.

## CRITIQUES OF STUDENT ONE INTERVIEW/ BIOGRAPHICAL PROFILES

How do my writing students fare with their first assignment? A few beginners submit profiles that, for the most part, successfully execute the profile form, but most don't succeed at all. The most common faults are excessive praise that smacks of public relations promos or the inopportune choice of professionals at the start or decline of their careers.

The student work displayed is mostly first drafts written a few weeks into the course as the first assignment. In their defense, I point out these beginning magazine writers not only are developing proficient reporting skills, but are getting used to writing to requirements of an article form. Because of their inexperience as journalists and pressures of short class deadlines, I'll confine my criticism to a common beginner flaw in their work. They all have winning, timely "openers" but they omit totally, or scantily state, facts about childhood, education, and early formulative influences. You'll understand the damaging effects of these omissions with examples.

For instance, in "Woman Traveler," by Esther Paige, the relevant biography is completely missing.

### WOMAN TRAVELER

As the publisher of *Hotel & Travel Index*, Melinda Bush stands out within the travel industry. She has spent 20 years in the publishing and advertising business.

"It's like being a part of a cult," she says, "traveling to Bangkok, Manila, Sydney, Mexico or Rio."

She is blond and blue eyed, appearing about forty (she wouldn't give her age). Her well tailored clothes accent her thin frame.

Leaning over slightly and tilting her head, she says, "You must be willing to be on the go all the time—living in hotels and out of suitcases." Mrs. Bush has worked at *Hotel & Travel Index* for five years attaining a leadership position. She is quick to point out, "I could never have done it on my own."

She is one of the few women publishers in the travel industry and the first at Ziff-Davis Publishing Company. There are approximately 60 employees at Ziff-Davis, 12 companies in various countries, and five here in the United States.

Mrs. Bush's background involves nearly twenty years of marketing and advertising experience in the leisure products fields. She had devoted several years to targeting consumer and business issues in the travel and hotel industries.

"It's like being in the foreign service," she says, "totally dedicated to moving around the world." Named the "1980 Woman of the Year in Travel" by D.A.T.O.

(Discover America Travel Organizations), she is an active member and fellow of the Institute of Certified Travel Agents (ICTA), the prestigious travel agent educational organization; a member of the American Management Association (AMA), the highly regarded aviation industry's *Wings Club,* and the *Advertising Women of New York.*

A frequent speaker and panelist at Industry associations and conventions, she serves on the Marketing and International Travel Committees of the American Hotel & Motel Association (AH&MA), directs the Travel Industry Committee of the Hotel Sales Management Association International (HSMA), and chairs the Cornell University/Hotel & Travel Index work studies program in hotel sales and marketing. Through interviews in the print and broadcasting media, Mrs. Bush has become a spokeswoman on sound travel advice for business, meeting and pleasure travel, as well as the changing consumer trends and lifestyles that affect the hotel and travel industries.

"The pleasures of seeing the world far outweigh having a family," she says. "I would much rather be on a plane, heading for a city conference, than taking a delicious meal out of the oven while the family is watching TV or sitting around the fireplace."

A graduate of the University of Colorado, Mrs. Bush is listed in "Who's Who in American Women."

Her eyes brighten but she nods her head in disbelief, never thinking the day would come when she would say to another staff member, "No, you take the trip to Hawaii."

Ms. Paige chose a ripe profile subject: Melinda Bush, one of the few woman publishers of an important travel guidebook, who just won an award. Bush's vivid quotes capture the dedication that gained her the recognition—"It's like being in the foreign service . . . totally dedicated to moving around the world," or "You must be willing to be on the go all the time—living in hotels and out of suitcases." Yet after Bush's impressive credentials, timely prize, and expressions of commitment, the piece disintegrates into a "Who's Who" resume of her club memberships, lecture specialties, and professional committees. A rehash of Bush's resume leaves the reader wondering what early experiences formed her insatiable desire for travel and financial independence over traditional female expectations of home, children, and economic dependency. By leaving out illuminations of Bush's biography, the profile appears like the happy face on travel brochures with whom none of us can identify.

Jerri Senior's profile of A.T. & T. district manager, Mary Bennett, exhibits a near-perfect example of the profile opener—A (present achievement), B (the road to it), A (present accolade), but then fails to reveal its subject's past.

Mary Bennett of Piscataway, N.J. has been climbing the corporate ladder at American Telephone and Telegraph Company (AT&T). Shortly after her husband died, Ms. Bennett joined AT&T as a general clerk. Eleven years and eight promotions later she is a district manager and winner of Bell System's 1980 national Black Achievers in Industry Award. She says, "It's a hectic life. But if you are self directed and have lots of stamina, the rewards are there and you can get them."

It took excessive drive for Ms. Bennett to successfully manage a fast track career and single parenthood simultaneously. She says, "When Floyd died I was determined not to let our dreams die with him. I had no alternative, I had to go for the money." Ms. Bennett knew she could not be successful on an 8-5 schedule. However, to do more required the cooperation and support of her children. She decided to make the family a company. Each child became a major stockholder and she became their living investment portfolio. The dividends have started to come in. Ms. Bennett has purchased homes for two of her three children and expects to be able to buy a third in the near future.

Fast promotional tracks are not carefully laid out for aspiring corporate moguls. They depend on individual initiative. Mary says, "I looked to see where I wanted to go and then focused on getting there with my whole being. As soon as I received one promotion I began programming for the next." Fast moving executives are said to thrive on challenges. However, many make concessions that often lead to emotional deficits. Reflecting Ms. Bennett says, "There were times when I thought of remarrying. But, I couldn't find anyone to buy my program. I'm on the road 35 percent of the time and the other 65 percent I'm steeped in conferences and reports. At the end of a day I need that input that says all's right with the world."

Mary travels from state to state with a team of staff specialists. They advise managers of AT&T's operating companies who wish to develop new policies and to institute cost saving work procedures. Although Ms. Bennett has a college education she does not have a college degree. She says, "As a continuing education student I took whatever courses were needed to get my next promotion." Fast tracking requires ability and commitment. Ms. Bennett says, "I developed a reputation of being able to deliver on time and in good fashion. This attracted mentors, but it cost me time that could have been spent with my children. I gave them lots of love but I'm not sure I gave them enough of me." Mary must have given them more than she thinks. Her two oldest children have joined her at AT&T and are working on fast tracks of their own.

Through the international World Vision Agency, Mary Bennett has adopted eleven-year-old Fantiu. Next year they will meet for the first time when Mary vacations in Kenya. About her future at AT&T she says, "The gatekeepers don't make it easy for you but women who are successful don't retreat. Before I retire, I will become the first black woman to head a division at AT&T." Based on her record, I think she is going to make it.

Ms. Senior starts with a paradox—a lady from New Jersey climbing a major corporation's ladder, then the fast track from clerk to district manager, timely Bell award, and Bennett's reaction to her success. The writing is succinct. Then the profile retells the corporate climb again and again from the perspective of her family tragedy, personal sacrifices, relevant education obtained en route, and her future. The reader never learns what in Bennett's girlhood or marriage strengthened her resolve—"When Floyd died . . . not to let our dreams die with him." The writer could have spotlighted the wellsprings of Bennett's drive for a better profile.

Eugene Draper's conversationally written profile of leather designer Carlos Falchi touches on his past, but not in enough detail. Like the last work, this starts with a paradox and then replays the rags to riches theme with more facts. The early anecdote is just another variation on that theme.

## STREET VENDOR TO HAUTE COUTURE

In 1970 Carlos Falchi, a long, shaggy-haired, non-English speaking Brasilien living in Manhattan, borrowed $100 from a cousin and bought some snake and lizard skins. He took them back to his apartment on the lower East side, "Behind the Merit gas station on Houston Street," he describes it. Heeding the natural tendencies of the textures and colors of the skins to blend in a unique design, he put together a few wallets and belts. The next day he took them to Washington Square Park and sold them. He made just enough money to pay his rent and his cousin.

Today Carlos Falchi lives in two floors of the old Tiffany building on Central Park South. He has 13,000 sq. ft. of loft space on West 23rd Street where 25 employees produce his handbags, portfolios, address books and other high fashion specialty items. The factory supplies stores like Bendel's, Bergdorf Goodman's, Bonwit Teller, and Brown's of London. Prices for the handbags start at $350 in these and other stores from Los Angeles to Tokyo. Ali McGraw chose a Falchi bag to use in the film *Convoy* with Kris Kristofferson. Mick Jagger, Miles Davis and others have worn Falchi capes and belts in their performances.

Falchi credits his wife Mary for pointing him in the fashion business. "She bought a belt one day that she didn't like. We got some snake skins and I made one that she loved. Then I started selling them on the street and to friends." Falchi was then working for a film company splicing film. His boss owned a boutique and asked him to supply him with some belts. The belts sold well and he did some silk kaftans with money his boss put up for materials. The kaftans caught the eye of Airto Moreira, who was the percussionist for Miles Davis, and Falchi was asked by Davis to design his wardrobe. "Miles Davis was a unique experience," says Falchi. "We became friends and I learned a lot from him." He left his film splicing job and started working for Bow-Wow Productions who had the lease on New York's Beacon Theatre. While there he designed costumes for top rock and roll performers. "I was working with my idols," he says, "I lived some very important moments."

When Bow-Wow folded Falchi dropped off six address books he had done for the accessories buyer at Bendel's. He was telephoned that afternoon with an order for a dozen more. Before long Bendel's was carrying a complete line of handbags and high fashion accessories. Other stores began ordering from him and he rented loft space and bought a few old Singer sewing machines to keep up with the demand. "The factory became my home. I was there from 8 A.M. to midnight. Many nights I just slept there." If his wife urged him to spend more time at home, Falchi says, "I would move in a sewing machine and a cutter. I was always experimenting. My home became a factory."

Currently, Falchi is starting to do home furnishings; tables, spreads, wall hangings, and collages with reptile skins. Two years ago a trip to Japan started a long-term export program with Isetan, one of Japan's largest and best-known retail chains. He also met Hanae Mori, the Japanese designer, and has recently designed three boa constrictor jackets for her Spring haute couture show in Tokyo.

Falchi began designing when he was 16 by doing postage stamps for the Government Post Office in Rio de Janeiro. He created many of the country's new stamps and was instrumental in getting a post office museum established in Brazil. He came to New York in his early twenties without friends, money, or knowledge of the English language. Looking back, Falchi says, "I always knew I would do something special."

With annual sales contracts approaching $1 million, and new contracts coming all the time (he has just agreed to do catalog items for many of the stores he supplies) Falchi is becoming interested in teaching design. He is involved in plans of the Pocketbook Workers Association to open a school and is interested in teaching a course of design at New York's Fashion Institute. He has traveled to Atlanta and Dallas to lecture on design in colleges in those cities.

"I want to get closer to the art," he says. "I am very excited about the murals I am doing." The next thing he has in mind are canvases. "I've never worked in synthetics," he says, "I'd like to try oils."

When beginner writers are too reluctant to ask personal biographical details, the resulting profiles become portraits of figures of inevitable success. Or, in Falchi's case, without money, friends, or the country's language, talent will out.

I understand the beginner's desire to keep a subject's imperfections out of print. In early profiles, like one on Joan Kennedy and later Eunice Kennedy Shriver, I exhibited, as one friend said, a penchant for leaving my best quotes "on the cutting-room floor." Because of a middle class upbringing, I had learned not to disparage others in public. My profile subjects were willing to expose weaknesses, but I had trouble incorporating them in my final copy. I was too protective of my subjects. I wanted them to look good. Once, when I showed a version of my profile of Emmy-winning television producer Arthur Barron to a friend, Barbara Connell, who'd worked for him, she urged me to revise, saying, "But it's his weaknesses that make him human, and it's his humanity that makes him lovable." Rewritten with the title, "A Documentary of Birth and Death," the piece appeared in *New York Magazine*. If some of my best students do not include the raw edges of their subjects' past that show what made them, neither did I. Eventually I learned to put back the scraps from the cutting-room floor because I came to value truthful reporting more than my subject's approval.

## ADVICE FOR THE PROFILE FORM

In summary, the following suggestions may help you avoid the pitfalls of the one interview/biographical profile form:

**1.** Choose a subject who's professionally established so you won't resort to inflated writing.

**2.** Go as a professional journalist to the interview to find the best answers to the topics the form demands rather than as a person who wants to be liked.

**3.** Probe for personal biographical facts to understand what drives your subject. Don't accept your subject's view of himself without digging.

**4.** Remember the structural requirements of the short profile as you organize and write up your material—an opener about the person's timely uniqueness, how achieved, endorsement by a prominent industry member, your subject's life-style; followed by a logically structured, revealing chronology of early life to future hopes.

# V How to Find the Right Magazine Markets for Your Article Ideas & How to Negotiate an Assignment

A preceding chapter urged you to explore your personal and immediate resources for fresh saleable article ideas. The last gave directions for the research and construction of the short profile form, so you can turn access to a newsworthy person into a by-lined article. This chapter helps you find receptive publications for your article ideas and explains how to negotiate an assignment. The next chapter will teach you a form to report a new consumer product or service.

## HOW TO LOCATE YOUR MARKETS

You'll discover the appropriate national or local publication to query by answering these simple questions: "Who's it for?", "Who needs it?", "What's it about?"

### "Who's It For?"
Your query will stand a chance for editorial consideration if you forward it to a national publication whose average reader would be interested in your topic. The national women's magazines and men's magazines divvy up their targeted audience by sex, age, education, income, and marital status. Send a query of concern to young women to *Seventeen*. If of interest to the college girl or someone her age in the work force, try *Mademoiselle*. To *Glamour*, for the college graduate entering the work world or just beyond entry level; to *Cosmopolitan*, for the single working girl without a college education in the upper twenties to low thirties. If pertinent to the well-educated, high-salaried executive woman, to *Savvy* or *Working Woman*. For an older, more sophisticated woman with ample disposable income, mail it to *Harper's Bazaar* or *Vogue*. Or should you try editors at *Family Circle, Woman's Day,* or *Good Housekeeping*, which cater to practical-minded gingham-curtain homemakers? Or *Redbook*, which appeals to the young married woman, or *McCall's*, geared for women in suburbia? If you define your article's potential female reader by age, interests, and career—or home-orientation, you'll match your query with the right magazine.

Use the same marketing strategy with men's magazines. Identify the readership your query fits. Newer entrants like *GQ* and its offspring, *M* and *MGF*, begun as fashion guides for men, are broadening their editorial content to satisfy the interests of the age groups they serve. *MGF* gives advice on fashion and personals to young men eighteen to twenty-nine in a first or second job who, with $30,000 or less a year, are experimenting with their clothes and life-style. *GQ's* $40,000 a year single, thirty-year-old has time and inclination to pursue books, films, women, and personal financial management. *M's* for older wealthier readers. *Esquire,* which yuppies to executives with receding hairlines read, has always reflected the "with it" educated male with inherited or acquired class. *Penthouse* and *Playboy* attract, I've always thought, part of the thirties-plus group who are making it without a sheepskin. Decide which male magazine reader by his age, income, education, and preoccupations would be most receptive to your query. Then forward it to his publication.

Queries to national magazines whose mastheads are jammed with names of staff writers or contributing editors get the greatest consideration when there is a change in top editors. Free-lance queries are more welcome during a changeover, because a new editor likely wants to cultivate a new brood of writers whose loyalties are not linked to his or her predecessor or the publication's old image.

Yet even at the best-matched publication, don't expect an easy sale. At the "nationals," you, as a free-lance writer, compete for limited editorial space not only with salaried members of the editorial staff, but with free-lance writers like you all over the country. All you may gain from drafting a well-written query for a national publication may be a bruised ego, a form rejection, and wasted time. As a beginner, the odds for publication improve if you try local outlets. At neighborhood, city, and regional publications, you have less competition for more editorial space resulting from greater frequency of publication.

## "Who Needs It?"

You'll track down the likeliest local outlet if you figure out what readership area needs to know the information in your proposed article. Research your options for print in the hometown of your profile subject, the community your issue concerns, or the neighborhood of the reported service. One student, Wesley Davidson, sold her class profile of Jennings Michael Burch, author of the novel, *They Cage the Animals at Night,* chosen as two book club alternates, to a local magazine, *Westchester Spotlight,* which covers Chappaqua where Burch lives. Another student placed a thoroughly researched article on the astronomical garage costs for west side car owners in the Manhattan paper that serves these residents, *The Westsider.* Still another, Marc Schultz, wrote for class a survey of Japanese stores in Fort Lee, New Jersey, which got all of page two—minus ads—of the local Jersey county paper, *The Palisadian.* For a topic with a strong local tie-in, don't hesitate to query your area paper or magazine. Local outlets pay much less than national magazines, but the achievement of your name in print and a first publication credit may be worth the modest fee.

## "What's It About?"

If you can't match your query by the average reader's profile with a suitable national publication or by a geographical hook with a local outlet, you have another range of options available, embodied in the question, "What's it about?" If you don't choose to query a publication on the basis of its national or local readership interest, the subject you want to write about may suggest other choices.

You have the best chance for acceptance of your query because of its subject at the newer magazines, because the vast majority starting up are subject-oriented. These days, the newest magazines often cater to some special interest, like *Circus,* for young rock music fans; *Ultrasport,* for endurance sport enthusiasts; or *Manhattan Inc.,* for Manhattan businessmen. You can get a "foot in the door" more quickly by querying new magazines, because their editors have not yet developed a stable of writers. But before you submit ideas to new publications discovered in the magazine racks, try to buy, borrow, or check out issues from the library to verify the contents of the actual editorial pages, target audience, and tone. If the publication is based outside a large metropolis, scrutinize the dates of issues to make sure there are no skips. A missed publication date suggests incompetent management by the magazine's publisher, a disorganized accounting system, or just not enough money in the magazine's bank account. Whether the fault is with management, accounting procedures, or insufficient funding, the result could mean long delays in payments to writers. Avoid start-up publications where amateur fiscal practices could cause you more aggravation and loss of time than the publication credit's value.

What you seek at a magazine focused on your journalistic interest is an editor who thinks like you, to whom you can give other queries for a steady stream of assignments. Rarely at first though do you luck into an editor consistently excited about the same article ideas as you, so persist. You are more likely to find that likeminded empathetic editor if you try to place your queries by their subject with the specialty publications than by any other means.

Some say you get your "lucky break" by "knowing someone," but I have gained entree to publications more on the merit of my ideas than by "connections." For instance, I developed a contact to *American Health,* which has given me the opportunity to specialize in articles on sports medicine, by chance during a run in Central Park. At that time, I had written on controversies in the fitness movement for official race programs, city sports publications, and regional running magazines. These pieces had led to one-time commissions for *The Village Voice, The New York Times, Esquire,* and *Harper's Bazaar.* But nothing like steady assignments from a receptive editor who thinks the proposed article ideas are just as important to publish for the public as I do. A group of runners I joined one weekend contained the head of the accounting firm that was handling *American Health.* He told me about the magazine and whom to contact. Once I met with the editors, I began to funnel more of my ideas on new developments in sports medicine to the section editor of "The Fitness Report." Eventually, because of the frequency of my publications in the magazine, I earned the masthead credit, Contributing Editor. Then I branched out briefly to a new publication devoted to reporting the latest in sports medicine for the amateur interested in high performance, *Superfit;* and sports specialty magazines like *The Runner.* Once you've defined your specialty, you can narrow in on the publications based on it, allied to it, or that designate it a regular section of the magazine.

In summary, your query's appeal to the typical reader of a national magazine, local paper, specialized magazine, or a special section of a magazine may direct you to the right editorial market.

# HOW TO NEGOTIATE AN ASSIGNMENT

*"What Is A Commission?"* If an editor likes a query enough to request you write the proposed article, take a moment to feel lucky, pleased, and proud. Then, assume the role of a tough negotiator. Once, a former student found a message from a *Cosmopolitan* editor on her phone machine. Before she returned the call, she got out her notes on my lecture, "How to negotiate an assignment." With the notebook open before her, she asked for terms during that editorial conference with words she'd never before spoken. She felt the number of negotiating points she covered made her appear more professional. She didn't win them all, but she raised the possibility she might gain more the next negotiation because she named them at the first one.

*Fee.* An editor may want a beginner to do an article "on speculation" without promise of a kill fee should the piece be rejected. *Kill fees* range from half the acceptance fee to as little as one-fifth. But why should you invest time, reputation, and ego in an article's research and writing unless a magazine will take some financial risk with promise of a kill fee and a commission. Even a beginner deserves some financial compensation for invested effort. A commission means you and the editor agree to a fee based on the amount and duration of the research, length of the assigned article, and any other considerations, like an exclusive interview. To determine a reasonable fee, ask, "What's the scale for this type of article?" Then quickly estimate the time necessary to complete it and voice your price.

*Fee Schedule.* Fees are paid upon the article's acceptance, publication, or after the issue appears. If you know in advance when the magazine's check should arrive, you can notify the magazine's business office of any delay.

*Rights.* In return for the magazine's promised payment, sell only First North American serial rights to the assigning editor. By stipulating the sale of only these one-time rights to publish your article in North America, you reserve chance profits from purchase of the piece by a foreign periodical, movie or television sale, or book rights for yourself. If your piece is unacceptable and still unpublishable after revision, and you receive a kill fee, the publication rights you agreed to sell revert back to you.

Some magazines require the writer to sign "work for hire" agreements. Under such agreements, all rights are reserved by the purchasing publication. If you can't extricate yourself from this requirement, you might acquiesce for the money, the exposure, or the chance to have "your say."

*Expenses.* You and the editor should agree, in the preliminary negotiation, on the limit of your expense monies. Also, you should find out if the publication will reimburse you for all the types of expenses required by your research. Such expenses may be long distance calls, meals, travel, lodgings, entrance fees. Sometimes, if a publication won't compensate for certain necessary research outlays, you have to seek a commission elsewhere.

*Expense Schedule.* Will the magazine give you an advance for your expenses separate from your fee later, pay upon receipt of restaurant checks and other vouchers, or pay expenses upon submission of the article, or what? You should ask this and be certain you understand the payment procedure and the duration of time till reimbursement will reach you after editorial authorization.

*Deadline.* Agree to one you know you can make. If you have other commitments and must delay work on the assigned article, tell the editor. If you promise a due date you can make and deliver on time, you will build the editor's confidence in you as a reliable writer "who delivers." Don't agree to unrealistic deadlines.

*Word Length.* Don't assume you know the word length; ask the editor, "How long should the article be?" Stay within your assigned word count. You can be off fifty words more or less, but not much more. If you exceed an assigned word limit, you may pay an unexpected price. Once, I was assigned a 150-word *American Health* "Fitness Report" article, but I turned in 750 words. And not even interviews with name runners like Grete Waitz and Craig Virgin in the piece could prevent my assigning editor from rejecting it. So learn from my mistakes. Needless to say, I have not deviated from assigned word length for *American Health* articles since.

*Theme.* During negotiations, you and the editor should verify the slant of the commissioned article. Sometimes, writers promise articles they cannot deliver because the editor never expressed the assigned approach to the material, nor did the writer venture to clarify it. Avoid such self-sabotage and elicit from the editor confirmation of the approach in your query or amendment of it in ways suitable for that publication. During the long era Mary Cantwell was Senior Editor—Features at *Mademoiselle*, she wrote me a letter that detailed the points to cover in the assigned article on women's sports injuries. When I received the letter, I called her. I explained I didn't think I could get an accurate answer to one specified point. I didn't presume I could find out whether blacks were more fleet-footed and Chinese better gymnasts. I knew of no evidence certifying race as an attributable advantage in sports performance. The *Mademoiselle* editor was flexible. She asked me to get what I could on the subject. In writing the assignment, I gave minimal space to the question of race as an advantage in sports performance, but I felt comfortable doing so because I had cleared my approach with the editor before I started to work on the article.

*Letter of Agreement.* Once you and the editor have agreed on matters of fee, kill fee, fee schedule, rights, expenses, expense schedule, deadline, word length, and theme, ask for a letter of agreement stating all points negotiated. Often editors don't want to take the time to write it, so offer to do it yourself. If you record in a letter your understanding of the negotiated agreement, you will avoid misunderstandings later. Keep a copy of the forwarded agreement letter for your records.

# VI The Service Article Form: How to Report a New Consumer Product or Service

The next basic type of article form you're going to learn is the service article. The 800-1000 word service article reports a new consumer product or service. Mainstream women's magazines like *Redbook, Ladies' Home Journal,* and *Savvy,* as well as men's publications like *Esquire,* have published service articles on a range of subjects from tips to taxpayers to the latest data copier machines, to variations of the new shoulder bag for men. Dailies and Sunday supplements use this adaptable form to survey shopping malls, health clubs, recipes, cosmetics, wines, nursery schools. It's easy to think up saleable service ideas. You've only to walk around your neighborhood or area of work to bump into some new service or product worth writing about for some local, citywide, or national publication.

Service articles are fun to do and very instructive. They teach you—as no other magazine form does—to take notes on concrete detail and to marshall just the facts in your limited word space. And if you learn to report and write more factually from efforts to master this article form, your writing will improve.

If you know in advance the type of information readers of the service form expect, you'll better tune your research to get the facts required for a lively write-up on the latest product model or recently opened service establishment available to anyone with sufficient funds to pay for it.

## INTRODUCTION: THE FOCUS

Introductions to service articles give readers a reason to delve into the article. The reason unually identifies a reader problem which the article's new service or trendy merchandise will solve. For example, the problem may be physical, financial, or personal.

Jane Goldman's *New York* article, "Ay, There's the Rub," published in the February 25, 1985, issue, argues strongly for the reader's attention with a very convincing reason at the start. The writer zeroes in on a common physical complaint and its new trendy treatment:

> How's your lower back—kind of strained and aching? Shoulders hunched? Neck tight and stiff? Think how it would feel to have those muscles kneaded, stroked, and coaxed into letting go, your tensions dissolving, your poor, cramped body surrendering in bliss. That's the promise of a professional massage. Don't snicker—I'm talking about *legitimate* massage, a modern version of the old laying on of hands. Proponents say it not only relaxes, but increases circulation, improves muscle tone, and helps heal old injuries and prevent new ones.

In the lead to a survey of the services of Manhattan masseurs, the writer inquires about the health of the reader's back and promises a sensuously described solution for relief of any spinal aches and strains. If your introduction can pinpoint the reader's problem the reported service is designed to treat, your reader will be immediately riveted.

One of my students, Andrea Messina, Research Editor for *House Beautiful,* launched her service piece, "Snip, Snip, Snip, Snip, Snip, Snip, Snip," printed in the Manhattan newspaper, *Chelsea Clinton News,* with another type of reader appeal.

> A haircut in Manhattan can be a real clip job. A wash-cut-and-blow-dry hovers around $25-$35, though it can run upwards of $50, excluding tax and tips. But there are some top-of-the-line salons that offer high-quality cuts for about the price of a decent comb.
>
> What's the catch? These are training sessions for salon assistants or regular hairdressers who want to perfect their technique or learn newer styles. They are advised by staff instructors at all times so the cuts take longer than regular ones, from 1½ to 3 hours. You must also be ready for a style change, not just a trim. Given all that, the popularity of the "model nights," as some salons call the sessions, indicates a true bargain.
>
> Here's a look at a few of the better-known salons that offer cut-rate cuts. Except where noted, a wash-cut-and-blow-dry is $5; tipping is left to the model's discretion.

This introduces a money-saving service for budget-minded readers in need of less exorbitantly priced haircuts. The reason for the service article is always justified in the introduction by the purpose of the new goods or service for the consumer.

Service article openings canvass for reader's time by focusing on new solutions to old problems, new answers to shared needs, or new goods for ordinary predicaments. A July, 1980, *Esquire* service piece, "Carried Away," begins:

> GOT YOUR HANDS FULL WITH THE PARAPHERNALIA OF DAILY LIVING? There's an easy solution that you can strap on your back or sling over your shoulder. From medieval hunting sacks to the postman's pouch, the shoulder bag is one of the oldest accessories. Now it's done up in napa leather, parachute cloth, or canvas.

The article introduces the over-burdened *Esquire* "Man Around Town," gym enthusiast, jet-setter and "Urban Trekker" to a new fashion device—the male shoulder bag—to solve his dilemma.

Again, the service article opening wins readers by highlighting a reason the new product or service will solve a predicament or fill a need for the potential purchaser.

# THE BODY: RESEARCH REQUIREMENTS

The body of the service article defines the product or experience of the service and evaluates it. This section of the article demands a lot of preplanning on the part of the reporter "to get it all." Also, preplanning your research will protect you against losing control of an interview when a store proprietor or product manager spins off in some self-promotion jive, and from losing your purpose under bombarding stimuli in a crowded new restaurant or a busy department store.

To avoid repeating interviews or site visits, list your questions before you begin the article's research. Think up the questions a reader wants answered, write them down, organize them in some logical order, and then call for appointments. One of my students hadn't thought through the reader's needs for a piece on a new West Side branch of a downtown lighting store and had to return four times to "have it all." So thoroughly prepare your research questions to make your location trip your first and only.

Whether the featured service is a new restaurant or survey of roller skating discos, the research should try to answer certain questions generic to all service pieces. For instance, who are the clients? If they aren't famous, you can etch their social status by clothes, gestures, phrases, or other revealing traits. I had an easy time filling in this answer for a February, 1984, piece on the West Side supermarket, Fairway, for *Good Housekeeping's* "New York Metro" section. Many regulars who come to Fairway for the freshest produce in town at discount prices are famous. So I just listed their names:

> Theatre stars Eli Wallach and his wife Anne Jackson, Celeste Holm, Ralph Bellamy, Tony Randall, Mariel Hemingway, Angela Lansbury, . . . number among Fairway's aficionados . . . Elliott Gould's aunt led him there by the hand. . . .

Besides telling the reader who uses the service, obtain such gauges as the behavior (knowledge, promptness, courtesy) of attendants (clerks, waiters, shopkeepers), prices, typical offerings (menu, model variations), specialties (attachments, specialty dishes). Get the establishment's or product's history to illuminate its uniqueness, such as the chef's past employments to shed light on his food style. Help the reader determine whether or not he or she wants it by delineating its uses. A *Family Circle* article on California wines mentioned menus to complement these table spirits.

Describe the product or service in detail to help the reader decide whether it fits his or her tastes. In the case of service establishments, give the colors, spatial arrangement, type of decor, furniture, lighting. In the case of a product, relate materials, feel, size, appearance; these questions apply to a wound-up toy as well as to a food dish. Ask what's relevant to your article research. If your piece heralds a new product, inquire about its durability, structural soundness, advantages, available repair outlets, guarantees. Secure enough information so the reader can judge whether the purchase or bill would be a worthwhile expense.

If you react with sizzling enthusiasm or distaste to your reported service or product, put that in your research notes and the reasons so that you can share that viewpoint with supporting evidence in your write-up. Because you are reporting a new goods, service, or merchandise trend, you have an obligation to the reader to evaluate it. In a *New York* restaurant survey, "A Lincoln Center Quartet," September 29, 1980, critic Barbara Costikyan describes her opinion of the menu's black sausage vividly:

> ($4.50 for two knackwurst-size pieces) . . . comes to the table with skins crackling and splitting from broiling, insides moist, damp, clumpy, and dead-rich. This is the sausage-lover's grail. I would kill for it.

Besides recording your opinion, jot down on-the-scene quotes from disenchanted or delighted bystanders. Quotes from users or participants will enliven your writing later. Omit, however, biased opinions by the manufacturer, salesperson, proprietor, or waiter.

You must report the negative criticism or derogatory comment about a product or service, to be believed. If your service reportage is simply all cotton candy, you invite readers' skepticism because you've produced an unobjective piece. So include the marring blemish or slight defect for credibility, even if you're going to give a rave.

## The Body: Structure: Types

Once you've defined the consumer's problem that your service article will solve, and you've netted enough information to satisfy readers' questions, you're ready to decide on a structure for the body of the piece. If you're concentrating on one service, such as a store specializing in cookbooks, or one special item, such as the newest mousse for men's hair, the remaining article is essentially a review of that single establishment or merchandise.

### Introduction and List of Outlets

More likely, you're dealing with several examples of the same service. There are three formats to handle a report on different varieties of one service. The simplest method is to follow the introduction with a list of examples of the one service, as Ms. Campbell did in her piece, "Dinner At Eight." She listed briefly the places on Restaurant Row for quick dinner reservations under the headings, "South Side Of Street" and "North Side Of Street." Her listing identified the restaurant by name, address, phone number, distinctive cuisine, available liquor and "moderate" to "expensive" price range. Writers have employed such lists to locate sources of the same product for surveys of the most succulent, tenderest chickens sold, foreign and domestic brand mustards, and store-bought peanut butter.

### First-Person Narrative
A second structure for a survey of samples of the same service is the first-person narrative. Readers enjoy firsthand opinion by writers on services like exercise classes, centers for reliable cardiovascular fitness tests, and safe saunas. If you think your opinion of the surveyed services could be important to the reader, try this format.

### In-Depth Reporting of Different Examples
So far, mentioned formats include the one service or product reviewed, introduction to the service or product and listed outlets, or first-person tour of the same service at different places. The final choice of structure requires more control and skill in the article's planning, research, and writing. After the opener, you convey different examples of one service by in-depth reportage. In, "Ay, There's the Rub," Ms. Goldman profiled exemplary masseurs, differentiated by different strokes, different schools, or on hand at famous health clubs or beauty salons.

I applied this construction design in my August, 1982, *Esquire* coverline article, "Special Places: Where to Go the Distance." After my introduction inveigled the runner who was "tired of the shorter races, like the traditional five-miler or the newer '10K' (to) seek more adventure and . . . the challenge of toughing it through the 26.2 mile marathon," I surveyed, as the coverline said, "Where to Marathon." I distinguished each marathon from the next by focus. I featured the Boston Marathon, the "oldest continuous race of its kind in the world," for its history; the London Marathon, for its historical course; New York City Marathon, for being the most superbly organized; and the Honolulu Marathon as a "splendid reason for a winter vacation." When you report in-depth similar samples of the same service, try to differentiate one from the next by your slant in the writing of each.

You can differentiate each example of the same service not only by dominant focus, but by choice detail supporting it, tailored to the tastes of that magazine's average reader. For instance, as I began to decide which details supported my slant for each major marathon surveyed, I remembered *Esquire's* Service Features Editor, Anita Leclerc, advised, "We like to give our readers an edge." So I imagined I could best give the *Esquire* entrant an edge on his competitors if I described each marathon's course conditions. My premise: the more familiar the reader was with the race course, the better race performance he could achieve. Here's how the chosen details of the London Marathon race course reinforced the historical theme of that article section:

## LONDON

If you're planning a trip to London next spring, book your flight with British Airways, which, as a major marathon sponsor, will guarantee your entry in the best foot man's tour of London's most prized landmarks. The surprisingly flat course begins on the historic lawns of the Royal Observatory in Greenwich. Then, as no other marathon course can boast, it slices through the prime meridian, taking you from the Eastern to the Western Hemisphere to head along the banks of the Thames. At six miles, you'll circle the *Cutty Sark,* the most famous and the fastest of the racing China clippers, which is moored in sight of the *Gypsy Moth IV,* the ship Sir Francis Chichester single-handedly sailed around the world. Then you cut through the boisterous suburbs of Lewisham and Southwark, where you'll hear the old maritime cheer "Go for her. Go get her, mate!"

Racers reach the half-marathon mark at the base of Tower Bridge. Across this nineteenth-century drawbridge you'll pass over the ancient and treacherously slippery cobblestones fronting the Tower of London, the nine-centuries-old fortified casket of the crown jewels. Then the course snakes through the East End—the cockney region—and up and back through the desolate, bleak waterfront area of the Isle of Dogs. At the loop's end, past the twenty-mile mark, are your rewards, the epitome of British tourist attractions—Buckingham Palace, Westminster Abbey, Big Ben, Parliament—and, after crossing Westminster Bridge, the jubilation at the finish.

I also chose course details that appealed not only to the tastes of the typical *Esquire* racer to distinguish each marathon from the next, but I also appealed to the average reader's affluence, which, from studying previous issues, enabled the *Esquire* man to go to a hotel and—if necessary—rent an armored car. With the typical reader's income in mind, I put in choice perks of each marathon—the picnic and free massage available after the Honolulu Marathon and the guaranteed entry to the New York City Marathon for the reader willing to join the New York Road Runners Club's "$1,000 Marathon Circle."

To review: organize your service article and write your opener. Then, depending on the number and type of examples, either describe and evaluate one consumer item, or structure it as an introduction and listings of its outlets, first-person narrative of trial experiences with the surveyed service, or distinguishing close-ups of examples of the same consumer product or service.

## Conversational Voice

Write your service piece in a conversational tone, as if you're confiding to a friend. Use the second person "you" to achieve an informal, intimate ring. The "you" allows the author to speak directly to the reader. Ms. Campbell reported that when she started writing a service article imagining that she was talking to her sister, the writing got "too conversational." I don't mean that "conversational," just language that reflects the way you speak every day, probably with slightly more precision and greater clarity than you customarily use.

You can also choose to do your reportage in the first or third person—"he," "she," "fellow diner" or the like. Whichever you use, be consistent. These different voices also mix. First and third person singular blend, as do second and third, in the same article, but the "I" and "you" voice in one piece can be jarring if the writer doesn't employ the "I" voice for a clear purpose.

If you report the service through the persona of an "I," the reader can experience vicariously whatever the "I" does. But the first person can also intrude on the flow of the piece by needlessly rambling or calling attention to the writer for no reason. If you decide to use the first-person anecdote, specify credentials that give your opinion authenticity. Or try to find similar anecdotes to yours that others have experienced and report them as the anonymous "customer," or "a woman," or some such persona. Above all, keep the tone of your service piece that of a friendly conversation.

## SAMPLE SERVICE ARTICLE

I'll demonstrate the service form with an example from my published work. Unlike the majority of my published articles, I didn't suggest this service idea. After an exploratory lunch with a couple of *New York* editors, fall, 1978, I received a call from a third a few weeks later. "Hi," she said, and introduced herself. "I understand you know all there is to know about running." She needed a service article on how to choose your running shoes by the next Wednesday. Because it was a "rush job," I negotiated a kill fee of 50 percent. If I invested the effort to research and write the assigned piece in six days, I wanted decent compensation whether the article was published or not.

I researched the assignment from a variety of perspectives. I spent a morning with a well-known Manhattan podiatrist and I also obtained complaints about running shoes from injured runners in his waiting room. I did a long phone interview with an internationally known podiatrist, Dr. Richard O. Schuster, now a regular columnist for *The Runner*. Besides those who treat the sufferers of poor shoe choices, I managed to interview Gary Muhrcke, a shoe seller who was also a winner of the first New York City Marathon. Muhrcke, for years, sold runners' shoes out of a van at an entrance to Central Park before he established his now-famous Manhattan chain of running stores, Super Runners Shop. Muhrcke was a connoisseur of manufacturers' defects.

The night before my deadline, I finished a first draft around eleven and placed a long-distance call to Chicago, where Dr. Schuster was attending a medical conference. Earlier, he had given me permission to call "any time" to check the accuracy of my information. When I reached him in his hotel room, his voice told me he must have been sound asleep before the phone's ring. But when I announced my name, purpose, and apologies for the hour, Dr. Schuster, gentleman that he is, said, "Go right ahead and read, dearie." As I did, he corrected my medical inaccuracies with gentle tact.

I delivered a crisper, tightened version, as a result of endless revision through the night, to *New York's* offices the next day. I didn't learn of the piece's rejection for a week. The staff had cut it to give space to another article about dating-mating patterns at a water fountain on a frequented runners' path.

But I had worked enough on the article to believe its valuable shoe information would help many brand new converts to the running boom choose the right pair for their maiden miles. So I called another city magazine, *Cue,* which since has become absorbed by *New York.* By a stroke of luck, the Editor-in-Chief knew me by name. She remembered, though I didn't at first, that I had once babysat for her during my years at Bryn Mawr College. We met again when I dropped off the piece at *Cue's* editorial offices.

I heard nothing for a week or two from *Cue.* Then I left town to do an interview with football player Franco Harris in Atlantic City for my *Glamour* article, "What's It Like to Be the Child of an Interracial Marriage?" I recall standing on one foot, then another, by a pay phone outside a Resorts International Hotel casino, shouting to hear my own voice over the din of gambling tables, as I made my deal for rights, fee, and pay schedule during a long-distance call to *Cue's* Editor-in-Chief.

The bright Indian summer's day that *Cue's* October 27, 1978 issue reached the newsstands, I discovered the latest copy hanging by a clothespin from a midtown Manhattan stand's display line. To my thrill, the cover bore the words, "How to Buy Running Shoes" as part of the magazine's promotional pitch to spectators of the forthcoming New York City Marathon. When I confided my thrill about a coverline on the new *Cue* to the newsdealer, he let me read a copy. To my relief, the piece had been published almost verbatim.

### FLEET FOOTED
### by Barbara Kevles

You only need one piece of equipment to be a year-round runner: the right pair of shoes. It's important to wear well-made, good-fitting shoes because injuries all through the foot and leg—toes, arch, ankle, calf, shin, knee, hip—can be traced to improper foot placement during running. Tennis, basketball, or spiked track shoes were not designed for the dynamics of running.

Though running shoes can sometimes cost more than $40, expect to lay out roughly $20 to $30 plus tax for your first pair. Happily, a more expensive price tag does not guarantee a better shoe; fit, not price, should determine your choice.

Don't order shoes by phone or buy the model worn by the latest Boston Marathon winner. Go to a sports or running shop and try on different models. Bring along socks if you wear them, and remember your socks can add ½ inch to your shoe size.

Look for the shoe that best follows the contours of your foot when you stand or, preferably, run in place. The beginner's foot slides slightly forward in the shoe after making initial ground contact at the heel, so any good-fitting shoe will allow a ½-inch space between your big toe and the shoe's tip. An ample toebox prevents bruised, bloody toenails. While allowing for forward motion, the shoe should grasp your foot snugly, but not tightly, under the laces. Make sure the heel cup does not slip up or down as you step. An overly loose or too-wide shoe can cause blisters or injury.

Once you find a running shoe that hugs your foot with ease, scrutinize its construction. A good shoe is made to protect you against impact shock. A runner's foot absorbs the shock of two to three times body weight with every footfall and each foot strikes the ground 5,000 times in one hour of running. The best shoes safely cushion your feet against this beating with a minimum of ½-inch soles and thicker heel lifts.

As important as cushioning is, however, famed sports podiatrist Dr. Richard O. Schuster considers the sole's flexibility more crucial. The metatarsal joint system lying across the ball of the foot acts like a hinge for the toes. If it cannot flex easily because of a stiff sole, you will strain the all-important Achilles tendon. Make sure the shoe's sole bends easily in half at the sole's widest point.

By contrast, rigidity becomes a plus in judging a heel counter (the semi-rigid support band in the back of the shoe). This device helps the foot's heel to remain firmly positioned against the shoe's heel. A weak heel counter gives you the feeling you're running on Jell-O and this instability makes you prone to leg injury.

To further increase stability, avoid excessively flared or narrow heels. The ideal heel is only slightly wider than the base of the shoe. Also, avoid shoes with cutouts under the arch in favor of shanks that lie flush against the ground for better arch support. Salespeople may offer advice, but don't accept any opinion unless the giver has earned the right to counsel by racking up a weekly minimum of 40 miles in various shoes over the years.

Once you've selected a pair of well-constructed running shoes that fit, inspect them for manufacturer's defects such as bunching of inner stitching, off-center tongue placement, or imbalance. Check that shoes stand straight on a flat surface, slanting neither inward nor outward; an imbalanced shoe alone can cause foot or knee strain and any number of other runner's problems.

Be aware that shoes rated tops by major national running magazines may contain more, not fewer, defects. To take advantage of endorsements, manufacturers sometimes greatly increase production at the sacrifice of quality control.

Take care to break in your new shoes gradually on short to longer runs. In time, your shoes may convince you that you are the winged god Mercury, but you will need to log many miles and long training hours before the start of your first marathon.

## Analysis

Now I'll demonstrate how this example of the service form meets the form's requirements.

The article demonstrates the simplest structural format—introduction to one product—running shoes—and a list of places for their purchase (omitted). Published during the late seventies running boom, the opener appeals for the attention of new converts to the fitness movement by focusing on a common amateur problem—choosing "the right pair of shoes" to prevent injuries from "improper foot placement during running."

The rest of the introduction helps consumers solve the problem with guidelines for shoe selection based on budget, the running foot's functional needs, and product durability. Purchase tips advise on such concrete features of the product as price, purchase location, proper clothing, and posture for a fitting, forefoot space allowances, heel snugness, cushioning, flexibility, heel counter stability, arch construction, optimal vertical rear shoe alignment.

The number of product features succinctly conveyed helps comprehend the reason I constantly revised through the long night prior to submission to slice away repetition and place like shoe features together. The form's reliance on reported details about the service should help clarify, as I said before, what you can gain by attempting it. If you attempt to research the necessary details of the product or service featured in your piece, your writing will improve because of the concreteness of the language required to communicate the features.

The piece earns credibility by alluding to possibilities of poor quality control of shoes manufactured to take commercial advantage of national running magazine endorsements.

It ends by warning readers against investing the well-made, comfortable-fitting pair of their choice with unattainable dreams for athletic achievement, founded only on the feel of good shoe leather.

The historically few old and new Manhattan running stores at the time were listed by name, address, and store perks promised for opening day.

## CRITIQUES OF STUDENT SERVICE ARTICLES

Students often astonish me with their performances in the service article. Still, even the best share certain common errors in execution of the form. The following excerpts from student works display some of these typical beginner mistakes. An awareness of these errors may help prevent you from making the same ones.

Beginners often forget to answer the reader's initial question, "Why should I read this?" In the first paragraph, they don't clearly state a reader's problem that the reported service satisfies. The following first paragraph from Carol Sweeney's "Honduras, A Simple Pleasure," is an example of the weak beginning. As you'll see, it doesn't strongly define the problem of the sophisticated traveler in need of a simple vacation spot, which the primitive pleasures of Honduras could solve.

Saturday Review recently published a listing of travel ideas. Among these, Honduras rated as a novel option for the sophisticated traveler. Don't be fooled! This is not Perrier with a twist and backgammon by the pool. No, you need not brush up your French, brush out your wardrobe, or brush on your charm. In fact be prepared to brush your teeth with Coca Cola, brush shoulders with burros and chickens and perhaps face a brush with death at the hands of a freewheeling bus driver.

Nowhere in this facilely phrased introduction does the writer reveal the country's special tourist attractions that are the reason for the reader interest in the piece and possible purchase of this consumer item—a trip to Honduras. Honduras' tourist lures are scattered through the piece: "spectacular mountains . . ."; "long white sandy beaches on the Caribbean Sea"; "Mayan ruins"; "the mercado . . . the heartbeat of the city (where buses and burros from outlying villages lumber in before daybreak, top-heavy with the freshest fruits, vegetables, pottery . . . animals . . . in various stages of slaughter . . ."; "generous people lacking in the . . . animosity toward tourists so apparent in other Third World countries"; and many more. The appeals of the simple Honduran country life are hidden in succeeding paragraphs. These should be summarized and showcased in the front window to give passersby a reason to enter, peruse, even purchase the merchandised travel service.

If at the start the service article doesn't name the reader's problem and the solution the reported service provides, the lack of a sharp beginning focus may not only cost the article readers, but hurt the subsequent writing. Without a stated theme, the remaining writing may ramble from details supporting the theme to ones irrelevant to it. At the beginning, enumerate the reader's problem your featured service will resolve, as protection against padding the piece with superfluous details unrelated to your focus. Your beginning focus serves both as a magnet for readers and as an aid for the writer. It helps you maintain thematic unity in the body of the service article.

Besides an unfocused start, students sometimes fail to distinguish one example of the service from the next. Vaguely written details are the source of this pitfall. As a result, different representative types of the same service seem the same. Excerpts from "Treat Yourself to Refreshing, Light Meals!" illustrate the failure of abstract details to distinguish types:

Examples of this trend toward light, natural meals can be seen at Curds 'n Whey on 43rd Street between Lexington and Third Avenues and at Au Natural on Second Avenue at 55th Street.

*Curds 'n Whey* is a vegetarian restaurant, with the exception of tuna fish for some sandwiches. Don't let the word "vegetarian" scare you. The food is delicious.

Curds 'n Whey starts the day with breakfast at 7:30 a.m. This enables you to stop in before heading for the office to enjoy natural cereals, fruit, yogurt, whole grained baked goods, and juices.

Lunch begins at 11:00 a.m. with salads, sandwiches, quiche, soup, fresh fruits and vegetables, juices, freshly baked breads and cakes, and some hot vegetarian entrees. This menu remains the same until closing at 7:00 p.m.

· · ·

*Au Natural* is a moderately vegetarian restaurant, offering the public freshly prepared foods and light meals . . . The menu includes lots of salads, yogurts, soup, quiche, juices, pastries, and some fish, veal and chicken entrees.

Strong contrasts between these restaurants for light, natural meals are not apparent. Without specifics like ingredients of dishes, their appearance, portion, taste, freshness, the reader is confused about the differences between the two places. The reader is not sure which is which. Sometimes, inexperienced beginners believe that vague lists of general features of the sampled service can convey its distinctions. On the contrary, vague lists blot out individuality. If beginners don't spend more time to immerse themselves in the details worth describing, they risk boring readers with an abstract encyclopedic list for the one service where each example sounds repetitious and interchangeable with the next. Try to remember the particulars of being there, and if you can recapture your experience of those distinctive details in the writing about the product or service, your piece will distinguish various types of it by palatable differences.

Besides describing the service's features in indistinguishable generalities, the writer of "Refreshing, Light Meals" falls prey to another beginner problem. The writer uses one of the owners of Curds 'n Whey as the judge of the fare.

Barbara Riccio, one of the owners, says that their most popular foods are spinach salad, tuna fish, strawberries, vanilla and chocolate yogurts, soups, and hot vegetarian entrees.

Owners, salesclerks, vendors who profit from favorable publicity of their consumer service are not the best sources for fair evaluation of it. Rather, opinions by you, other customers, or clients are preferred and more trustworthy.

You've been briefed on three types of beginner mistakes in writing service articles that you should take care not to duplicate. Jane Arend's "Carry-Out Cuisine" doesn't make one. Her survey of available Manhattan outlets for prepared take-home food fills all the form's requirements—an opening focused on a dilemma of numerous readers which the featured service solves, vivid detail to differentiate one example of the service from the next, and evaluations by reliable critics. The opening and first two carry-out cuisine outlets will demonstrate:

# CARRY-OUT CUISINE
## by Jane Arend

For the cook who is weakened and worn by the hot weather, held up late at the office, or just plain sick of cooking, carry-out cuisine must be considered as being beyond price. Obviously, a meal assembled from one of Manhattan's finest charcuteries will never qualify as the most prudent of economies, but neither will it sink to the dismal despair of a corner delicatessen's dried-out chicken, rubbery cold cuts, and commercial cole slaw.

Charcuterie has been defined by Jane Grigson, in her book, *The Art of Charcuterie*, as "the cooked meat of the pig." Thus, each of the shops listed stocks notably sizeable selections of all kinds of ham, sausages, bacons, and other pork products. With one exception, they also carry various types of pate, cheese, salad, bread, assorted cooked meats and poultry, and dessert. In other words, they can offer one-stop shopping with imaginative, well-cooked pick-up provender.

One note: At-home staples, for further menu enhancement, might include favorite chilled libations, and fresh greens, such as romaine or watercress; both useful for salad and entree adornment.

Listed geographically, a few of Gotham's best charcuteries.

## WALL ST. AREA
## THE BIG KITCHEN
Address: World Trade Center, Main Floor, Vesey and Fulton Sts.
Phone: 938-1153
Hours: Monday-Friday 11:30-4:30, Saturday and Sunday 11:30-5:00
No credit cards, no delivery.
Specialties: Fresh barbequed spareribs, $4.75. Chicken, $2.35.
Pike and spinach pate, $3.98 lb. Seven varieties of quiche (best seller, spinach souffle/ham quiche), $4.95. Hot vegetable pies and pastry shells filled with either beef or turkey may be ordered by calling their special number, 938-1197. They are famous for their delicious turnovers stuffed with veal and tomatoes, $2.50; with chicken curry, $2.30; or with sausage and peppers, $2.10.

The Big Kitchen is sprawling and bustling. Thirty cheeses are on display. A fine French chevre covered with either fennel or thyme is featured daily. The breads and pastries, from the same kitchen that serves the rooftop Windows on the World Dining Rooms, have received triple star ratings from several prestigious food critics, including Mimi Sheraton of *The New York Times*.

SOHO

**Dean and DeLuca**
Address: 121 Prince St.
Phone: 254-7774
Hours: Monday-Saturday 10-7, Sunday 10-6.
No credit cards, charges, or deliveries.
Specialties: Sweetbread and spinach pate, $6.50 lb. Chicken toscana salad, $6.00 lb. Homemade raspberry mayonnaise, $2.50 pint. An exquisitely chosen selection of cheeses. Individual pyramids of Montrachet are $4.00. Desserts are masterpieces of patisserie art. For a small taste, finger dacquoise are $.80 each, and green grape tarts, $1.50.
Dean and DeLuca is the nearest thing to a real Parisian charcuterie in the city. Chamber music softly plays in the background, and every fruit and vegetable is lovingly arranged in low, wicker baskets. The personnel is informative, patient, and soft-spoken.

Ms. Arend's introduction warmly woos the reader worn by weather, job, or housework to consider the solace of immodestly priced charcuterie in its pure form and variations. So the writer identifies a reader's need, the services to cure it, its advantages, and possibilities.

Two well-chosen outlets for charcuterie fare are sharply contrasted by the consumer information describing them. Besides the logistics—name, address, phone, hours, credit cards, delivery—the particulars of The Big Kitchen are specialties, prices, popular dishes, famous ones, display space, daily offerings, clients, name critics' judgments.

In addition to location and business procedures, the second charcuterie differs by its specialties, decor, and the approach of the personnel.

## ADVICE FOR THE SERVICE FORM

Ms. Arend's piece shows successful service articles are within a beginner's reach. To eliminate common errors in execution of the service form, keep in mind the following:

1. Plan your research by jotting down every conceivable question any reader could ask about the reported product or service before you make your first appointment or visit.

2. For a survey of several examples of the same service; a) be sure to select ones distinctively different, b) stay on the premises or investigate the product thoroughly to obtain enough concrete distinguishing details to contrast the representative sample or service with the next.

3. Note the problem or predicament or need the product or service solves and translate that insight into the opener's defined focus. It will give the reader a reason for delving further and preserve your writing from distracting detours.

4. Choose only concrete details about your service that reinforce your thematic focus.

5. Use criticisms—pro or con—from sources other than the vendor, salesclerk, waiter, owner, or manufacturer, for credibility.

# VII How to Get & Prepare for an Interview

A previous chapter gave you strategies for discovering markets and negotiating commissions. The last one introduced you to the article form most suitable for reporting new consumer products or services. This chapter explains how to obtain interviews and prepare for one. The next teaches you the form for writing about a completely new issue or a new development in a well-reported subject. This type article is based on information gained from one interview with one expert.

## HOW TO SECURE AN INTERVIEW

When faced with having to get an interview, many of my beginner students are overwhelmed by fear. This fear is so strong, it stops them from making a single call to request an interview. If the prospect of arranging an interview evokes similar terror and paralysis in you, combat the problem by using the approach ultramarathoner Stu Mittleman developed during his first New York Six-Day Run. Asked how he made it through that awesome 144 hour competition, Mittleman, three-time American record holder at 100 miles, said, "I broke the race up into manageable parts, decided on a goal for each, and concentrated on one aim at a time."

So, handle what may be a nerve-wracking "first" for you the same way. Divvy up the arrangements and preparations for an interview into a number of tasks, each with a defined goal. Control your fear of phoning someone for an interview by focusing on each challenge en route one at a time. For a successful outcome, decide, "Whom do I contact?" "What should I say?" Once you have a firm appointment, resolve, "Where will I research my questions?" and, "How will I record the interview?" If you concentrate on completing each task the best you can, you will cross a finish line you never thought you'd reach.

### "Whom Do I Contact?"

Call the person you want to interview directly. If that's not possible, write a letter. As a last resort, try to establish contact at an event like a game, concert, or speaking engagement where your expert or celebrity is scheduled.

A phone call is the most effective method because it gives you immediate access and an answer right away. So your first challenge is getting the right number. The number can be for your party, an organization that can give your party's home or office number, or an agent who can make the appointment for you.

Your search may be over when you open your local phone book. One of my students, Nancy Koester, a writer and editor for the Lutheran Church in America, got to Pete Seeger, the acclaimed folksinger, by calling a record company, Folkways Music Publishers, Inc., which gave her the number for Seeger's agent. But she could have also looked up Seeger's name in the Manhattan telephone directory, where it is listed with the agent's address and same phone number Ms. Koester received from the record company. The agent promised to forward her request to Seeger if she would send it in a letter. "I got an answer within ten days." Ms. Koester reports. Her profile of another well-known folksinger, with back-up quotes by Seeger, was published in newspapers in two midwestern cities where the singer performed.

If you can't find your subject listed locally or through the long-distance operator, think of an institution or company with which the person is connected. If your expert teaches or studies somewhere, the college or university switchboard operator likely will put your call through to your expert's office, department secretary, or dorm. One student who chose to profile Amy Eilberg, who was to become the first woman to be ordained a conservative rabbi, contacted her through the Communications Department of her university, the Jewish Theological Seminary of America. Often educational institutions will help set up an interview because a faculty or student mentioned in the press offers the institution free publicity. When I received the *Cosmopolitan* assignment later published as "Notes Of A West Point Woman," I called the Public Affairs Office at The U.S. Military Academy at West Point to ask for aid in casting the interview.

"Whom do I call?" is often answered by, "Who could benefit from the publicity?" For the home number of TV comedy writer Gail Parent for the *Working Woman* interview titled, "Gail Parent Is Alive And Living In Los Angeles," I dialed the publisher of her novel, *Sheila Levine Is Dead and Living In New York,* and requested the publicity department. To reach eight-time Oscar winner, the late Edith Head, I phoned Universal Pictures' west coast studios where the famous costume designer was readying for the studio production of *Airport 77.*

Besides the phonebook or potential beneficiary of the publicity, a celebrity's publicist, personal representative, or agent may provide the necessary tieline. When the first film Jeanne Moreau directed, *Lumière,* premiered in New York, I tracked down a number for her east coast agent through the French Film Office. The afternoon I arrived at Manhattan's Hotel Pierre for the interview, I discovered the agent awaiting me with bad news. Moreau was ill with a high fever, unable to take medicine because of her allergy to antibiotics, and would leave for the west coast as soon as she was well. I returned to my apartment quite devastated, but I rallied when my current boyfriend said to me, "You're going to fight, aren't you?" I needed his urging to marshall my spirits and rethink my options to restage the cancelled interview. The next day, I called the publicity office for Paramount Pictures, which was distributing *The Last Tycoon,* in which Moreau had a cameo role. Not only did Paramount agree to arrange the interview with Moreau in L.A., but consented to provide the plane tickets and hotel if *Working Woman* would cover sundry expenses.

When Moreau and I finally met a month later, she asked me why I had pursued her 3,000 miles for an interview. And I explained that all the creative women of achievement I had ever met—and I ticked off their names: Anne Sexton, the Pulitzer Prize-winning poet; Diane Arbus, the famous photographer—had killed themselves. And I wondered what satisfactions there were for her as a working professional woman, what sustained her, why she kept on living, if not for the conventional satisfaction of husband and children.

My ability to gain access to celebrities was recognized and valued by *Working Woman*'s editors. When one of the editors went on vacation to the Mideast, other members of the staff circulated this joke around the office: "Betty-Jane's riding in the blazing hot desert to an undisclosed destination, when from nowhere appears a camel courier, who hands her a note with the urgent message, "Barbara Kevles wants to interview you."

If you can't find your subject's number or obtain it through an employer, publisher, agent, or other interested third party, take a chance and attend a public event where the person you seek to interview will appear. There, you might confront your quarry face to face with your request or use the meeting to secure quotes to combine with peripheral materials in the written article.

### Present Your Credentials Honestly

Never present false credentials to gain entree to the press room or front row of a concert, political rally, or game. A former student in pursuit of a Russian chess master told an inquiring ticket taker, "Oh, I think I'd like to sell my story to *People.*" And when she returned from the ladies room, she said, "I'm writing it for *People.*" Finally, she told a fellow journalist, "I'm from *People.*" When I questioned her reasons in class for her false front, she admitted, "I was really beginning to believe I was from *People.*" Whatever fantasies you have about a future sale, without a firm assignment, you must answer gatekeepers honestly, saying, "I'm doing this on speculation. I hope to sell it to. . . ." The magazine world is a small professional world. Word of disreputable practices like falsification of press credentials could get back to the very publication you want to buy your article. So, don't give phoney credentials; the lie may do more harm than good.

Rather than spring your request for an interview without an introduction at a hectic noisy public event, it's slower, but often more effective, to work through channels that have a self-interest in the publicity resulting from the published interview. So persevere. One of the subjects of a *People* profile told me after the article's publication, "I couldn't have bought the publicity in a million years."

## "What Should I Say?"

Once the agent, publicity department, or promoter gives you the right number, you may wonder, "What am I going to say?" Many beginners, particularly those lacking publication credits, are uncomfortable about soliciting an interview because they have the wrong attitude. They think they are asking for a favor. In truth, it's just the opposite. You are proposing to do someone a big favor by offering that person the chance for publicity free of charge. In exchange for a celebrity's time, you are contributing your preparation, your time for the interview, your work reworking the material into publishable form, and your hard efforts to gain publication of the piece. You are taking all the financial risks for this energy expenditure at no cost to the subject of your interview. Realize that publicists are paid substantial fees for what you are offering to do for nothing. But publicity agents cannot take credit for their work with a published by-line, nor are they free to say what they wish, which are your benefits as a free-lance writer. But for these rewards of recognition and editorial freedom, you assume a lot of responsibility for a much lesser fee. So when you dial the number of your interview, remember you will be doing the favor.

Your subject may block your request in one of a number of ways. Most people will want to know the name of the publication that commissioned the article. So if you have an assignment, say, "I'm calling for an interview for . . . ," and name the publication. Then add, "I've been assigned to do a piece on . . . ," and name the subject of the article, and note the assigning editor's name and title. If you don't have a commission, don't identify yourself saying, "I'm a journalism student and. . . ." or, "I haven't published before, but. . . ." Rather state, "I'm a free-lance writer," and drop the name of a publication with, "I hope to publish in. . . ." Following these directions, my student who phoned the Jewish Theological Seminary of America for the Eilberg interview said, "I hope to publish the interview in *The Westsider*." Mention of the local paper got him the appointment. He eventually sold the piece to *Savvy*.

Besides information about the article's eventual publication, prospective subjects want to know something about the reporter. If the word, "free-lance," creates disquieting modulations over the wire, give a number where you can be reached at home or at work and past publication credits. By offering the subject a method to contact you and a brief resume of published credits or place of work, you present yourself as a reliable, trustworthy, professional writer.

### Right to Manuscript Review

Besides information about the publication and your credentials, a celebrity may request editorial review prior to manuscript submission in exchange for cooperation. He or she may say, "Can I see the article before you submit it?" Basically, the source is asking for control over the piece's content. I field this attempt at censorship by answering, "I'll call and check any facts and quotes for accuracy, rest assured." You'll be surprised that a famous person who may demand to see the whole text often will back off if you promise partial review. If you define reasonable perimeters for shared authority over the published material, the expert or famous person will usually agree to the interview. Show trust in your subject, and your subject will respond with trust in you.

Inform subjects, though, if the published interview will consist mainly of their answers to questions prefaced by a short introduction, that you will send it to them to initial each page. The reason is clear. When a published article is comprised primarily of direct quotes, your source has to approve his or her quoted words for print to protect you and the magazine against possible libel. When you forward the manuscript for initialing, stipulate your ground rules. The person can only correct errors of fact. The writer controls the area of interpretation, such as what quotes are included, omitted, their order, allotted space and other prerogatives. Under these terms I left my interview with Liv Ullmann at her Manhattan hotel prior to its delivery at *Working Woman's* offices. When I retrieved it, I found Ullmann had not corrected anything but two misspellings. She told me, "Many people write about a part of me. But your interview has a beginning, middle, and end. It's me." Fact checking gives you the gratification of instant feedback by an informed authority. Don't be threatened by a request for editorial review of an article to be published as an interview, as long as you clearly state your ground rules.

When experts, such as medical doctors, request the right of review over my final copy, I consent gladly. They fear damage to their professional reputation, should an article attribute inaccurate information. I agree to allow them to verify all technical information in advance of submission, not only to protect their reputation, but mine as well. Often I will tell an expert, "I don't want to appear the fool in print." As a math teacher's daughter whose childhood dinners often consisted of trying to find the right answers, I have an enormous respect for factual accuracy. And I would feel pained if something published with my by-line carried inaccuracies.

My verbal guarantee of editorial review before submission often persuades a reluctant expert to cooperate. A vice-president of a famous Manhattan institute for sports medicine confessed he would give me the interview because he knew I did check copy with my expert. If I didn't, he warned me, "I've consulted with my lawyer, and I could sue you." I followed my usual review procedure before submission. In addition, I kept him informed of the editor's simplifications and elisions of highly technical material, so he was aware of the editing changes weeks before the article's publication.

Medical experts particularly distrust journalists because magazine writing for mass audiences generally oversimplifies complex medical data. In turning medical jargon into lay language, an uninformed editor may distort or create errors in the text. With the awareness of the problem of accurately reporting complex topics, do persuade an expert interviewed to check the facts in your submitted copy so that any faults in the published article are not yours. Whatever condensations occur because of space or editing requirements, it's your responsibility to confirm their accuracy with your expert. So ask to see edited proofs for this consultation with your source. Such blue ribbon treatment will assure an expert's good recommendation of your work to future sources.

Besides overcoming a subject's natural distrust of a stranger or an expert's justifiable fears of being misquoted, you may confront problems from the air-tight schedule, a subject's self-worth, restrictions for privacy, and a shakedown for an interview fee—all for the sake of getting the interview.

If you must convince a very busy executive or over-booked doctor to award you precious free time, be as flexible as possible. Allow the candidate the upper hand and choice of convenient day and time. If an appointment-packed expert or overburdened shop owner resists, volunteer to arrive as early in the morning or late at night as necessary. If employed, suggest "any time" on the weekend. Such adaptability usually convinces someone of your sincere interest in the interview and wears down defenses of those who believe they have "no time" at all.

Ask for a day and time to meet, but don't specify how many hours. Don't scare your subject off with a time estimate for all your questions. Be confident that once someone agrees to be interviewed, that person will make the time to complete your research, should one meeting not cover it all. So in that initial call, don't quibble about something you can negotiate later. You may lose your interview because of that minor dispute.

In certain situations, you may detect that the subject's protests about lack of time for an interview hide feelings of unworthiness of attention. Such was my hunch about the resistance with which Pulitzer poet Anne Sexton greeted my request for an interview for *The Paris Review*. I asked her directly during researches for a *Look* profile—the poet's first for a national magazine. I remember pleading my case in her first-floor porch study saying, "But the interview will help somebody," which mirrored the reason with which her first therapist had motivated her to write poems. I think I pointed to the framed bookjacket of her first book of poems, *To Bedlam and Part Way Back,* above her mantle. Also, Anne Sexton may have had initial reluctance to the "Writers at Work" series because she wasn't, at that time, as worldly in the politics of the poetry world; she didn't understand with what prestige *The Paris Review* interviews are regarded. When I returned for the questions and answers for the published piece, "Anne Sexton: The Art of Poetry XV," later twice anthologized, thumbed volumes of *The Paris Review* lined the top of her study radiator. If you sense a subject wavers because of feelings of unworthiness or naivete about the importance of the requested interview, perhaps you can win consent by persuading the person that an interview about his or her life and work will help others.

Besides suspicions of the reporter, the medium, external pressures, and personal ones against an interview, some may counter your request with reservations about their privacy. In such instances, you may have to resort to flattery. That was the gist of an unexpected lecture I received from *People* editor Cran Jones. He recommended I use compliments to obtain the cooperation of recalcitrant subjects. I was fidgety throughout this lecture. I'm very honest and it's hard for me to give unfelt or false flatteries. But I had a chance to use this strategy that very afternoon, and it worked. I called a well-known restaurateur for consent to an interview and a potential list of famous guests for a dinner party whose names might make the photo captions sparkle. After agreeing to a *People* story, the potential host understandably didn't want to give out such a list, though similar star-studded captions had already graced another national magazine story. So I tried my editor's suggested approach. I went on about the mouth-watering food he'd prepared for the photographed dinner, and so on. By the time I folded in all my compliments between his named guests, the list totaled some forty famous celebrities. To my chagrin, my project was rejected by my editor because of a current surplus of *Host* stories already written and photographed in the inventory. But I learned, if you must prod a subject to cooperate, spew forth flatteries that hopefully are grounded in some truth, and your enthusiastic compliments may convince a four-star subject of your project's merits.

During tentative discussion of an interview, you may have to wade through not only personal distrust, malignment of your medium, time pressures, self-doubts and reserve, but also demands for a fee. Refuse to pay. If you pay for an interview, the truth of your reporting can be questioned. A paid informant may create facts under the formula, "The more information given the higher the fee." Save for the agent who markets your work to a publication, nobody deserves a penny of your commission. Also, deny any request for a kick-back for the reasons given earlier. You are doing all the work to conceive, research, and write the article.

Once I had to turn down a request for a pay-off by the agent of a world class runner I wanted to interview. The agent, his superior, and I were meeting at a posh Manhattan restaurant purposely so that the agent could give me the runner's hotel number for the next day. During the discussion, the agent suddenly tried to force me to pay for the interview. The agent argued that agents have to make a living, too. I had not come to that meeting prepared to argue that demand. I remember responding, "But you couldn't pay to get . . . into this type of high class magazine." I explained this kind of magazine would never do a profile of a world class runner, so my piece would be a way to promote the runner in that class publication among that type of readership. The agent and the top brass didn't buy my argument. Finally, when I tired of repeating my ethical position that truth of fact could be undermined by paid informants, I met their power to negotiate an interview for a world class competitor with my own. "Fred said to give me the interview," I snapped loudly. And I repeated, "Fred said to give it to me." I got the number.

Weeks later I saw Fred Lebow, Director of the New York City Marathon, who asked, "Did you say, 'Fred said to give me the interview,' to....?", and he named the agent. I answered without hesitation, "I did." I reminded Fred that with this article, as with about a dozen past, he had told me whom to interview and told me to say he had suggested the interview. He couldn't argue that, so we dropped the subject. In retrospect, I add you can only argue forcefully against fees for interviews if you are prepared to give up the interview for the sake of principle. If so, argue either you will take the interview on your terms or not at all. Your position is unassailable because you are ready to bear the consequences.

You can successfully deal with a subject's fear of strangers, of journalistic distortion, lack of time, of confidence, reserve, or attempt at a "shakedown," but some may simply refuse.

Always be prepared for a no. When your preferred interview subject won't see you, either try to find a substitute, or, in the instance of a profile assignment on a famous person, interview "around the person." If you want to question associates, family, friends, and other sources, try to consult your subject who refuses access for a list. If you proceed without prior approval, your selected sources may check with your subject for permission for the interview or for discussion of touchy areas. So don't call up your subject's intimates surreptitiously unless your subject will never see you. If there's a chance for your subject's cooperation and you arrange peripheral interviews without his or her prior knowledge, your secretive research may backfire and become the reason a wavering subject will never grant you the interview.

When I began work on what became my Joan Kennedy cover story for *Good Housekeeping*, Joan Kennedy didn't want to be interviewed. She had received unfavorable publicity because of the miniskirt she'd worn to President Richard Nixon's inauguration. So, through a congressional aide to her then husband, Senator Edward M. Kennedy, I elicited a list of phone numbers and addresses of family and friends who'd known her at various stages of her life. Eventually Joan Kennedy decided to let me interview her because of recommendations by the members of her circle who had seen me. Also, I suspect, she wanted to know the reporter's opinion of her friends and what those friends thought of her. Don't lose heart if you have to initiate your research on a celebrity with interviews of the surrounding circle. Their positive response to your desire for comprehensive knowledge of your subject, your honesty and high-minded objectives can only build good will toward you and may lead to a few hours with your assigned subject after all.

Besides a firm no, another equally distressing obstacle may impede access. Subjects will say yes, but delay confirmation of a time and day for the interview. I became so exasperated with the daily refusals for "A Talk With A Hollywood Legend," which was the subtitle of the interview with Edith Head, I threatened to return to New York at the end of the week without it. Shortly after I announced my plan to her secretary, Edith Head agreed to see me the first day of production for *Airport 77,* a multimillion-dollar disaster thriller, rather than lose the opportunity for a magazine interview. When we did the interview during a lunch break at her Universal lot office, I began to understand the delay. She had had to do so much last-minute work on the film's costumes, the eight-time Oscar winner said, "I'm under terrific pressures. I'm under such pressures that at the drop of a hat, I'd crash through the ceiling, if I could."

Don't become so focused on firming up an appointment that you begin to believe the whole world revolves around you and your arrangements. This happened to me during researches for the Joan Kennedy profile. Before I had her consent to what evolved into a series of interviews, I had some trying moments. Once, while quartered at the Jefferson Hotel in Washington, D.C., I experienced a delay in the processing of these arrangements that I interpreted as an irrevocable setback. I had tried for hours to get through to the Senator's Press Secretary, Richard Drayne. In a panic, I called a supportive Washingtonian. After recounting my morning of frustrating, never-answered calls, I asked in a weepy child's voice, "Do you think I've lost the story?" Quietly, my friend asked, "Have you seen the morning paper?" I admitted I hadn't opened *The New York Times* which had accompanied my breakfast tray. Then my friend proceeded to inform me that Senator Kennedy had just come out publicly against a major weapons system—the A.B.M.—in a just-released report. My friend capped his news update with, "Kennedy's office is swamped with calls from media from all over the country. Nobody can get through to his press secretary. Barbara, he's busy!" I have never forgotten that ringing observation. In times when auxiliaries to the famed cannot be reached or cannot fix a firm interview time, realize others have their busy lives to lead and that you and your request are not a major priority for them. In such agonizing waits, patience is your only recourse. Still, I sometimes lose perspective and think an unreturned call is a final rebuff. In these moments when I am leaning towards paranoia, I repeat to myself, "He's busy," and take a deep breath and try to relax while I decide when to try again.

The wait for a confirmation is less trying, though, than the problems from a cancellation. For instance, I received a travel advance from *Seventeen* for a trip to Boston to interview Kathleen Kennedy, but after a preliminary meeting, the eldest daughter of the late Senator Robert F. Kennedy called me at my hotel to announce she decided not to do the interview. She explained she'd rather be interviewed for *The Atlantic* or *Harper's* than *Seventeen,* or write something herself for that type of publication. I called *Seventeen's* Editor, Ray Robinson, and related the news. Then I put in a call to Joan Kennedy, Kathleen's aunt, at her Cape Cod home. She accepted the call despite the historic events of that day. When I explained my reason, she promised to get her niece to keep the interview.

Early the next morning, Kathleen called and invited me to her dormitory room for our planned talk. Later, I read a newspaper and learned my call had reached Joan Kennedy the night her then husband had been exonerated of any wrongdoing in the drowning of an aide in his car at Chappaquiddick.

This section has enumerated some of the common stratagems used to deny interviews, so you can defeat them. If all fails, find a more cooperative subject for your assignment.

## HOW TO PREPARE FOR AN INTERVIEW

### "Where Will I Research My Questions?"

Do the necessary research for your interview and plan your questions in advance to guarantee good results. As coaches often tell beginner competitors, "If you've trained, you'll do well. Your race performance can only be as good as your preparation." Similarly, the results of your interview will reflect how well you prepared for it. Do your homework before the interview—not during— if you expect good quotes, useable background information, or a published "Q.&A."

To prepare for the interview, you can turn to print sources, the intimate circle around the famous person, and your own resources for help with your questions and eventual article.

#### Print Sources

First, I strongly recommend you study articles similar to your assignment previously published by the commissioning publication. A review of these models will help you understand the sort of topics, questions, and basic information expected in yours. As I told you a few chapters ago, when I needed to familiarize myself with a type of assignment I'd never written, or with the unfamiliar ways a publication handled a form, I'd review previous pieces in back issues, just as I'm suggesting you do. To aid my research, I'd jot down the exact questions I found other writers asked or queries their materials implied to obtain similar information for my assignment.

Besides the assigning magazine's published examples of the form, a second print source to consult for factual materials are the newspaper or magazine articles about your famous profile subject or celebrity interview, or publishings by your expert.

Agents, press representatives, local libraries, or institutions affiliated with your subject are excellent supply depots for this second type of necessary periodical research. Once I had scheduled an appointment with the actress and newly debuted film director, Jeanne Moreau, I called for permission and then went to the French Film Office where I machine copied the files on Moreau. The stored clippings provided a fertile storehouse of materials about the early controversies in Moreau's film and stage career and much biographical information as well. For needed research on Joan Kennedy, I was both given copies of filed clippings and allowed to make additional selections from the press folders in Senator Kennedy's office, which I photocopied on the premises. When about to head for Cambridge to interview the oldest daughter of the recently assassinated Robert F. Kennedy for the piece, "Kathleen Kennedy: 'Everything that happens has to change you,' " I burrowed through yearly reference guides to published periodicals for listings of relevant clippings housed in a television network's library, retrieved the pertinent magazines from the shelves, and photostated the selected articles. In any library, start your general clipping research with the *Readers' Guide To Periodical Literature*. Then ask the librarian if there are any indexes of journals or other published materials related to your article's subject.

Existing clips are excellent references to help you devise chronologies of your subject's life and work or, by their repeated facts, to alert you about the importance of certain themes. Let them suggest areas of primary importance to research, questions, facts to check or investigate. But don't accept any reported facts or quotes without question. Verify any published quote's accuracy or any fact before lifting it verbatim for your article.

Always ask your celebrity or expert if there are misinterpreted facts in past articles. Even if you cannot divine any inaccuracies, include the question, "What are the common myths about you?", or, "What's been misreported?" Your evident desire to correct past reporters' gaffes—at least from your subject's point of view—may earn your subject's greater candor. Still, even if an authority tries to embellish or rectify facts in ways the published record confirms as untruthful, you can, nevertheless, use this material. Biased facts indicated by the writer as such can expose your subject's vanities or prejudices. Untruths can be as revealing as confirmed facts.

Finally, other writers' clippings can inspire hunches about a subject's character or motivation or can reveal controversies within an expert's field. Use these intuitions to develop some very tough questions. Then, when your subject has relaxed during your question period, mete them out very gently. Once I was interviewing New York City Marathon founder, Fred Lebow, about the commercialization of running for my *Village Voice* article. I was extremely uncomfortable about inquiring about "under-the-table fees" to elite marathoners. So before I did, I prefaced by saying, "Look, I don't want to ask these questions, but I feel I must because of my article's theme." I knew I had to get Lebow's answers even if the questions antagonized him, because I had seen the figures for runners' expenses in the New York City Marathon's annual budget. So with profuse apologies for asking, I pushed these questions out. My admission of discomfort helped get the information I wanted. The display of personal vulnerability disarmed Lebow, brought out his courtliness, and made him more interested in easing my discomfort than protecting his professional interests as Director of the New York City Marathon. He later wrote of, at times, being too candid with the press, and I always thought that this time—with his open discussion of "so-called" under-the-table fees—was one of them. So admission of reluctance to ask difficult interview questions can prove beneficial rather than detrimental to the outcome of the interview. But if you don't prepare for the interview by steeping yourself in published background on your topic, you won't know enough or have the courage to ask the "toughies."

Besides examples of the form in the assigning publication and articles published on the topic, a third print source to consider is any book by your expert, about your celebrity, or articles by your expert in professional journals. Doctors—those with medical degrees or Ph.D.s—often have journal reprints or are willing to send you photocopies of their papers. The beginning summaries or stated results are often intelligible to a lay person. If not, you can request an explanation of the paper's results in lay terms during the interview. Be sure, of course, to take the paper with you for reference. Always request a resume prior to or during the interview. You'll invariably have to consult a resume about the precise title of an authority's current position, affiliated institution, past education, and degrees.

In summary, consult the three print sources—models in the assigning magazines, clippings about your subject, and published material by your authority to devise pithy questions and gain needed background information.

### The "Inner Circle"

When working on a profile or celebrity interview, it's wise to elicit from the subject a list of intimates—friends, associates, family—to talk to prior to the actual interview. Sources other than the subject of your article often will produce items formerly withheld from print or never stated publicly. Preparatory to my taped conversations with Judy Collins which, in edited version, formed the published piece, " 'I've Looked at Both Sides Now . . .'," the folksinger gave me a list of five friends who knew her well in different areas of her life. These interviews helped me understand the conventional wife she'd tried to be, the breakup of her marriage, its effect on her career and development as a singer, and much previously unreported material. By soliciting interviews with celebrities, associates, or friends, you can learn about forgotten experiences, major influences, or painful turning points a subject might not remember without your probing.

### Your Personal Resources

In addition to your market, published works by or about your subjects, and their inner circle, the last and best source for interview questions is yourself. Give yourself some time. Consult your proposal. Think over the questions you want answered before the day of the interview. Add these to your list culled from outside sources. I always take the time to pull all I've learned about a person or topic into a typed list of questions, which I renumber in logical order and retype in preparation for my interview. You may not ask all your questions, but at least you'll have these guidelines for use of the interview time.

## "How Will I Record the Interview?"

In the final stage of preparation, be it for a background interview or with the assigned subject of the piece, you have to decide the recording method most suited to the conditions under which the interview will take place, and your deadline. You have three means available—taping an interview, typing it, or writing it up by hand. You can employ any of these methods alone or in combination.

I use a tape recorder when the final article will be printed as questions and answers. After the taping, I will transcribe the tapes, or, by prior arrangements with the editor, a transcription service will copy the taped conversation. But the spoken word is never as succinct as the written, so you will have to edit your transcripts into publishable form. You may condense quotes, rearrange them, change words to make language more vivid or concrete. But never invent ideas the person interviewed never said and never change connotations of words to mean things the person interviewed never meant. The published interview is both a transcription and edited version of the original tapings.

Because a typed interview is an instantaneous transcript, often I will take notes on an interview over the phone or in person by typing. I can type as fast as anyone can talk. To make the deadline for my first *People* interview, "In Her Own Words: Dr. Janet Hardy explains an increase in teenage pregnancies," I typed the responses of Dr. Hardy, codirector of the Johns Hopkins Medical Institutions Clinic for The Comprehensive Adolescent Pregnancy Program, one long morning and afternoon in her Baltimore office and turned in the edited interview, complete with introduction, to my *People* editor in New York two days later. The piece went to press the day it was submitted. This recording method allows you to meet rush deadlines because of the clarity of your research notes and ease with which you can transform them into publishable copy.

When, because of convenience or deadline pressures, you decide to type an interview, inform the expert what to expect. Otherwise, you might have problems. Not every expert will consent to speak over the racket of a typewriter. Once, I met a surgeon who refused to let me use an office typewriter. He had been in surgery for hours prior to the interview, and he just didn't want to put up with the noise of my recording method. But I pointed out that I had advised him during discussion of the appointment of my method and I had not brought any audio recording equipment. Furthermore, the interview that Friday was due at the editor's office the coming Monday. He reluctantly withdrew his protest and carried his secretary's IBM electric into his office. By typing the ensuing interview, I was able to make the deadline for my first article for *Harper's Bazaar,* "Choose The Sport That's Right For You." Next time I called to interview another surgeon at the same institute for sports medicine, the second doctor warned me in advance I would have to tape it or write in in longhand, because he had heard his colleague's complaints about the typewriter's clatter.

As a last resort, I will record the interview by hand on unlined, five by eight inch index cards. In such cases, I will bring different-colored pens to scratch out prepared questions whose answers spontaneously arise in the interview, to underline undeveloped ideas I want to return to later with more questions, and to mark poignant or powerful quotes that I want to remember to use in the article. I prefer index cards because later I can withdraw those related to one topic from the consecutive-numbered pack when I hit that subject in my draft, and then reinsert the cards so I maintain the original flow of the interview by keeping my notes in the order I recorded them. The cards are also sturdy enough so I don't need a clipboard to write against when following a subject at an event.

Some of my students both tape-record and take notes by hand during an interview. I don't combine techniques. I will either tape, type, or write the interview. Choose whatever method suits you, the form of the published piece, your deadline, your source's personal preference, and the degree of mobility under which the interview will be conducted.

# VIII The One Issue/ One Interview Article Form: How to Write Up a New Issue or a New Development in an Old Field

Now that you've learned numerous methods to secure and prepare for interviews, you'll find access to newsworthy profile subjects or sources for new consumer products or services will be easier to gain. Your improved skills will help you better research not only the article forms previously studied, but the next one as well. This form—the one issue/one interview—serves as the best vehicle to write up a timely interview with an expert who possesses new information about an old subject or a brand new issue. This versatile form, which can accommodate dramatic breakthroughs in old or new fields, crops up in a short 200-600-word version or in a longer one which can reach upwards to 1500-2000 words.

To help you understand this article form, I'll give examples of the form, explain the type of material it best handles, and describe publications to query with your own issue/interviews.

## DEFINITION:
## ROLE OF EXPERT

Adaptable for the gamut of light to serious topics, this article form enlivens the spectrum from national to city to neighborhood publications. For example, *Vogue's* "Health" page frequently heralds medical advances with one issue interviews, as did a short one in the July 1985 issue about a new treatment for a familiar cancer. Titled, "Breast cancer: less surgery is in," the one issue article reported new successful results with partial rather than total mastectomy and quoted the project chairman's judgment of the new treatment method.

During the form's presentation of the new subject or old one, the expert not only may evaluate the development, but, often with brand new issues, explain it. For example, the same *Vogue's* "Health Style" page carried another in this form called "good fat, bad fat." The piece explored a new issue—the relationship between the site of excess body fat and disease—and a researcher elaborated the risks from too much in the upper body.

In this form, experts quoted not only interpret the news about the old subject area or new issue, but, as the source, may give it. The same summer month, *Harper's Bazaar's* one issue/interview, "Good Sense About Sex From Dr. Ruth," announced a syndicated radio-TV therapist's enlightened methods to counsel sexually aware teenagers on the old topic of sex and birth control.

## DEFINITION:
## FOCUS OF ISSUE FOR PUBLICATION

Now that you are aware of the roles experts can play in the one issue/one interview form, we'll turn to its second characteristic—the issue's focus for the publication's particular readership.

National magazines employ this article form for new developments of concern to national audiences in broad subjects like psychology or medicine, and regional publications turn to this form for new issues of local interest in general fields like business, education, or literature with a local or special focus for the publication's readership. For instance, *Manhattan, Inc.,* frequently uses one issue articles for local financial news, as did its October 1984 report on new hikes in Manhattan limo rentals, and for business trends of local concern like, in the same issue, a piece about a local firm's national survey of white-collar employees' average yearly personal calls. In the regional version, general issues or local events are all angled toward the publication's regional or specialized audience.

Dailies and weekend supplements also cater to special readership interests by amplifying events in politics, sports, or the cultural scene with single issue interviews. Frequently, *The New York Times Book Review* pairs a review with an interview with the new publication's author about his views of the book, his work life, or psyche, to give further insight into the analyzed work. Again, the timely subject at issue for the single expert's analysis or presentation is pegged to the interests of the readers of that specialty or metropolitan publication.

While the news at issue in one interview articles in national magazines appeals to the mass market audience, and the form in specialized or metropolitan publications focuses more on readers' particular or regional interests, the focus of subjects capsuled in this form in neighborhood weeklies narrows even further, to pinpoint local happenings or other cares of the paper's community audience. Long Island papers like "the Tribune," the abbreviated name on the inside pages of *The Jericho Tribune;* or, the other, *The Syosset Tribune,* employ the short one issue form to report community interests, such as, developments in a Syosset school board meeting over the old issue of new school roofs or roof repairs, or the Nassau County District Attorney's new charges under the national Environmental Conservation Law against a Syosset petrochemicals company for Unlawful Possession of Hazardous Wastes and Storage of Hazardous Waste without a Permit.

For all levels of circulation, this form highlights what's currently at issue for the publication's readers; the recognized expert chosen for his or her relevant local, city, or national credibility serves to give or gauge the developing news about the old or new subject.

### Advantages of Form for Technique

The one issue/one interview allows you the chance to perfect a writing skill different from the ones you've acquired from article forms learned thus far. In past chapters, study of the profile prompted you to do your research by means of an interview to gain fresh saleable materials; study of the service article encouraged you to collect concrete detail to improve your writing by making your words less vague and more factual. Study of the one issue/interview form will help you understand the different functions quotes perform, why and when to use them, how to introduce them, and when to substitute your own words instead. These skills are essential to writing magazine articles. Quotes will appear in every form of magazine journalism you attempt. They heighten the immediacy, entertainment, and most importantly, the credibility of your writing. The technical understanding you can gain about the work of quotes from mastery of the one issue/one interview form can improve every future article you write.

## CHOOSING YOUR SUBJECT: REQUIREMENTS FOR YOUR TOPIC

Requirements for a topic for the one issue interview differ from those for other forms. Its definition stresses two criteria that can help you search for a suitable issue. First, the subject has to have news value. Hence, an issue related to a new subject or news development in an old field often satisfies this requirement for timeliness. Second, your news has to be about a field of information like those in the previously mentioned published examples such as medicine, health, psychology, business, sociology, publishing, education, and environmental conservation. When casting about for a subject remember that, as a rule, you write best about whatever passionately interests you. You'll discover the territory of information to mine for a timely issue if you just think for a moment, 'What field do I know, or care to know better?'

For example, one of my students employed at a middle echelon publishing job has a real fear of flying. She found out about a local behavior modification clinic that helps aviaphobics like her. So, she's in the process of trying to market a query for an interview with the clinic's director on the issue of how fear of flying inhibits young executives from taking the next step up the career ladder to better paying, more responsible jobs that involve air travel. Her proposed article, which stems from her deeply felt phobia and professional dilemma, catches a new issue in the traditional field of business psychology of timely interest to growing numbers of women executives who subscribe to the national magazines devoted to working women.

Another student matched an immediate private interest of hers with a new issue in an old medical specialty. Right after the birth of her baby, she had taken a course in infant first-aid. She realized other first-time mothers might want to read about her teacher's advice, too. The national women's magazine she queried was impressed enough with her one issue/interview proposal, but would commission the subject only if she ghosted it in the style of a monthly columnist. At first, she said, "No." The next day she phoned back and accepted the assignment to write about this new subject in an old field in his format to get a publication credit for her resume.

Another student recognized the cherished territory of information to survey for an issue didn't have to be one of vital interest to her, but could belong to someone close to her. She turned to a family member, a veterinarian, and interviewed him about new developments in his professional specialty.

If your curiosities lean toward medical subjects, call the most accessible research center, hospital department, or reputable university laboratory, and ask a staff member's help in pinpointing a relevant issue based on the lab's latest published research. If psychology or sociology is your bailiwick, turn on the TV talk shows to see what expert is seeking publicity for a newly published book with an apt approach that evokes your sympathies. Or phone up a local organization of a cause you share, such as the Audubon society, and ask, "What's new and noteworthy?" Likely the staff's update on a shared issue will generate your enthusiasm for an article for which they would be glad to secure an expert in hopes of free fund-raising publicity. So if you honestly admit the area of passionate concern to you, that focus will route you in the direction of a local research institute, the TV dials, nonprofit organization, or someplace where knowledgeable staff may unsheath a timely issue in a field of information you personally would like to investigate further.

Sometimes, when you begin to focus most of your free-lance work in one field of information, as I have with sports medicine, valid topics for one issue/interviews will find you. In December 1983, on a People Express from Washington, DC to Newark, this happened to me: A white-haired gentleman with red boutonniere in the next seat turned out to be Dr. John Bland, a professor at the University of Vermont's College of Medicine. That day he had given the lecture annually sponsored by the National Hospital for Orthopedics and Rehabilitation on his work with reversing osteoarthritis. He mentioned publication of his research in the June 1983 issue of *The American Journal of Medicine*. Instantly, I started an interview and scribbled his answers on the front and back of a brown manila envelope, which was all the paper I had handy.

The following Tuesday, less than seventy-two hours after that chance meeting on a People Express, I reached *American Health* Senior Editor, Steve Kiesling, and enthusiastically proposed a "Fitness Report" article on Bland's work. I confess, at the time I didn't know enough to tell one type of arthritis from the next. Nor was I aware, as I discovered in *The American Journal Of Medicine* article, that osteoarthritis is so common, we stand a one-in-three chance of developing it by age thirty and nine-in-ten chance by age seventy-five. I didn't comprehend the disease's prevalence nor the scientific knowledge underpinning Bland's research when I pitched the piece, but I had enough grounding in my area of sports medicine to recognize the conclusions were newsworthy. Like the *Vogue* piece on breast cancer, mine about a new treatment method for a major form of crippling arthritis, perceived to be irreversible, explored a new issue of a medical advance in a known field.

First published in *American Health's* July/August 1984 issue, the piece, "Stiff Joints: Come Again to Cartilage," was reprinted two years later in Frank Rosato's West Publishing Company textbook, *Physical Fitness,* in which the theme was the connection between fitness and staying well.

## REQUIREMENTS FOR YOUR EXPERT: CREDENTIALS

How can you be sure the expert who offers you a timely issue in a substantive field is truly qualified? Your evaluation of the expert's credentials is crucial. The information and accuracy of the final draft will be based wholly on knowledge of your authority. To help you select a qualified source and analyst, the following survey of credentials of different spokespeople in randomly chosen one issues will show you the types of qualifications you can rely on to verify that your expert has the knowledge for your article and the credibility to be publicly believable. These credentials typify ones used for the well-known authority with special knowledge in the academic world, professional expertise in business, health, and other fields of information, or an inside track on local developments.

For instance, in the *Vogue* one issue/article on breast cancer, the medical authority quoted had these credits trailing his name:

Bernard Fisher, M.D., of the University of Pittsburgh, a leader in cancer research and chairman of the National Surgical Adjuvant Breast Project, presented two landmark studies on breast surgery in *The New England Journal of Medicine.*

Fisher has in-depth knowledge of the issues and accreditation by virtue of his educational degree, academic affiliation, professional reputation, landmark research project, his supervisory role in the research, and its publication. Should an expert inform you of or be the source of new controversial findings, right away check for his or her educational specialty, university affiliation, rank, and relevant journal publishings, to confirm the credibility and authority of your source on the suggested issue.

When you seek a professional outside academia, look for someone with a say on a news development in an old or new field whose work life and professional specialization justify the person's opinions as reputable. So *New York's* financial writer, Dan Dorfman, in an August 12, 1985 column, "The Bottom Line: The Doomsday Man," identifies his stockmarket analyst who advises, " 'This is the time to sell all stocks. . . .,' " in this manner:

> That's the word that investment strategist Richard J. Hoffman is relaying to his roughly 100 institutional clients.
>
>                                    . . .
>
> Hoffman, 44, was the chief investment strategist at Merrill Lynch between 1976 and 1983. He's now doing the same thing on his own, through R. J. Hoffman & Company of West Orange, New Jersey. Hoffman is obviously doing something right: His clients, who include leading banks, insurance companies, and investment advisers, pay him an average of $25,000 a year each (or about $2.5 million in all) for his investment thinking.

According to Dorfman, Hoffman's superior savvy is founded on his area of professional specialization, numbers and kinds of clients, current age, former employment position, employer, length of tenure, company now, client fee, and total fees. Just as you want academics with education and research in the relevant issue and its field, so you should seek professionals whose pertinent work experience and proven success with clientele authorize their views on the issue.

When selecting an expert, say, in mental health, who's a popular media figure, try to find someone whose authority is not only confirmed by a listing on the TV or radio page, but by published work as well. Dr. Ruth Westheimer, the featured spokesperson in *Harper's Bazaar's*, "Good Sense About Sex. . . .," seems ideal:

> referred to as "Dr. Ruth," she advises thousands of teenage callers during her nationally syndicated, phone-in radio program, *Sexually Speaking*, and her Lifetime cable TV show, *Good Sex!* She personally talks to them on lecture tours and has written a sexual information guide for young people, *First Love* (Warner), to be published later this year.

Though Dr. Ruth Westheimer's professional education is never spelled out, her radio, cable TV, and book credits give her credibility and guarantee her expertise through public practice of her profession via the media, lecture tours, and authorship. A pop media expert who has published is a better informed, more believable source for a one issue article than one who hasn't.

Your first-choice insider for regional one issues usually is a participant in the event or researched trend. So, in *Manhattan, Inc.*'s report on the expected rise in the price of limo rentals, the commentator is the director of administration at the Taxi and Limousine Commission, where new registration fees of some 30,000 nonmedallion vehicles are driving up limo costs. *The Jericho Tribune*'s update on the Syosset school board issue likewise used an involved eyewitness—the Superintendent of Buildings and Grounds—to analyze the extent of the roof leaks and water damage to school ceilings, windows, and floors. So for issues slated for local, regional, or specialty publications, the person with the vantage from the right job or appointed position likely will be in the know and able to give or gauge the news development.

In summary, informed, recognized experts for national, city, or community issues, certified by educational specialty, professional affiliation, publications, professional specialization, work experience, clients, or current job may serve as your own issue's primary source and, later, be identified as its spokesperson or analyst. When you contact a potential candidate, ask for a brief resume over the phone and request a copy by mail, because any editor you query will demand this essential information for a commission. So try to line up an expert whose superior knowledge or insight into the issue is confirmed by significant laboratory or clinical research, work specialization, published articles or a book, job vantage, or similar important credential, which you can also use as certification in your article.

## REQUIREMENTS FOR YOUR EXPERT: CONVERSATIONAL LANGUAGE

But if the expert privy to ground-breaking research, a new trend, or news event can't communicate the issue in conversational language, you may have to scrap the article or salvage the commission by finding a more articulate substitute.

Test whether your specialist has the ability to convey technical jargon in words accessible to you and the reader. During preliminary conversations, ask your expert to summarize the findings, new view, or news development for your query. If replies are feathered with vague generalities or monosyllables, cancel out and look elsewhere. You can't risk dealing with an uncommunicative authority or one fearful of speaking openly in the press, because your interview materials, in effect, are your first draft.

Most likely, each time you speak with your expert you'll receive pertinent information for the article. So let me give guidelines to monitor the language of these preliminaries. Also, apply them when you do the main interview to fulfill the form's requirements listed in the following section. Always make sure your expert's responses are put in everyday words. If not, interrupt and suggest, "Could you phrase that in language the common reader can understand?" If the expert persists with technical terms, then take the lead and translate the answers on the spot into words your reader can recognize. Say, "You mean ..., and then enunciate in a conversational manner what the expert's specialized words intend. After a few "simultaneous translations," experts usually take the hint and speak as they normally may to a busdriver or grocer. If the specialist occasionally strays into jargon, your intercession will push the interview back on the right language track. No matter how important the expert may be in a professional field, that specialist will cooperate because he or she knows the more useable answers you leave with, the longer the piece, and the greater the publicity.

If an expert refuses to take direction or lacks the ability to simplify, then you have to translate the rhetoric as you proceed, answer by answer. In this case, make sure your expert corrects or approves without modifications the translations as you do them. Should the expert say nothing, ask, "Do you mean this?" every time you revise an answer. Only record your paraphrases of the expert's jargon on the grounds that these are what the expert would say if he or she had your gift for expressing complex technical information simply. Through these means, you leave the interview with answers phrased in readable prose and confirmed for accuracy by your expert.

Many beginner writers feel if they can't make sense of a one issue interview with an expert who spewed forth in professional rhetoric, it's the writer's fault. The beginner feels he or she should have known more about the expert's field. If you come prepared for an interview, and the expert sticks to jargon, then your ensuing confusion is the fault of the expert.

If you are not conversant with the field of your expert, that is to your advantage, because neither is your reader. An anecdote will point up how a writer's naivete gives an edge in researching new vistas. When, in the mid-seventies, I first interviewed New York Road Runners Club President Fred Lebow, for my premiere piece on running, "Women: Going the Distance, Closing the Gap," for the 1977 *"Official Program: New York City Marathon,"* Lebow, who founded and continues as Director of the NYC Marathon, asked incredulously, "Do you know anything about running?" Though I had been assigned to write the major program piece for this world-famous event on women runners, I shook my head, "No." Then, with his usual insight, Lebow said, "Well, you'll have to tell it to yourself first before you can write it." He meant, I think, I'd have to understand my material enough to be able to say it to myself first before I could write the article. So, I've learned as long as you know what you don't know or don't understand about your expert's answers or the assigned issue, you know all you need to in order to proceed with your interview.

For example, I recall that during many months of research for a one issue article, a source called to announce a medical discovery, which he conveyed by reading the titles of research abstracts being sent to important medical conferences. When he hung up, I realized I hadn't understood a word. Knowing I could reach him the following week, I made up a list of questions, starting with a request for the definitions of the words in the titles of those papers. Knowing what I didn't know led to a productive interview and publication.

Here are the facts. From October to December, 1984, I was researching my article on the pioneer discovery of a new cause and treatment of chronic monilia, later published in *American Health,* April 1984, as "Rx: Monilia: Vanquishing Beasty Yeasties." Just before the Thanksgiving weekend, the chief researcher on the project, immunologist Dr. Steven Witkin of Cornell University Medical College (NY), phoned to tell me the latest lab findings, which I could get, he said, from the titles of three abstracts he would read me. Two were for the Society for Gynecologic Investigation's March 1985 Phoenix conference, and the third was for the Federation of American Societies for Experimental Biology Anaheim, California, conference, April 1985. Then he excitedly dictated as I typed the FASEB abstract's title, "DETECTION AND TREATMENT OF A MACROPHAGE DEFECT IN WOMEN WITH RECURRENT CANDIDA VAGINITIS"; then, both listings for the SGI forum including a paper called, "REVERSAL BY INTERLEUKIN 2 OF A LYMPHOCYTE PROLIFERATION DEFECT IN WOMEN WITH RECURRENT VAGINITIS."

After the holidays, when I asked Witkin for translations, he gasped. Words like lymphocyte and related ones like prostaglandins seemed as elementary to him as the sun, moon, and stars. At first, he seemed unable to reach down to my level, but gradually he got used to simplifying his language. Actually, he and I did so much interviewing as the research progressed that he would instantly switch, when speaking to me, to lay language of a fairytale, with metaphors of "invaders . . . mounted a defense . . . call to arms. . . ." and the like. Because of his brilliant simplification of highly technical science, I could write in my final submission about monilia, the gynecological problem which hits one woman in four who visit gynecologists:

> . . . Normally, your white blood cells known as T lymphocytes stop the spread of yeast by multiplying many times and engulfing the invaders. But in lab tests, T cells from women with a minimum of three infections the past year mounted a small defense or none at all. . . .

What follows is what the papers for those conferences were about.

> Further research ruled out problems in the T cells. When Cornell investigators combined patient white cells and yeast with the hormone interleukin 2 (IL2), the T cells now were able to respond with their normal rate of replication. Obviously, something was inhibiting them. . . . Explains Witkin, "We knew from animal experiments that IL2 which your T cells secrete to increase their forces can be blocked by prostaglandins. These are catalysts which produce inflammatory reactions in your body.
> So patients who wished—31 so far—were put on doses of the most effective . . . prostaglandin inhibitor—ibuprofen—to boost their white blood cells. . . .

The *American Health* editor, Robert Barnett, who pared my piece for publication, commended me on the impressive amount of technical knowledge I had mastered. But then I had had many good lectures in lucid lay language.

Avoid specialists who express their news, views, or new information in rhetoric for ones who can use ordinary speech. I did not always follow this advice. I created editorial difficulties once because I actually argued for technical terms and suffered the penalty. Here's what happened. I was commissioned to do the *Harper's Bazaar* one issue/interview, "Choose The Sport That Is Right For You," which matched different physical female weaknesses with proper or improper sport choices, for publication in the May 1980 *Bazaar.*

*Bazaar's* Health Editor, Denise Fortino, reviewed my submission and told me certain technical medical portions would have to be simplified to fit the magazine's style. I argued feminist politics. I said many women who suffer ankle sprains went to male doctors who played the role of all-knowing male authority. But technical facts, I said, would give these readers a better understanding of their injury and ways to measure the doctor's handling of their case. But according to a readers' survey quoted by my editor, the most physical exertion the majority of readers had was from riding their bikes. I was arguing, albeit, for the needs of a very small minority of readers. Rightly, my editor changed the complex medical descriptions of sports injuries.

So learn from what happened to me. If your expert seduces you with technical or abstruse expressions, expect to have your editor rework your sentences into more readable prose. In truth, Dr. Barton Nisonson, orthopedic consultant to Lenox Hill Hospital's Institute for Sports Medicine and Athletic Trauma (NY), had been reluctant to be so technical, but I had pressed him to against his better judgment. So I got my proper comeuppance. After the publication in *Bazaar,* I realized I could have accomplished my feminist purpose and given readers the same medical insight, not in simplistic, but simpler prose. But professional humiliation can spur you, as it did me, to write more colloquially the next time. When I did another commissioned women's sports piece for *Harper's Bazaar* the following year, the published piece was comprised of 90 percent my words from the submitted manuscript.

So far, the chapter has introduced you to the one issue/one interview form's definition, and explained the qualifications for selection of a well-focused, timely issue in a new or old field of information, and the required credentials for a recognized, articulate informed source. Now to proceed with the form's research requirements.

## RESEARCH REQUIREMENTS

If you learn the type of information the one issue form needs, you'll be better equipped to tap your source to get it. Familiarity with the general requirements of the one issue article's start, contents, structural models, and uses of quotes can help you plan your research questions and press for greater clarity in their answers.

## The Opening

The beginning of the one issue article covers the basic information promised by the definition of this form. In brief, the beginning announces a timely issue of interest to a specific readership. Some examples and discussion of these sample beginnings of one issue articles in national and metropolitan magazines will demonstrate the kind of information to secure. As you read these sample beginnings of one issue articles, ask yourself the questions the form's definition needs to have filled in the opening paragraphs: "What's new?," "What's at issue?", "What's the audience of this publication the issue is aiming for?", and for your own mastery of the form, "What is the technical device?"

*Harper's Bazaar's* one issue/article, "Good Sense About Sex From Dr. Ruth," by Eileen Stukane is launched with a single indirect question:

> You may wonder and worry about whether your teenager is sexually active, but today the question of when "sex" starts is no longer the biggest parental concern. Adolescents are making their own choices and the real issue facing many adults is whether their son or daughter is having a relationship for the right reason—and with contraception.
>
> A recent study from the Alan Guttmacher Institute in New York City reveals that adolescents in five other industrialized countries (The Netherlands, Sweden, France, Canada and England/Wales) have far fewer pregnancies and abortions than American teens although they are just as sexually experienced. The reason: The other countries are concerned not with the morality of early sex, but rather with the prevention of pregnancy through an attitude of openness, sex education and free or low-cost birth control.
>
> These findings fuel Dr. Ruth Westheimer's drive to enlighten parents and adolescents as young people discover their sexual selves.

Let's address the information requirements for this type of article's opening, couched in those questions, one at a time. The news at issue is expressed in the first paragraph: ". . . the question of when 'sex' starts is no longer the biggest parental concern . . . the real issue . . . is whether their son or daughter is having a relationship for the right reason—and with contraception." The new issue of "parental concern" is the current change in young people's sexual mores, for which the featured therapist will offer enlightened counseling. This national magazine article uses "You," meaning the reader, but the article's target is parents of adolescents. The device at the start is a paradox—a contrast between what a concerned parent may worry about with an adolescent interested in the opposite sex, and what is true of adolescent sex today.

In summary, the *Bazaar* piece points up a timely nagging problem emerging from a new social trend, shared in many countries by parents of adolescents, and recommends expert counsel for it.

The next sample beginning from a one issue article published in a national magazine encompasses a larger target audience, a new issue in a different traditional field, and another device, but you'll note this beginning takes the same structural approach to organizing its information—statement of a problem, a reason, and possible solution. The one issue article, "Fish—For Health," which appeared in July 1985, in *Bazaar's* newsstand rival, *Vogue,* begins:

> The more we learn about nutrition and fitness, the smarter we become about eating... which helps to explain why fish consumption is at an all-time high. Now, research gives a new reason for choosing fish: it may be "preventive medicine," actually *lowering* the risk of heart disease, offering some asthma and arthritis relief, and—this research is still in the most preliminary stage—even reducing the risk of breast cancer.

Again, let's turn to the promises in the form's definition—timeliness, an issue, particular audience focus, and (for beginners in need of technique), identification of the device—for our discussion of the *Vogue* one issue article's beginning. The piece opens with the device of a social observation about a new nutrition trend and an example, "The more we learn about nutrition and fitness, the smarter we become about eating." This timely nutritional interest in eating smarter to be fit is exemplified in "fish consumption... at an all-time high." The "we" to whom this observation and the article is addressed are all *Vogue's* "Health Style" page readers concerned with making smarter food choices to stay in shape.

In essence, this national magazine article follows the format of problem, solution, reason in this fashion. It narrows in on a new nutritional problem emerging from the fitness movement—how to eat for fitness—suggests its readers, as its title states, choose "Fish—For Health," then gives the research endorsing this dietary change.

The next one issue article is not about a national trend in childrearing or health, but one of local interest to New York City business executives. Yet this opening also mirrors the structural design—problem, solution, reasons—you have seen in the preceding two samples of the form's start. *Manhattan, Inc.,* another 1985 National Magazine Award winner, drew readers' attention to a new budgetary issue and its causes in "Limousine Prices Stretching Out." It advised users to increase or limit their budget for this luxury expense because of the expected hike in limo rentals.

> That is the likely result of an intensive effort by the Taxi & Limousine Commission to nail some 30,000 nonmedallion vehicles that should be registered but are not.

Owners will have to pay the commission $250 per car per year and $50 per driver per year. Those costs will probably be passed on to consumers, who have been using car services and limousines in record numbers because empty taxis are often impossible to find.

. . .

Again, our analysis will reveal the opening succeeds because it follows the stipulations implicit in the form's definition. The piece addresses "those" executives with expense accounts or salaries for whom stretch limo rentals are a fact of business life. The piece reports a new business development, the predicted price hike of rented limos, recommends solutions, and explains the maze of changes in city administration of these luxury vehicles responsible for this new business budget issue. The introduction could be described as a condition and results or statement of a cause and effects.

From these sample beginnings of one issue articles for national and metropolitan publications, it's obvious that you can get a head start on your beginning if before, during, and after the interview you ask, "What's the problem underlying the new issue?", "What's its cause or reason?", "What are solutions?", "Why?", "What readers will want to know about it?" You've seen several ways to introduce a one issue article about a trend or event—a paradox, observation and example, cause and effect, and you likely can think of many more. Whatever your method, if your beginning identifies a timely issue of interest to readers, your opening will give the reader a reason to read on.

## THE BODY: RESEARCH REQUIREMENTS AND TYPES OF STRUCTURES

Study of different structures for the one issue article and the type facts that fill them may help you focus and expand your list of questions. You may gain more information than the assigned space permits, but you will better understand your topic and write a more-informed article as a result.

Short summaries of one issue articles from the fields of health, finance, and literature from national and weekly publications will show possible organizational strategies and suggest the necessary research for the body of your one issue article.

The structure of my *American Health* article, "Rx: Monilia," about repeated yeast infections, is based on a structure and the same factual ground often touched by articles on new medical issues in other national magazines. The main body of the piece gives patient symptoms, definition of the infection, its prevalence, chronic signs, new research on the cause of chronic infections, new treatment method, the reason, results, dose of medicine, practical precautions to avoid the infection. In summary, the structure follows that of a comprehensive medical analysis of a problem and its solution—diagnosis, cause, treatment, results, preventive measures.

In researching new scientific findings, be sure to include critical questions readers will want answered and report the expert's defense in your piece. So in my *American Health* article, "Stiff Joints: Come Again to Cartilage," I asked Dr. Bland whether surgery might have speeded the recovery of mobility rather than the year of a vitamin/exercise/aspirin regimen it took for the bedridden professor's new cartilage to grow. His reply appears in my piece. " 'Surgery might have been faster,' admits Bland, but 'nothing beats your own joints.' " Remember, just as I cautioned you to criticize the new product or service reported, I recommend you do the same with the news development or new issue for the same reason— to enhance the credibility of your writing.

The organization for a medical article is just a more complex version of the problem/solution structure prevalent in similar one issue/interviews about other fields. Dan Dorfman's "The Bottom Line: The Doomsday Man," in *New York* magazine introduces the problem of the all-time-high stock market, offers Hoffman's "sell all stocks" solution, and then follows with the strategist's reasons, including a Dow decline, pressures from climbing interest rates, a severe recession, and other economic indicators. The piece concludes with practical choices for conservative and aggressive investors. So the article adheres strictly to this outline—problem, the radical method of solving it, the reasons, and practical applications of the advice.

An interview with an author on his newly published work may require a different structure. Here is the synopsis of one very fine interview by Patricia T. O'Conner with Richard Lourie, titled " 'Burn Before Reading,' " from *The New York Times Book Review*, August 4, 1985, which appeared next to a review of Lourie's suspense novel, *First Loyalty*. As a substitute structure for the one about a problem, solution, and its application, O'Conner organizes telling details from the author's perspective of his novel, his professional work, personal life, and resume into variations on a theme. A summary of the interview will indicate its repetitive thematic structure.

The interview leads off with Lourie's anecdote about the motto in the interview's title. Accordingly, some Russian emigres in the United States "joke that their motto for passing along clandestine material is 'Top-secret—burn before reading,' " which Lourie claims characterizes his novel's atmosphere. The details of his reported biography: Lourie's work as translator of Polish and Russian works, his activity in their literary undergrounds; his residence in a " 'nerve center' " of emigre activity; friends like dissidents Andrei D. Sakharov and his wife; names of famous writers whose works he has translated—Czeslaw Milosz and others—all reflect this atmosphere. So the interview finds in the literary life and work of the reviewed author a repeated motif that sheds light on his reviewed novel. The structure of a repeated theme works well for a literary interview about the issues created by an author's newly published work.

But in researching and writing on newsworthy developments in an old field or in new ones, I suggest you consider a definition of the new issue, the problem that precipitates the issue, the reasons, and solutions, as a general outline. Your efforts to fill in its particulars may help you plan, focus, obtain, and structure the information necessary for this article form's format.

So far you've learned the criteria for selecting a timely topic in a field of information and the qualifications for an informed, articulate spokesperson whose credentials will withstand scrutiny in the piece. In addition, this section has explained the form's introduction, design, and type of facts for the article's construction, to insure you devise adequate, objectively critical research questions.

## REQUIREMENTS FOR QUOTES

The final portion on requirements for this article form is devoted to quotes— their importance, their uses, how to make quotes out of your interview material, a warning against their abusive use, and advice about when to employ quotes or paraphrases.

### Quotes: General Purpose

Use quotes to increase the effectiveness of your reporting and the quality of your writing. They're very important to one issue articles. Quotes give the reported issue immediacy and can make your writing entertaining and credible. Quotes give immediacy because the comments by the expert allow the reader to experience or understand firsthand the new trend, update, or event directly through the expert's eyes, words, and viewpoints. Quotes entertain because they break up the impersonal voice of the author reporting the issue with personal, conversationally expressed messages from the expert to the reader. The one issue form mandates the expert's quotes for credibility because of the roles of the expert in this type of article. As spokesman or commentator, an expert may reveal or examine the new issue in direct quotation. So quotes are both necessary and a built-in advantage to the one issue form for both authenticating your reporting and vitalizing your writing about the issue.

### Quotes: Functions

Quotes in the one issue article, as well as other journalistic forms, are extensions of the functions of the expert. The following is a list of these tasks dictated by the expert's dual roles. As presenter of the issue, an expert in direct quote may define an issue, explain it, reveal a facet, elaborate, or give examples. As analyst, an expert may evaluate or summarize the issue. These tasks of the expert are the rightful work of quotes in this form and also illustrate what quotes do in general in nonfiction article writing.

Examples of quotes from published one issue articles will demonstrate their different services for the expert. Often, quotes by an expert are a more authoritative way of defining the topic than a simple paraphrase. For instance, as spokesperson on the issue of women's sports injuries caused by deficient athletic conditioning, Dr. Nisonson, in my *Bazaar* piece, defined the weak ankle vulnerable to sprains this way:

> "Those whose ankles have a tendency to turn in under them on uneven ground or who lose their support stepping on a branch or rock usually demonstrate chronic instability of the ankle," Dr. Nisonson observes.

The quote defines the tendency for chronic ankle instability by the evidence in a woman's physical movements. The quote serves as a succinct definition of a portion of the issue by the expert presenting it.

Besides defining a facet or the entire topic, quotes can give the expert's reasons to elucidate the issue presented. Here's one from Dan Dorfman's "The Bottom Line: The Doomsday Man," which ends a long analysis about the advisability of

> Another investment alternative: gold. Hoffman points out that there are cross-currents at work on gold. On the one hand, a deflationary trend—namely falling commodity prices—should weaken the price. On the other hand, given the worldwide recession he's predicting and the accompanying prospects of a worldwide banking crisis, the fear factor should drive gold prices higher.
>
> "My guess is gold will go higher because fear will get the upper hand," Hoffman says.

An expert's reasons for his or her views often are followed by an elaboration, which is another purpose that quotes fill to help the expert present the issue. The following quote from my *American Health,* July/August 1984 piece, "Stretching Out: If It Feels Too Good, Stop," exemplifies the use of a direct quote for this purpose. Watch for the reason first and then its elaboration by Dr. Joseph D'Amico, chairman of orthopedics at the New York College of Podiatric Medicine. First D'Amico explains why 88 percent of 540 25-mile-per-week joggers who stretched before runs had more leg pains than those who didn't stretch at all.

> "The wrong people do stretching excercise," says D'Amico. "Those who need to don't do enough because stretching doesn't make them feel comfortable. And those who can stretch with ease overdo it and become more prone to injury. If a naturally loose-jointed runner flexes more than necessary, the muscles have to

work harder to propel the body forward. That extra workload may lead to muscle inflammation."

The last quote shows an expert presenting the issue and giving a reason for his study's results and then further explanation.

Besides, quotes allow an authority to reveal an issue or give examples. A direct quote in the Richard Lourie *New York Times Book Review* interview illustrates these uses. The first reveals insight into the atmosphere of his novel and the motto, " 'Top secret—burn before reading.' "

> Richard Lourie, the author of *First Loyalty,* said in a recent interview. "That's the atmosphere of the whole thing, fun and funny but serious. It's a smart Russian joke on the recognition of their own paranoia."

Later on, Lourie gives an example of this atmosphere from his life in a community where relatives of Andrei D. Sakharov and his wife, Yelena G. Bonner, who are friends of Mr. Lourie, live.

> "[The family] did get a postcard very recently from Bonner," he said. "It seems like certain letters were traced three or four times very heavily, and there was a secondary message in that fact. For example, if she writes 'I' and emphasizes 'I'—you don't even need 'I' in Russian—that may mean that what she's saying of herself is not necessarily true of Sakharov."

You see how both quotes—one, a revelation; the other, an example—bring immediacy to the literary issue of the novel's atmosphere and readers' understanding of it because the quotes permit the expert to speak directly to the reader without third-party interference by the interviewer.

You've watched quotes work for the expert to define, give reasons, elaborate, reveal, offer an example, in order to present the issue. Two more samples will illustrate how quotes act for the expert who, as analyst of the issue, can evaluate it or summarize. In *Manhattan, Inc.*'s reported national survey by Accountemps, a local New York City firm, of total annual personal calls by employees, Marc Silbert, an Accountemps vice-president, evaluates the sixty-two hours total chitchat yearly spent free-of-charge by white collar employees on the job as "one of America's largest phantom job benefits."

Besides evaluating the issue, the expert performing an issue analysis may draw conclusions at the article's end. In the final paragraph of the *Bazaar* piece about "The Teen Scene: Good Sense About Sex," Dr. Ruth's quote summarizes her enlightened policy regarding talks between parents and adolescents about sex:

> "In the happiest families, communication is always open between parent and child, but ultimately a teen's aim is to become less dependent and form his *own* value sys-

tem," she stresses. "Parents are really just a stage in that growth toward independent thinking and sexual maturity."

The quote is the expert's summation of the attitude that makes for "Good Sense" between parents and their growing children "About Sex." A summary in direct quotes gives the expert the opportunity for a final analysis of the issue.

This last section has tutored you in the ways quotes serve the dual roles of the expert in presenting and analyzing the issue. I suggest you plan questions for the expert that highlight these multiple roles. If relevant, don't hesitate to volunteer any of the following questions during the interview at the proper moment:

"Can you define this?" "Can you give a reason?" "Can you elaborate?" "Can you shed any insight?" "Can you give an example?" "How do you evaluate this?" "Will you summarize the issue?"

If you push the expert to better phrase raw quotes in the interview rather than accept them unquestioningly, your effort will supply a wealth of sharper, more articulate quotes for the article.

When, after review of your research notes, you decide which portions to make direct quotes by the expert in the written article, you can introduce these quotations within the one issue article in two ways. One, you can preface the quote with a summary of its theme, as Dorfman did preceding Hoffman's reason for choosing gold as a sound investment. Or, you can simply insert the quote without any introductory lead. Without a lead-in, however, the quote may not fit smoothly into the exposition. An abstract summary of the quote's theme eliminates jarring the reader because it provides a smooth stepping-stone to move from one idea in the article to the next. But you be the judge and do whatever you think is best to insert your quotes as you write your article.

## Quotes: Methods for Construction

Now I want to address the issue of the methods and ethics of rewriting your expert's words for quotation in the article. When, for instance, my student read her draft of the interview with her family member about new developments in veterinary medicine, I criticized the piece for too many technical words. She claimed, "But there were many more." Did she do the right thing in rewriting her authority's words to make them more conversational? I would argue yes.

I believe in rewriting the expert's answers to clarify and heighten the intended meaning. You can condense the expert's answers, rearrange the order of the sequence in which the answers were given, switch or reverse phrases in sentences, remove repetition, delete extraneous words, or drop superfluous ideas to change the spoken to the written word. But you can't invent ideas the expert never said nor tamper with the connotation of the authority's thoughts. I want to stress again unequivocably: You can substitute your words for vague or overly general terms by the expert to intensify the meaning, make the thought more vivid, or make the idea clearer. Your raison d'etre is to communicate the expert's truth more exactly and more accurately than the expert, who speaks in jargon, rhetoric, or technical obfuscations, may have the verbal skills to do. Yet you cannot create ideas the expert never expressed for attribution, nor can you alter the meaning of your authority's words to mirror your viewpoint. You must report the authority's information accurately. When you have finished your one issue article, always call the authority and read back all quotes—not for approval, but for verification of their accuracy.

## Quotes: Abusive Use

On the other hand, I want to warn you against overly relying on an authority's quotes to write your one issue article. If you use extended quotes by your expert simply rearranged, you are abdicating your responsibility as the writer. You are withholding from the reader your particular focus because all your article does is repeat your expert. Your writing may lapse into platitudes and undocumented facts because you have not used available techniques to impose your views on the materials. If your views guide you in organizing and writing the article, you will avoid such pitfalls as cliches and vague references for this reason. Your views of the issue will help extract a personal focus from the interview material, because your views will shape the raw data into the article's premise, argument, contradictions, judgments, summaries, in concert with your position. By shaping the materials, I mean not only giving the ideas a structure and order, but I also mean allotting more space to some ideas over others. By eliminating or paring ideas, you deemphasize, diminish, or enhance the importance of chosen reported facts. So you relinquish the writer's hard responsibility for synthesizing the research to articulate a point of view when you indulge in overextended quotes. You may wish to refrain from indicating your position publicly, but the price is rambling, undocumented cliche writing. Furthermore, you disappoint your readers who look to a writer for a special filter that is wholly yours through which to view the issue. It's my belief that as a magazine writer it's your viewpoint along with demonstration of sterling integrity that gets your articles published.

## Quotes: Appropriate Employment

This conclusion brings up another need of the beginning writer. You may wish for some rule to consult in decisions about when to quote your expert directly and when to summarize. My rule of thumb is this: Use the expert to say ideas only an expert could say, because you as the writer have no authority to voice them. Summarize in your voice factual information that you as the writer have more skill to say more concisely than the expert did. Usually, an expert will express this pertinent factual material in uninteresting, disorganized fashion. Such interview materials need the writer's ability for succinct orderly compression.

For instance, if the information is simply a list of facts, you might opt for indirect quotation, as in the following example from an October 1979, *Mademoiselle,* "Health Guide" piece, "The Cystitis Connection." The expert is Dr. W. Reid Pitts, Jr., Assistant Professor of Urology (Clinical) at Cornell University Medical College, The New York Hospital.

> If your cystitis seems to be recurring frequently, Dr. Pitts recommends seeing a urologist who can determine if there is any physical cause (reflux of urine from the bladder to the kidney, malformation or position of the kidneys, urethral abnormalities, etc.) for your repeated bouts of infection.

The list of probable causes for repeated cystitis seems suited to indirect quotation.

In general, in decisions about whether to use a quote or not, try to remember the dual roles of the expert and the services quotes perform as extensions of these roles—such as define, explain, elaborate, reveal, give an example, judge, or summarize. Let the reader know what the expert said in direct quotes when the authority's words justify an information function of the expert's roles. If a quote performs one of these tasks, it might be wiser to put it in direct quotation. But apply such advice case by case, because you are the ultimate arbiter on your problem.

## SAMPLE ONE ISSUE/ONE INTERVIEW ARTICLE

The section just concluded informed you about requirements for the one issue/one interview form's topic, expert, the introduction, structure, factual contents, and direct quotations. To show you these essentials in practice, the last part of this chapter contains a sample one issue article from my published works and excerpts from student attempts at the form.

I received and executed the commissioned one issue/one interview article, "How to Find the Right Sport for Your Body," published in *Mademoiselle,* April 1979, despite several editorial misunderstandings. I'll briefly review them.

When I approached *Mademoiselle,* I was just developing my specialty in articles about sports medicine. I was narrowing the theme of women runners and their problems "Closing the Gap" with men's performance times to that of women's sports injuries due to their unequal athletic conditioning. So in the late seventies, I was foraging for a mainstream women's publication with a strong feminist slant on sports medicine. When I reached the secretary at the office of *Mademoiselle's* Senior Editor for Features, Mary Cantwell, I requested an appointment and rattled off as qualifications my recent credits—THE OFFICIAL PROGRAM: NEW YORK CITY MARATHON; *The Village Voice;* OFFICIAL PROGRAM: MINI MARATHON; and some names of some esoteric running magazines—and got the scheduled meeting.

En route I remembered I had known the name of Mary Cantwell as a long-lived name editor in women's magazines since my freshman days at Bryn Mawr.

During my long presentation of article ideas, Cantwell's secretary often interrupted. But as Cantwell signed letters, nodded agreement, or suggested meeting times, she performed these jobs like a besieged hausfrau rather than a senior editor preening during the rule over her domain. With each article suggested, I drew out of a bulging manila envelope some glossy medical journal extract to confirm my thesis or my expert's authority in the field. I must have seemed like one of those bag ladies who roam New York streets with all their worldly goods in paper shopping bags. I remember showing a glossy article by Dr. James A. Nicholas, Director of Lenox Hill Hospital's Institute of Sports Medicine and Athletic Trauma, about women's sports injuries.

In time, her secretary called to arrange a second editorial conference at Condé Nast. I was to bring a specific extract. She gave me the wrong reference, as I discovered upon arrival. The conference couldn't take place as a result, so Cantwell, as apology, took me to lunch. I had to return the next day with the right article to discuss the *Mademoiselle* feature assignment. The next week, the most thematically detailed agreement letter I'd ever received arrived. I was to report the sports injuries women are prone to purely because they are women or a physical type. Yet as I mentioned in a past chapter, I was disturbed by one assigned guideline and the omission of purchased rights. (The fee purchased First North American serial rights only, Cantwell told me by phone later, but she had neglected that fact in the agreement.)

It's worth reexamining the point of disagreement to show you the flexibility you can expect from an editor. In my reply, I agreed to explore the greater numbers of black runners, which Cantwell had euphemistically called "ethnicity," but from a broader perspective. I wrote:

> As for ethnicity and athleticism and whether physical reasons explain perhaps a preponderance of black runners (I will have the expert check this), I would like to broaden this suggestion to the question of race and athletics. I wonder whether orientals, blacks, Indians or Caucasians have any advantage in a particular sport because of racial body builds. I don't know, but I'd like to try this approach if that is all right.

As I said before, the editor acquiesced to my broader sociological reinterpretation of her point about "ethnicity." She also gave me the extended deadline I requested.

When I called Lenox Hill Hospital's Institute of Sports Medicine and Athletic Trauma for an appointment with its director, the Assistant Director who handles these requests shuttled me to a research assistant, Meredith Melvin. I doubted I could use anyone in such a low-ranking position, not for the lack of a prestigious title, but for the lack of depth of knowledge and sufficient clinical practice in the subject of the interview.

I needn't have worried. Besides reviewing the medical journals to which the sports institute subscribed, Melvin often administered the institute's fitness tests. She was so au courant on research in sports medicine the institute often sent her on media interviews to places like *Vogue* and CBS-TV. A vocal feminist, Melvin had presented a paper at a recent medical conference that attacked restrictive chauvinistic views of women's sports potential and their greater vulnerability to sports injuries. So Melvin was an ideal spokesperson for the interview—informed with up-to-date knowledge of the topic, an articulate veteran of many press conferences, a feminist, and a recognized expert within her profession.

An hour interview at my home stretched to double the time limit. At my dining table, I typed her answers as fast as she formulated them. She had prepared a researched approach to the subject which I tactfully disabused her of to avoid a lecture of unuseable rhetoric. When I reread our results, I recognized some information needed clarification. With much verbal tugging, Melvin returned for another hour and a half for "pick up" questions.

I did the interviews on a Tuesday and Thursday, and delivered the final 2,000-word manuscript by the following Tuesday. Cantwell called that afternoon to say the piece was accepted, but she wanted the material requested in her agreement letter about the relationship of body types and sports injuries. I was bound to give it to her, but Melvin wasn't and refused. She felt the institute's director, Dr. James A. Nicholas, had done so much research on the topic, she couldn't make the compromise and submit to oversimplified statements about such a complex subject. I supported her position as a lay scholar, but, as the assigned journalist, I had an assignment to fulfill.

So I called Mary Cantwell and, in an agonized voice, said, "You're the editor. What do you need?" Armed with her response, I approached the institute's Assistant Director. He gave me names of two former institute associates. I interviewed long distance in Los Angeles one who had been a past consultant to the New York Knicks and New York Jets. Then I wrote out the assigned points and phoned in the information Cantwell had insisted on.

I heard nothing from *Mademoiselle*'s editorial offices. Weeks later I called to check the accuracy of available edited copy. I was told the article was in page proofs. A copy was messengered to me. I called Melvin and read the entire piece. My expert wanted two words changed—"rotor," which was misspelled, to "rotator," and "flex," which was incorrect, to "extend." When I phoned in the corrections, the piece was at the printers and on the presses. The following one issue/interview article is the one that appeared in *Mademoiselle,* April 1979, with the two errata intact.

# HOW TO FIND THE RIGHT SPORT FOR YOUR BODY

## By Barbara Kevles

There are no guarantees that everyone has the capability to be a great athlete. At least two dozen variables affect sports performance. But if you have certain physical characteristics, your chances for playing and winning in a sport can be increased. And even if you don't excel, there is no reason to stop doing something you like. Orthopedic surgeon, Dr. Marc Friedman, former fellow at the Lenox Hill Hospital's Institute of Sports Medicine and Athletic Trauma and consultant to the New York Knicks and the New York Jets, suggests the following physical characteristics may match you to your sport.

UPPER BODY STRENGTH If you can lift two heavy bags of groceries and carry them up a flight of stairs, you have strength in your upper body. You might be good at baseball, bowling, canoeing, golf, judo, swimming.

SMALL BODY FRAME Anything less than a size seven or eight. You might be good at ballet, diving, gymnastics, modern dance, tumbling.

LARGE BONE STRUCTURE Anything above a size eleven or twelve. You might be good at basketball, football, hockey, water polo.

STRONG LEGS If you can walk all day and still disco at night, you have strong legs. You might be good at ballet, basketball, biking, horseback riding, skating, hiking, skiing, soccer.

LONG ARMS If you stand up and your arms extend beyond the middle of your thigh, you have long arms. You might be good at badminton, canoeing, fencing, handball, paddleball, any racquet sport, volleyball.

FLEXIBILITY You can tell how flexible you are with simple tests devised by Dr. James A. Nicholas, Director of Lenox Hill Hospital's Institute of Sports Medicine and Athletic Trauma. Keep your knees straight and see if you can place your palms flat on the floor, or with knees straight, see if you can rotate your feet 90 degrees so they form a straight line. If so, you might be good at ballet, basketball, diving, fencing, gymnastics, modern dance, swimming.

### . . . and play it safely

As more women change from sports spectators to participants we wondered whether the new female athlete is more prone to injury because women are weaker, softer, frailer, more pliant creatures. We posed the question to women's sports specialist, Meredith Melvin, researcher at Lenox Hill Hospital's Institute of Sports Medicine and Athletic Trauma in Manhattan. To our relief, Ms. Melvin refused to concede athletics are more dangerous for women than men because of a woman's genetic inheritance. "Injuries occur frequently not because of women's standard biological and anatomical differences from men," Ms. Melvin assured us, "but because of women's inequality in physical conditioning. Under athletic stress, women with underdeveloped muscles are more predisposed to injury."

Ms. Melvin gave an example of a sports injury caused by women's poor conditioning. "The anatomical fact that women have half the muscle mass of men makes them exceptionally weak in the upper torso, particularly in the shoulders and arms. And because of societal brainwashing, women haven't developed what muscles they have in these areas." Accordingly, the beginner woman athlete is likely to suffer "thrower's shoulder." You know it by a razor pain in the shoulder when you lift your arm. Ms. Melvin explained the reason. "The pain results from a 'muscle pull,' which is a partial tear of the rotor cuff muscles. These muscles cap the top of the upper arm bone, the humerus, in the shoulder joint so as to stabilize the arm's rotary motion. Injury to the rotor cuff muscles interferes with the entire movement of the arm. When a woman is out of shape, any sudden pitch of a baseball, the swing of a squash racquet too hard or a swim stroke executed too sharply can produce 'thrower's shoulder.' "

The most common female sports injury from poorly developed muscles is "runner's knee," technically called "chondromalacia." Walking or jogging, you will feel pain right under your kneecap and know you have the badge of the beginner athlete. Ms. Melvin described it medically. "With the leg's movement, your kneecap rides up and down in a groove on the femur, the upper thigh bone. When the kneecap slides out of its track, its undersurface of cartilage becomes irritated and inflamed, which translates into this specifically-located pain under the knee." In the past, Ms. Melvin pointed out, medical experts attributed women's greater incidence of chondromalacia to female anatomy. Because a woman is constructed with a wider pelvis for reproduction, "the thigh bone joins the pelvic bone at a steeper angle than in a man. Consequently, the quadriceps, the muscles attaching fom the pelvis along the femur to just below the knee, pull the kneecap at a sharper angle than a man's quadriceps, which better parallel the groove of the kneecap." But Ms. Melvin stressed the quadriceps' odd pull on the female knee was not the primary cause of women's knee problems. "Women with complaints of chondromalacia symptoms chronically exhibit weak quadriceps. If the quadriceps which keep the kneecap on track are weak, the kneecap becomes unstable and slides out of its groove." Two types of knee injuries result. Subluxation, a repeated partial dislocation of the kneecap, appears among women basketball players, dancers and quite frequently runners because, Ms. Melvin said, "Running is the sport chosen by women who haven't been athletic since high school gym class and who've been swept up by the fitness craze." The more serious knee injury, complete dislocation of the kneecap from its track, happens more to athletes with weak quadriceps who fall during a hockey game, a ski competition or roller-skating derby. In these cases, surgery may be required to realign the knee.

Not only female anatomy, but also female physiology, has been misunderstood in sports medicine, according to Ms. Melvin. Women's greater ligament elasticity—long considered a cause of athletic injury—may simply be another symptom of underdeveloped muscles in women. Ms. Melvin defined ligaments as "the fibrous structures which hold bones side by side and together at the joints." Then she delineated how with untrained muscles a woman's looser ligaments increase the danger of injury. "Ligaments function passively in the body," Ms. Melvin said, "unlike muscles which are active. So if these passive structures have more elastic give, as they do in women, these conditions demand stronger muscles to do more of the work to keep the bones in place. Under athletic stress untrained women athletes risk more injury at the joints because their muscles can't perform at sufficient levels to compensate for their loose ligaments."

For this reason, the second highest ranking injury among women athletes is the ankle sprain (or "torn ligament"). Frequently, Ms. Melvin finds patients with this injury show "a partial shearing of the anterior talo fibular ligament, which attaches from the tallus in the ankle's cavity to the lower leg." If you have a sprained ankle, you'll notice swelling around the ankle, pain at each step, and tenderness under and around the protruding knob of bone just below the calf. The ankle's torn ligament results from overstress, Ms. Melvin claims, because the body's muscles which link the leg to the trunk—the hip flexors and abductors—are not developed enough to meet the ankle's demands in athletic performance.

But with well-developed muscles, women's inherently looser ligaments give them greater flexibility and a decided advantage over men in such physically demanding activities as ballet and gymnastics. Ms. Melvin said, "Because of the greater ligament laxity, women possess a greater range of motion at the hip, knee and lower leg, which enables women to execute the turned out foot positions so essential to ballet steps and some of the unparalleled tricks of a gymnast of the caliber of a Nadia Comaneci. Also, the greater flexibility at the hip means a ballerina can isolate her leg to kick higher and wider than, for instance, a football player, who must lean forward with his whole pelvis to leadoff with a kick."

But for untrained women, such flexibility can mean vulnerability not only to torn ligaments, but to tendonitis—an inflammation of the fibrous material attaching the body's muscles to its bones. According to Ms. Melvin, when a muscle is weak, that laxness can precipitate an injured tendon because "if the body requires a weak muscle to pull or contract, the tendon must expend more effort for the task." Ms. Melvin cited this imbalance as a "primary cause—though not the only one" of "tennis elbow."

Women with this injury feel excruciating pain focused in their elbow, but a wrist movement or grip of a racquet can also stimulate the pain. "You lose a lot of your grip power with tennis elbow," Ms. Melvin said, "because the inflamed tendons in your elbow attach to muscles that move the wrist and fingers." Poor conditioning in the upper extremities makes women athletes prey to tendonitis of the wrist, an inflammation of tendons from muscles which flex the fingers.

Yet all these athletic injuries—wrist tendonitis, tennis elbow, ankle sprains, runner's knee, thrower's shoulder—Ms. Melvin stressed, are not caused by women possessing less muscle mass than men, but by women simply being out of shape. "The fact women have half as much muscle mass as men doesn't mean women can't function free of injury in the gym or on the athletic field."

However, Ms. Melvin acknowledged that women athletes have an inherited biological liability in sports, which conditioning cannot solve. "When women get hit by a hockey puck or misplaced basketball, they are more susceptible to injury than men because of female body composition. On the average, female athletes possess 10 percent more body fat than their male counterparts. With typically smaller bodies, lighter frames and more fat, women don't withstand impact as well as men because fat doesn't absorb shock as well as the greater muscle mass borne by men. Consequently, women are apt to bruise more from blows in contact sports."

She revealed women's bruises take longer to heal. "The black and blue marks women athletes incur are larger and longer staying because women have a greater predisposition to "effusion" and "edema." She illustrated her terms. "Because women's capillaries are thinner than a man's, they break more easily under a blow, so that more capillary fluids spill and swell the skin as in a bruised ankle. This is 'effusion.' Then because greater numbers of capillaries spill open because of their greater fragility, larger quantities of blood run out and collect in the wrong place, which is called 'edema.' Women's black and blue marks take longer to disappear because women traditionally retain fluids in their bodies more than men."

From this vantage, she viewed the female breasts as simply "one more large, relatively exposed area to bruise." Yet she denied that a blow to the breasts causes cancer. "That myth is just a bunch of baloney. A bruise on the breasts is more painful than one located elsewhere on the body, but it's still just a bruise." She noted that often women as well as men competitors suffer irritated nipples and she cautioned that no one should let the irritation become so aggravated "that the nipple ruptures and bleeds because infection could result."

Asked whether any race had better protection against injury, Ms. Melvin answered candidly, "There is no good scientific evidence to document that any racial group has any inherent physical factor that better protects them from sports injury. There are too many past environmental factors that could predispose blacks to being first-place sprinters or Chinese to being first-class gymnasts. All you can do is tell someone to do the best with the body they have."

She underlined her theme, "Fitness is important for staying free of athletic injury not only for today, but also for tomorrow." She stressed that supple muscles not only protected the ligaments and tendons from injury, but the bones of the body as well. "Women don't realize that bones change their composition consistently every day. Calcium and other minerals within the bones are constantly being absorbed by the body, so that the bone is always making new cells to replace worn ones. It's as dynamic as the process of breathing. As women age, their bones become brittle because they lose more minerals than they replace. This is called 'osteoporosis.' The more out of condition a woman becomes, the less her muscles move the bones to encourage this cell replacement. So that an older woman who hasn't kept fit through a sport is more prone to osteoporosis, which predisposes bone fractures in her brittle extremities. Sporadic older women skiers are more likely to incur leg fractures than a woman the same age who'd kept in condition."

Were younger women more safe from injury because of being closer to their athletic prime? "We don't know what the prime age is for women athletes. We know a young girl has the most ligament laxity she'll ever have for gymnastics, but that advantage decreases with age. In terms of all other factors of athletic performance, we don't have enough statistics to say when women reach their athletic prime because in the past not enough women participated as much or in as many sports as women today or had the encouragement and facilities to test their athletic capacities to their limits." She advocated that rather than rely on her age, a woman should protect herself against athletic injury by strength-building exercises. She summarized, "Athletics are no more injurious to women than men. Women have every capability of being good athletes. They can compensate through conditioning for their lighter muscle mass, steeper pelvic-femur angle, looser ligaments, greater fat tissue, more fragile capillaries and lighter, smaller body frames. It's more dangerous for women not to be active in athletics than to participate."

So we discovered that women are weaker, softer, more pliant and frailer than men, but these factors are no longer valid excuses to exempt women from athletic competition for fear of bodily harm.

## Analysis

"How to Find the Right Sport For Your Body" demonstrates the fundamental design of the one issue/one interview article.

The work has two beginnings because of the editorial compromise I made to get the article published. The first is about body types and choice of sport. The second, which begins after the heading, ". . . and play it safely," introduces the main article by stating a timely issue in a field of interest to the publication's national female audience. The article's emerging issue in the new field of sports medicine is expressed this way: "we wondered whether the new female athlete is more prone to injury because women are weaker, softer, frailer, more pliant creatures." So the article's beginning satisfies the form's need for the right kind of developing issue by questioning whether women have a greater predisposition to athletic injury. The topic is timely because of the reported trend: "more women" have changed from "sports spectators to participants." The issue, which falls within the realm of modern sociology, appropriately focuses on a general field and topic of national concern to college-educated women in their early to mid-twenties who may read *Mademoiselle*. Of course, the underlying problem the article touches upon is whether *Mademoiselle*'s readers should join the burgeoning group of women athletes even though a sports injury due to their sex may be the inescapable initiation dues.

The article's expert is identified succinctly by her professional specialization ("women's sports specialist"), position ("researcher"), professional affiliation ("Lenox Hill Hospital's Institute of Sports Medicine and Athletic Trauma"), and by the institute's location ("Manhattan"). The affiliation with a nationally famous sports medicine institute enhances Melvin's public credibility and her research position and specialty underscore her knowledge of the article's topic.

Structurally, overall the piece follows the medical model mentioned for the one issue form—a survey of the problems, causes, and solution. Specifically, the article explores different kinds of women's sports injuries principally caused by inequitable physical conditioning by reviewing the common ones to major body sites—the shoulder, knee, ankle, elbow, wrist. Besides injuries due to inadequate conditioning, the work enumerates women athletes' liabilities because of body composition, race, or age. Within sections, each athletic injury is described by a medical definition, symptoms, cause, and, where relevant, degree of severity. In the final paragraphs, the issue of whether women should refrain from sports because of the physical risks of their sex is resolved. The expert advocates "a woman should protect herself against athletic injury by strength-building exercises." At the very end, I, as the writer, conclude by recalling the opening theme:

> So we discovered that women are weaker, softer, more pliant and frailer than men, but these factors are no longer valid excuses to exempt women from athletic competition for fear of bodily harm.

Always try to tie the dominant issue announced at the start of the one issue with some viewpoint of your own at the piece's end. At the close, the writer has the right to give an opinion on the issue that he or she has fairly and objectively reported prior. It's your chance for a say on the issue, so take the opportunity you've earned to give your views.

The article's quotes fit the purpose, goals, and permissible uses of quotes in the one issue form. The quotes purport generally to convey technical information and sociological insights that I, as the writer, have no authority to say. They aim to present the views of the sports specialist directly, without the writer's intercession, so that the reader may comprehend the topic from the expert's words firsthand. Unlike the simplifications appropriate for *Harper's Bazaar*'s fashion-conscious readers, the specialist's highly technical medical material and complex sociological positions expressed in ordinary words are suitable for *Mademoiselle*'s more intellectual college readership.

Besides filling the goals of quotes by giving immediacy to the writing and authenticity to the facts, the quotes perform the jobs of the expert as presenter and analyst of the issue. As illustrations will show, the quotes let the expert in presentation of the issue define it, give reasons, elaborate, offer examples, and reveal the issue. The direct quotations also allow the expert, as analyst of the issue, to evaluate and summarize.

Here in list form are direct quotes from "How to Find the Right Sport for Your Body" which work for the expert performing the roles dictated by the one issue form.

Quotes in the piece define, as the one for a "thrower's shoulder":

> "The pain results from a 'muscle pull,' which is a partial tear of the rotor cuff muscles. These muscles cap the tip of the upper arm bone, the humerus, in the shoulder joint so as to stabilize the arm's rotary motion."

They give reasons and elaborate on them, as the one for the cause of women's knee injuries due to poorly conditioned thigh muscles, rather than women's angular alignment of hip and knee:

> "Women with complaints of chondromalacia symptoms chronically exhibit weak quadriceps. If the quadriceps, which keep the kneecap on track are weak, the kneecap becomes unstable and slides out of its groove."

They give examples, like the sports motions that cause "thrower's shoulder":

> "When a woman is out of shape, any sudden pitch of a baseball, the swing of a squash racquet too hard or a swim stroke executed too sharply can produce 'thrower's shoulder.' "

They can reveal, as in the explanation for the female body part with the second-highest incidence of injury among women athletes:

> "Under athletic stress untrained women athletes risk more injury at the joints because their muscles can't perform at sufficient levels to compensate for their loose ligaments."

They can evaluate, as in:

"Athletics are no more injurious to women than men. Women have every capability of being good athletes. They can compensate through conditioning for their lighter muscle mass, steeper pelvic-femur angle, looser ligaments, greater fat tissue, more fragile capillaries and lighter, smaller body frames. It's more dangerous for women not to be active in athletics than to participate."

They can summarize the attitude of the expert toward the issue, as in:

"Injuries occur frequently not because of women's standard biological and anatomical differences from men . . . but because of women's inequality in physical conditioning."

These quotes serve the expert's functions as spokesperson and commentator on the issue assigned by the form. My article is not written entirely in quotes that camouflage the author's view under undigested facts, nor is it written devoid of quotes, which can bore the reader by an excess of heavy-handed undocumented opinion by the writer. If you wish to balance your vision of the issue with the expert's in quotation, then recognize the purposes, aims, and uses that quotes serve in the one issue form. Select quotes that perform the tasks for the expert as source and analyst of the issue for your article and combine them with your say on the issue at the close of the article.

## CRITIQUES OF STUDENT ONE ISSUE/ONE INTERVIEW ARTICLES

Beginner magazine writers often make one of three mistakes with the one issue article. They digress from the issue, lack a critical viewpoint, or quote the expert's rhetoric without discrimination. Excerpts or summaries from student tries at the form will illustrate these easily corrected errors. An article by a former student, Frank Hammel, about a timely nautical trend stayed on course most of the way, with the exception of one jarring detour. The piece dealt with the rejuvenated interest in wooden boats, despite four decades of fiberglass competitors, by exploring one representative wood-boat builder's quick commercial success—the reasons, his methods of wooden boat construction, waterproofing methods, and the prohibitive maintenance costs (which keep the comeback at quiet levels). The piece digressed when it veered into the expert's plans for expanded shop facilities, which did not pertain to the issue but rather to the expert's personal career growth. Make sure your facts illuminate the issue rather than extraneous themes relevant to your expert's personal profile. Stay on theme.

Another student's one issue article read like a public relations promotion because it reported only one side of the issue. The work questioned the timely issue of how much protection the martial arts give a liberated single urban woman. Every part of the reported interviews with a founder of a women's martial arts center and her instructors argued for karate's protective benefits, because of its power to reverse women's learned passivity, its assertiveness training, its potency as a military tactic, and its **adv**antage as a deterrent in street fighting. The one-sided report omitted karate's negative side, such as student problems with violent acts, or their injuries from its athletic training. When you research your issue, ask your expert questions both for and against the favorable position for objective reporting.

Besides making beginners' mistakes like thematic digressions or omission of criticisms, students sometimes accept the expert's jargon too uncritically. The following opening paragraphs of Ana Pacheco's "Psychic Healing" reveal this flaw.

> "I'm not opposed to Western medicine; however I do feel there are other ways of approaching the problems an individual may have," says Science of Mind Practitioner Julie Winter. A member of the Church of Religious Science, Winter has been practicing psychic healing in New York City for the last six years.
>
> Like a growing number of people, among them Elisabeth Kubler-Ross, author of *Death and Dying*, Winter has chosen an alternative route to helping people with their problems. With the methods practiced by members of the Church of Religious Science, she has helped people not only with physical ailments, but emotional ones as well. Psychic healing entails letting the person know what his mind is, what he may do with it, and what he can expect from it.
>
> Winter believes that each person contains the knowledge to heal his own body or circumstances. "One of the hardest things for an individual to do is know himself and change himself, but once he does, he can approach obstacles in his life more readily."

This discussion will stress the common pitfall in one issue articles of vague quotes, their possible causes, and measures to prevent them. The first quote, which begins, "I'm not opposed to Western medicine. . . . ," offers the writer a chance to use the expert as presenter of the issue of psychic healing, to define how this form of medicine differs from traditional Western medicine, but the vaguely expressed idea falls far from defining this issue. Similarly, the quote that starts, "One of the hardest things for an individual to do. . . . ," could be a quote that explains the reasons and methods of psychic healing. But the quote's language is so general that the quote could apply to a career change, change in behavior in relationships, and, least of all, to psychic healing.

If, during an interview, experts speak in generalized language, challenge them to say what they want as if they were talking to a street vendor. However, if you haven't researched your topic, you may lack the savvy to confront the expert on his style of expression because you are trying to master your subject at this first hearing. So, prior to an interview, immerse yourself in books, magazine or journal articles, pamphlets, or anything relevant to your newsbreaking issue. Then you'll have enough perspective on the content of the interview, so that you'll be able to hear when the expert needs your urging to break out of self-defeating rhetoric to speak in more humanized words about his or her expertise.

Following is a near-perfect student sample of the one issue/one interview form, "Teacher Burn-Out."

## TEACHER BURN-OUT
### By Frances Marie Sullivan

When Patricia Brown graduated from college in 1972, she was a bright, enthusiastic teacher, eagerly anticipating her first class. Seven years later, she is seeking a job in industry. Pat Brown, along with thousands of fellow educators, has become a victim of the latest epidemic in education—Teacher Burn-out.

Burn-out is not a new phenomenon, but its recent escalation can be traced to what Larry Sorensen, executive director of New York City-National Education Association, sees as "increasing problems. The school has become the substitute for parents, probation officers, you name it. The teacher must be all things to all students."

As a result, many teachers, angry at being the scapegoats for a general deteriorioration in education and frustrated at the lack of support from administrators and parents, have simply opted to leave the profession. According to a recent NEA poll, 33 percent of the teachers surveyed said they definitively or probably wouldn't choose teaching as a profession if they had it to do over again as opposed to 20 percent in 1974. "Many teachers," said Sorensen, "have simply decided it just isn't worth it."

Increased discipline problems, parent apathy, administrative harassment, and financial considerations, are all cited as major causes of burn-out. Violence toward teachers has also been increasing in recent years. In the school year 1968-69, 70,000 cases of teacher assault were reported; in 1978-79, that figure jumped to 110,000. One case in ten required medical attention. Although incidents were more frequent in large urban school systems, it's a nationwide problem. According to NEA statistics, there was a 3 percent increase in 1979 of attacks in "small world" or suburban systems.

Sorensen feels one of the major reasons for this behavior can be traced to a breakdown in discipline in the classroom. "Children need structure, direction. A student feels frustrated when he is not learning and takes out those frustrations by becoming a discipline problem." This opinion is supported by many teachers who, under threats of lawsuits, are relegated to mere classroom babysitters.

When a teacher does try to exert authority, she often finds herself bucking both parents and the school administration. "Parents," states Sorensen, "will often side against a teacher and in favor of their child. This attitude is sensed by the child and reflected when he comes to school." Lack of respect toward teachers—expressed through verbal abuse, increased absenteeism, and unprepared students—leaves many teachers feeling that education is no longer a priority.

But for school authorities, the motivation is often political. Says Sorensen, "Frequently, the administration will side with parents against a teacher either because it's easier or because it's less threatening to their own positions."

Many educators, therefore, feel that responsibility for failures in the system has been placed directly on them. Public furor over such issues as functional illiteracy, a phrase that is becoming as common as reading, 'riting, and 'rithmetic once was, has centered on the schools—specifically teachers.

Consequently, twenty states have instituted competency tests for teachers. One such test, in effect in New Jersey, is Thorough and Efficient Education. Its purpose is to provide equal education for every child regardless of race or economic background. In some systems, teachers are assigned to a committee which sets long term goals and achievement percentages. Students are tested at the end of the third, sixth, ninth, and twelth grades. If the prescribed percentage is not met, it reflects unfavorably on the school and teachers. Therefore, teachers who predict high achievement rates can, as one young teacher explained, "slit their own throats." So, to insure a safe margin, low estimates are often made.

While many state and local programs have proved beneficial, others create misleading results, needless paperwork, waste of money, and frustration for teachers. Increasingly, schools have been asked to perform duties that fall into the broad category of education without being given the staff or facilities to operate efficiently.

A good illustration is the law PL 94 142 which states that every handicapped student must be mainstreamed into a regular class whenever possible. This is often carried out without any inservice education to deal with these students. Teachers are not instructed in choosing the necessary institutional materials and classes are not made smaller so that a teacher may provide individualized attention to each student. Programs for special pupils must be developed in a teacher's spare time or with after school hours participation of parents.

These excessive demands placed on educational systems often have another effect—a sense of inadequacy for the teacher. "People go into teaching, not for the money, but for idealistic reasons," says Sorensen, "They feel they must help every student. When they realize they can't, they experience a severe sense of failure." The guilt many teachers feel at failing a child often erodes his or her self-confidence and leads to burn-out.

It is not only the multiple of factors inside the classroom that affect a teacher's attitude, but outside pressures as well. Money worries play a big part in career-change decisions. In a time of double-digit inflation, many educators are simply having a hard time making ends meet. Observes Sorensen, "If a teacher has a family, how does he or she provide for them financially? He sees his contemporaries in industry making double his salary, and he feels resentul—and he takes this resentment into the classroom."

How can you tell if a teacher is burning out? You can't. Burn-out is a stress reaction which is manifested according to the individual. Basically, says Sorensen, "There is a lack of enthusiasm. They feel it isn't worth it anymore. You can almost see it in their eyes."

The solution is, of course, to correct the causes. But, barring that, there is help for teachers.

The NEA and its branch associations offer counseling programs operated by specially trained therapists in teacher stress-related problems. Group therapy has been especially effective in this area.

"In a group," says Sorensen, "teachers can reinforce each other. They begin to see that the world isn't sitting on their shoulders. They also learn that the hostility they feel is normal, that it is just a reaction to the situation. With this knowledge, they can begin to deal with the stress situation."

Whether teachers can learn to cope with these increased job pressures is unknown. But if the present trends are not reversed, many educators are pessimistic about the future. As John Sawhill, former president of New York University, commented in the August issue of *Saturday Review,* "Our schools provide a key to the future of society. We must take control of them and nurture them if they are to be set right again. To do less is to invite disaster upon ourselves, our children, and our nation."

The discussion will reveal the reasons Ms. Sullivan's work meets the form's requirements. The opening paragraph introduces an escalating educational trend—teacher burn-out—with an illustrating anecdote. Next, the well-chosen expert earns credibility for his informed views by his high-ranking position and the vantage of his professional affiliation. His quotes, worded in ordinary conversational language, are extremely articulate. The article's structural design enunciates the problem, causes, and solution. The piece gives the varied reasons for the problem of teachers' burn-out: their scapegoat position for public education's deterioration, frustrations with pupil discipline, community disrespect for their profession, unrealistic expectations for test scores, insufficient job funding, and loss of personal idealism. The piece concludes with an interim solution—group therapy for the disheartened, disillusioned teachers. Finally, the quotes serve the expert's dual roles as spokesman and commentator on the issue by conveying definitions, reasons, elaborations, examples, revelations, evaluations, and summaries. Frances Marie Sullivan's one issue/interview on "Teacher Burn-Out" is a consummate delivery of the form's requirements for a pithy introduction to a timely issue in a field of information; a structured, well-researched examination of the issue; and intelligent, well-aimed quotes in everyday language.

## ADVICE FOR THE ONE ISSUE/ONE INTERVIEW FORM

To do as well, keep in mind some of the following points when selecting, researching, and writing your one issue/one interview.

1. Search a field of information of personal interest to you for a topic of timely urgency that you would like to investigate or know better.

2. Choose a recognized, articulate, informed authority whose credentials can give credibility to your query.

3. Prepare for the interview, so you can help your expert translate obtuse language into conversational words.

4. Listen to your expert's answers. Don't hesitate to ask your expert to rephrase jargon the moment you hear it.

5. Don't forget to criticize the expert's thesis during the interview and include the expert's refutation in your submission.

6. Outline your article so that every fact adds information to the issue under exploration. Stay on theme throughout.

7. In your article, don't forget to mention the pertinent credentials of the expert that convinced you of his or her inside track or up-to-date knowledge of

the topic and recognized authority.

8. Select quotes that perform the expert's role as presenter and analyst of the issue.

9. Write and rewrite until all vague rhetoric has disappeared from your prose and the expert's quotations.

10. Call your expert and read all quotes to verify their factual accuracy.

11. Give your opinion on the issue at the article's end. It's your right.

# IX How to Do an Interview

Other parts of this book may recommend particular interview questions for specific article forms. This section explains the aim of any interview, your role as an investigator, methods for taking control, strategies for dealing with uncooperative subjects, for throwing tough questions, staying the professional, evading digressions, and preventing interruptions. This list may sound as if the reporter is always cast as a prosecutor facing an unwilling witness. That's not so. In nearly twenty years of free-lance writing, many subjects of my research interviews have been generous, open, even entertaining. But difficult encounters can occur, so this section prepares you to handle them.

## AIM OF THE INTERVIEW AND IMPORTANCE OF PREPARED QUESTIONS TO ACHIEVE IT

Your aim as interviewer is to secure information. As this book has stressed before, the purpose of the interview is to secure fresh, unreported material that will make your piece saleable. So, before the interview, do the necessary background research and plan your questions. Prepared questions will help you control the interview's direction, maintain professional independence, and give you confidence. With a preconceived list, you'll have greater assurance because you'll know the aims you want to accomplish through the interview.

If you don't figure out the questions in advance, you can be easily led to your journalistic downfall. Without definite aims and a question list to fulfill them, you, like a former student, will be prey to whatever rhetoric your subject wishes to dole out. The student, who had interviewed the psychic healer, admitted in class that the expert had given her a lot of "verbiage." In trying to transform the interview into an article, the student confessed, "I felt like a high school student trying to pad a term paper." So, your prepared questions are not only your guidebook for the route of the interview, but your defense against powerful advocates of a cause or self-publicists. You'll be able to handle any strong personality in an interview as long as you think out beforehand what you want to find out from your subject, because you can be certain your subject knows what can be gained from you—publicity! Without your list, you risk an interview that offers nothing new. So come armed by research and questions ready to drill and extract marketable information.

## YOUR ROLE AS INTERVIEWER

Your understanding of your role in an interview will greatly enhance your chances for achieving your objectives. Your role as an interviewer is that of an investigator who tracks down and closely examines information. So feel free in an interview not only to inquire, but to probe in order to comprehend or verify the material as truthful.

As an investigative interviewer, you may, nonetheless, act as your subject's friend, psychiatrist, or confidant while performing your job as a journalist. A brief description of these parts will suffice because succeeding sections will elaborate on them. At the interview's start, you should show a friend's sensitivity and compassion as you initiate your quarry into the interview process. Further on, you may, as a psychiatrist, have to figure out your subject's roadblocks and ways to surmount them. Also at times, you may have to become your subject's confidant to get the truth as it would be told to a close friend. And as you don or doff these guises, you can never relinquish your role as interviewer or the goals of your investigation.

## METHODS FOR TAKING CONTROL OF THE INTERVIEW

At the start of the interview, establish your control by following this routine: take the attitude, not of an authoritarian, but of a collaborator, and inform your subject of the topics, though not the specific questions, for the interview. If you outline the topics in advance, your subject can get a "head start" and be thinking of answers for forthcoming questions. Secondly, if you define the points the interview will cover at its inception, you tacitly persuade your subject to commit the time to respond. By stating the perimeters of your questions, you get an implicit agreement from your subject to stay till their completion.

For instance, at the start of a long phone interview with the 1981 New York City Marathon women's division winner, Allison Roe, I read the then world women's marathon record holder the list of internationally famous road races I was reporting for a *Harper's Bazaar* article, "The Top Ten Races: How to Finish a Marathon." Once Roe told me the ones in which she had competed, I knew, as did my subject, the skeleton structure of the interview. As I typed her recollections of well-known 10K's and marathons, I would from time to time say, "We have only"—and give the number of races remaining—"left." My enthusiastic encouragement convinced Roe to continue the interview despite an appointment-packed day. This famous racer awarded me all the time needed—some two hours—to ask about all my assigned races, perhaps because I announced the topics of the interview at the start.

If, in the spirit of collaboration, you preview the interview topics, I believe that shared information relaxes a subject. If you forecast the topics, a subject feels more comfortable because he or she has some idea of what type questions to expect.

You can heighten a subject's sense of a cooperative effort if you report problems in recording the interview as you experience them. For instance, if you are taking research notes by hand and your subject speaks more quickly than you can write, ask the person to slow down. I often make this request. Interestingly enough, slowed speech doesn't break a person's thought sequence, but intensifies it, as the subject also begins to listen more carefully to his or her expressions. So rather than distress a subject, the request, "Please slow down," becomes a tantalizing compliment because your subject is watching you write down his or her every word.

Similarly, make the test of audio equipment at a taping a cooperative venture. Ask your subject to state the date, time, and place. Replay the recorded material to verify that the audio level and mike placement guarantee fidelity of the recorded interview. If necessary, make slight volume changes or relocate the mike, and do several audio tests to confirm that you've achieved optimal recording conditions. And each time you flip to a new side or thread up a new tape, repeat the audio test to avoid losing any part of the recorded interview through mechanical negligence. View these repeated checks as professional guarantees rather than displays of amateurism for which you must apologize. And if you verbalize the reasons for your tactics, disclosure of your equipment difficulties will help inspire candor from your subject to match yours.

Other methods of recording interviews have their particular mechnical problems. When typing an interview, if you reach the bottom of the page, let your subject know. Say, "Paper out," or whatever you wish, so the person will stop talking and resume only after you've inserted another sheet. If you are taping an interview by phone, not only inform your subject that the conversation is being recorded, but keep the person apprised of the mechanics of the recording, such as the necessity to test the audio, change a tape, or flip to another side.

Again, I stress, demonstrate your vulnerabilities—no matter how minute—to create the atmosphere for mutual openness.

So far, I've defined your aims and role in the interview as a probing investigator intent on accurate, saleable material, suggested methods to gain control from the start and recommended spontaneous honesty about minor hitches in the recording process to inspire the same candor in your subject.

## STRATEGIES FOR HANDLING
## UNCOOPERATIVE SUBJECTS

Now the chapter will address reasons for the breakdown of the collaboration and strategies to reconstruct it. When subjects won't permit access to the information you've set as an interview objective, you can regain their cooperation if you can figure out the reason for the loss of rapport. The following roadblocks commonly impede subjects from delivering requested information: personal problems, inexperience at interviewing, reluctance, unreadiness, rhetoric, or refusal. By knowing the possible obstacles in advance, you'll be prepared to surmount them *should they occur.*

Always monitor the answers you're getting and react instantly to any that are weak by probing for the cause. For instance, subjects may have personal problems that day or personal attitudes toward the role of the interviewer that are interfering with their answers. If the subject appears jittery and the discomfort persists through the initial questions, like a sensitive friend ask, "What's the matter?" One administrator of a foundation project responded that her daughter, the victim of a car accident, had just returned to college that day. For a few moments, I let that administrator veer off the interview's themes and air her worries. They obviously were uppermost in her mind and preventing any concentration on the interview. After she explored her daughter's physical and psychological difficulties the first day back at a college regimen, I gradually brought the woman to focus on my questions. By acknowledging a distress and permitting a person to talk it through, you relieve the immediate discomfort and enable your subject to concentrate on your needs in the interview with a clearer mind.

Another administrator of that foundation project responded to my friendly sympathetic inquiry with, "You are a writer and judging me." In that case, I tried to extinguish her fear of me as an independent authority by turning her attention to my dependency on her. I stressed how much she could help me by supplying certain information only she knew. Then, as the project administrator began giving me the facts and insights I wanted, she slowly recognized herself as the authority, at least, on the project, and her fear of me as her superior and judge disappeared. So, if your subject's answers seem vague, watered-down or unfocused, see if a personal problem rather than your questions is the cause.

Besides psychological stress, a subject's inexperience with interviews may prevent good responses. So don't hesitate to tutor the inexperienced subject in the effective format for answers. As I've noted elsewhere in this book, after you've asked a question, request your subject to incorporate it into the response. If you say, "What's the cause of. . . .?," then at the question's end, tack on the reminder, "And don't forget to say, 'The causes of . . . are. . . .' " If you repeat your request frequently enough, a subject will begin to follow your directive without your voicing it. Secondly, remember to interrupt when someone waxes into rhetoric of the trade. Politely recommend that the professional speak in everyday language, as he or she might to a telephone operator. Your coaching in the midst of the interview will not halt the flow of ideas, but rather make the exchange more vivid for both of you. And don't worry about irritating or hurting subjects. Their egos will withstand polite criticism. In fact, you'll find them ardent pupils of your tips for proper phrasing of answers because they want their quotes in print.

Besides a psychological problem or unfamiliarity with interview technique, a subject may be reluctant to answer a question for fear of public disapproval. Usually someone who hasn't done an interview may react this way. A student reported that her boss, who was a prominent administrator in an international business, declined to talk about his life prior to his present job. He pleaded he would "hurt too many people still living." In such a situation, I try to work out a compromise between the subject's wish for self-protection and a professional's desire to report all the facts truthfully. When a subject fears a disclosure may cause harm, I often reply, "I believe anything can be said tactfully in print." Then I persuade the subject to tell me the facts on the promise that together we will find "a way" to answer the question. So write an answer with your subject "aloud." Keep rewriting it until your subject finds it acceptable, as do you, within the perimeters of your question's demands.

But don't give up a question because it poses difficulties. Too often beginners, particularly with profile interviews, are pushovers for the wishes of their subjects. In such cases, care more about your self-respect as a professional than the approval of your subject. You are not there to please your interview subject. Don't turn your expert into a parent or another authority figure of the past. You don't have to please anyone; you simply have to perform a professional job and meet the journalistic standards of your craft, your assignment's requirements, and the interview's objectives.

If attempts at compromise fail, explain how the question relates to your article's theme and where the answer fits in the article as a means to stress to your subject its importance for the article's success. Don't, though, as the student did with her boss, give up a valid question by giving in to a subject's squeamishness about the past. When you plead your case, however, be firm without being overbearing. You don't want to antagonize your subject to the point that the person stops the interview.

If a subject won't compromise or accept arguments on behalf of the article's form, offer to attribute the material to an unidentified source, disguise it, or use a pseudonym. None has any advantage over the other. You may persuade a subject to permit self-incriminating or possibly harmful material by recommending the facts or opinion not be attributed to your subject. These unattributed remarks are what other journalists call "off-the-record." So ask if your subject wants to go "off the record." In such instances, I show the potential informant my interview cards where, in the margin next to the information, I place the letters, "N." and "A." I explain this means the answer will "Not be Attributed" to an identifiable source. The offer of protection of a source's identity sometimes shakes loose the remarks desired. By acknowledging a subject's desire for self-protection and by giving that source a shield, you may attain your aims.

Sometimes, it's wiser to offer to disguise a source's material. By this method you can often circumvent medical professionals who, out of professional ethics, want to protect a patient's identity. In these interviews, ask if you can alter the patient's name, residence, age or other particulars without modifying the medical facts. By this camouflage you protect the privacy of the doctor-patient relationship and at the same time obtain facsimiles of clinical examples to enliven your prose without distortion of the medical truths they describe.

If diplomacy, technical arguments, offers of "not-for-attribution," or a proposal to disguise a source's material fail, you have another device available. Sometimes during the contact call, subjects will agree to be interviewed only if you employ a pseudonym to represent their story. When you agree to this condition in advance or during an interview, tell your editor what you promised. Once I acquiesced to such a condition in the research for a *Glamour* article, "What's It Like To Be The Child of an Interracial Marriage?" Just prior to the article's publication, a *Glamour* copyeditor called for the names and numbers of my subjects, to check their quotes. I relayed them, along with my promise about a pseudonym for one subject, a child of black and Caucasian parents. The invented name so resembled the girl's real one, I had to climb a ladder, retrieve a file box holding my interview notes, and check my research for the real name and alias to be sure the published article contained the promised disguise. If you promise protection of a source's identity by use of a pseudonym, it's your obligation not only to inform the editor of this condition, but to verify it in the copy for publication. You may know that under the shield law, journalists have gone to jail rather than divulge a source promised protection. Keep such promises for the sake of honor and professional reputation.

Sometimes, compromise, persuasion, or offer to mask the identity of your source cannot succeed in getting a guarded subject to talk. The subject's fear may not be of self-indictment, but of inferiority. Those subjects are afraid to answer because they are afraid of giving uninteresting or boring answers. In such cases you may have to resort to flattery of them or their viewpoint. To inspire a person who fears, "I have nothing to say," to be articulate, show enthusiasm for any anecdote or personal statement, no matter how ordinary or banal. Greet any professional perception or elaboration of an issue with bursts of appreciation, smiles and exclamations like, "Oh, that's so interesting; tell me more." Eventually, your appreciative treatment will dispel your subject's defeating sense of worthlessness. Under a barrage of compliments, subjects usually gain confidence and begin to speak without restraint or hesitation, as interest in the topic gradually supersedes their draining self-absorption.

Oftimes, a subject's distress, innocence at interviewing, fear of exposure, or lack of confidence are not the reasons for a skipped answer. A subject may not have an answer because no one ever asked the question. When you sense someone simply can't think of an answer, wait and ask the same question a few minutes later. A brief respite may be all the subject needs to gather his or her thoughts into a decent response.

If you keep submitting a question in the same or similar phrases, a subject will often spontaneously answer one he or she find disturbing to contemplate. The following illustrates the possible reward of perseverance. Once, to reciprocate a generous editorial lunch, I invited *People* Senior Editor Cranston Jones to my home, in the tradition of my alma mater, for tea. Parenthetically I add, I have always interpreted this Bryn Mawr tradition as a permission for serving sumptuous, calorie-laden dessert food. During this afternoon fete, I took the opportunity to ask Cran Jones what gave him the stamina to work *People*'s schedule, where the hours seem very akin to the free-lance writer's trek. The editor sometimes stayed till two a.m. Saturday morning or later, and the same on Monday and Tuesday when the magazine was closing pages and sending them to the printer. Save for vacations, Cran Jones kept up this strenuous endurance schedule week after week at the obvious sacrifice of personal family life. So I was very curious about what mental attitude enabled him to "take it."

The first time I posed the question, replete with my explanation of the reasons which motivated me to ask it, Cran Jones didn't have an answer. So I filed it at the back of my mind and, a couple of minutes later, asked him again. He confessed, "I knew you would." He answered that he saw himself as someone climbing a mountain. And as he scaled the terrain, he was aware his ordeal would be over someday. His kids would graduate from college and these financial responsibilities that were so draining now would be drastically reduced. His sense that at a future termination point this strain to his endurance would be over gave him the courage now to go on. He could continue, he said, because he knew the journey would not last forever. Parenthetically, he added, "I wondered how you got the answers you did in profiles and now I see." He had indeed seen a practical demonstration on himself. I had probed, failed, returned to my question at another propitious moment, and probed again till I got the full answer. A tenacious grasp on a failed question will enable you to hoist it again into the discussion of the interview at a more propitious time, so that you may win the hard booty you seek from your formerly unprepared candidate by relentless tenacity. So, if someone doesn't have an answer for a question and can't think of one right away, wait. Let your subject marshall his or her resources and then ask again, and you may hook "the catch" of the day's interview.

Some candidates less honest than Cran Jones may not defer questions to which they have not found an answer, but offer pat replies. If that happens, don't put words in the mouth, say, of a politician with little time or inclination to think a question through. Once, a former student, Sarah Puri, interviewed a candidate running for the position of civil court judge for the local Manhattan paper, *Our Town*. When she inquired why the candidate thought it had happened that both liberal and conservative parties had endorsed him, the nominee replied, according to Ms. Puri, " 'Because these people know me.' " Then she says she probed, " 'Well, is it because. . . .' " and alluded to a fact in his record, " 'and because . . .?' " Ms. Puri later confessed, "I felt like I was writing his material for him." At first, I said, "If your subject approves your made-up answers attributed to him as truthful, you can use them." Then I rescinded that position entirely. I now hold, "You can intensify quotes, but you can't invent them." If an interview subject gives you pat answers, you can't invent answers the person never thought of and print them as his. Either you repeat your questions and try for better quotes or scrap the assignment.

Sometimes a subject avoids a question, not because of mood, naivete, fear of self-incrimination, lack of confidence, or unpreparedness, but out of the desire to manipulate the interview into a press release for self-promotion. When a celebrity or expert stubbornly refuses to answer reasonable questions, threaten to halt the interview. You can't let a subject censor your every question or exploit your professional purpose for publicity. Threat of lost press coverage usually inspires most V.I.P.s to be more candid and giving. They know their refusal to cooperate could result in bad press.

## ASKING TOUGH QUESTIONS

Till now, you've been given numerous strategies to handle unexpected problems in the interview, but you may create them—on purpose. I usually come to an interview with two or three difficult questions certain to disrupt its flow. I base these probes on certain hunches about my subject's character or motivation. These hunches arise from my intuition, which is what the practice of journalism (rather than study of it through books—even this one) will develop for you. When you've created a rapport with your subject, you can bring out one of these heavy-duty probes. As strategy, don't sling it on your subject without warning. Preface with a graceful request for help for you as a journalist, or for their cause by a good answer to a "toughie," or, by a shared personal experience, inspire a similar revelation from your subject.

When you have a difficult question to pose that potentially can embarrass a subject, you may wish to divulge your embarrassment in asking such a question and request the subject's help for your discomfort. The unpremeditated use of this strategy enabled me, as I recounted earlier, to question New York City Marathon founder, Fred Lebow, about then illegal "under-the-table fees." My admission of discomfort—actually I stammered when asking my questions—brought out Lebow's gentlemanliness and made him more interested in easing my embarrassment as his interviewer than protecting his professional turf as Director of the New York City Marathon. The article left such a wake of controversy that recently, when I first met top-of-the-line sports publicist, Joe Goldstein, at a New York City Marathon function, he remembered my name, saying, "Didn't you write an exposé in *The Village Voice?*" Goldstein said my piece was the first in a major media outlet to suggest "under-the-table fees" were paid to runners in the New York City Marathon. He recalled, "And Fred went berserk."

Besides prefacing difficult questions with a personal appeal for a subject's help, I may turn that appeal into the subject's aid for a representative cause. I may say, "This is a tough question, but I'm asking it to get a strong answer." I used this method repeatedly in interviews for my article, "Dispute on Wheelchair Athletes Stirs New York City Marathon," which appeared in *The New York Times,* Sunday, October 7, 1979, *Sports* Section. As a result of these maneuvers with questions for opponents and advocates of wheelchair participants in footraces, both factions thought theirs had won in the published piece, because the quotes obtained from each faction's representatives were so forceful as a result of my appeals.

If, in interviews about inflammatory topics or controversies, I precede hard questions with pleas for aid to the reporter or the subject's cause, I handle "toughies" in a biographical profile interview, or ones with a celebrity, somewhat differently. I may turn my subjects into my confidant to become theirs. I offer intimate, personal anecdotes similar to the type I wish to extract as preface to probing for theirs. I share any relevant life traumas or personal insights for three reasons. I don't want my subjects to feel alone or "the only one who has experienced this" as they reveal materials from their "private lives." Secondly, I give these intimate details willingly so subjects don't feel "milked" by a reporter's voyeurism or by the article's demands. Lastly, if subjects are strong enough for this type of self-exposure, I, nonetheless, want to buttress their strength with mine.

## MAINTAIN PROFESSIONALISM

Once when I explained to a class the part an investigative interviewer may play as a subject's confidant, one student asked, "How much of your life should you share in an interview?" I choose to reveal only those life stories or lessons that directly pertain to the interview's themes. Also, I don't attempt to extract private material from my subject outside the interview's framework. For instance, when I interviewed an American Marathon record holder who reputedly had separated from her husband because he secretly—without her knowledge—had been giving her steroids, I never broached the topic of steroids or her marital situation because these themes lay outside the province of my assigned article. You must adhere to the professional purpose of the interview. What you reveal about your own life or ask about your subject's must be motivated by valid professional aims.

The same student then asked, "Is the mark of a good interview that you and your subject become friends?" I told her, "Absolutely not!" Never try to develop a friendship with an interview subject until you have written your article and the piece has been published. Then you will discover if your subject wants to be friendly with you because of your value as a publicity vehicle or because of shared interests, compatible personalities, and similar life styles. You rarely can determine your subject's motives during the interview because the process demands the focus of interest be on your subject. An interview is basically a one-way conversation. After publication, you will find out whether the person interviewed wants to know your part of the conversation or whether his or her real interest is to have you only as a listener to satisfy a deep-rooted infantile narcissism.

How can you become friends with your subject before the interview's end if you have to act, at times, in the role of inquisitor? If you have to push, press, pinch till you hear the truth ring like pure crystal, you have to ignore a subject's discomfort at difficult questions, which may overstep his or her boundaries of personal decorum, in search of professional truth.

I hold there is a private and professional decorum. As an investigative reporter, you have to abide by professional tact and ask the tough questions in search of emotional divulgences or hidden facts needed for your article. Sometimes you will have to violate a subject's personal privacy to obtain your professional aims. At these times I know I would not ask these intrusive questions in ordinary conversation which, in an interview, are justified by the theme of the article.

For instance, I profusely apologized to Eunice Kennedy Shriver before I asked an intrusive question. I didn't want to, but I needed the information revolving around a very private memory for my *Ladies' Home Journal* profile. So, nearly crying over my painful recollections of the historic event, I said, "Can you describe how you learned of the shooting of your brother John that day of his assassination?" I said I wanted to dramatize how well she knew the possible dangers her husband, Sargent Shriver, faced for the 1976 Democratic presidential nomination by her memory of the assassination of her brother, John F. Kennedy, during his presidency.

Recalling the November day in '63 when her brother was fatally shot, Eunice Shriver answered, "I've never told anyone about that time," and she added, "but no one has ever asked." And she began, "I was downtown having lunch with Sarge. I was several months pregnant with Mark. . . . And Sarge was called to the phone. When he came back to the table, he told me, 'Your brother's been shot.' I asked, 'How serious is it?' He didn't know, but he said, 'We should leave.' And he asked me where I wanted to go. I said, 'The White House.' And we left immediately. I remember the streets of Washington were strangely silent. We went in by a back entranceway. I spoke privately to Bobby and he told me, 'It's very, very serious. That's about as clear as you can get.' And I told him, 'I don't think I'll go back home, I'll go to the Cape where Mother is.' And somehow I got hold of Teddy or he called me and we flew up to the Cape and stayed with Mother. It was clear when we left he was going to pass away."

"Did you believe it when you heard the news?"

"Of course you don't believe it. When I heard the news at the hotel, I wanted to get back and check it out. I remember the scene at the hotel and I remember not believing it and walking out of the hotel and everybody was quiet. Everybody had heard."

I used Eunice Kennedy Shriver's recollection in the profile, "The Kennedy Who Could be President (if she weren't a woman)," published during her husband's campaign for the party nomination for the office held by her brother at the time of his assassination.

Too often beginner writers skip over tough questions which invade a subject's privacy in order to be a "nice guy." But your goal is not to be liked, but to be truthful. The writer who wants to be a "nice guy" will be conned into writing a publicity release from the subject's viewpoint rather than an article from the objective stance of a journalist. Protect your writing from criticism of undue bias by asking the tough questions to drill through the grey, unsubstantiated facts to the unflattering anecdote or the human weakness that will give your piece credibility.

This section has covered the purpose of the interview, your role, methods for control, strategies for the unexpected and expected difficult moments needing "special care." Now some general pointers about appropriate instances to relax your control, enforce it, and proper decorum for the interview's end.

## AVOIDING DIGRESSIONS AND INTERRUPTIONS

Don't be so rigid that you can't share control with your interview subject. Allow the subject to elaborate on ideas or biographical periods as long as the material fits your thematic framework. Go with the flow of the interview as long as your subject's information serves the assigned slant. If your subject progresses beyond the commissioned focus, politely take control of the interview again. Apologize for the intrusion and say, "That's so interesting, but in the time remaining, I need to ask you about . . .," and then ask a direct question. Let your subject take charge of the interview's output only as long as those results reflect the purpose of the interview. Similarly, if you listen well and are thinking throughout the exchange, new questions inspired by revelations in the interview will occur to you. Ask only the ones that pertain.

Don't tolerate any interruptions. If the phone rings in the home or office of your subject, ask if someone else can "man the phone" till you've finished the interview. If the person must answer, tactfully suggest the return of the call another hour or day. Try to prevent or restrict any artificial interruptions of the interview that may harm the momentum of the exchange.

Of course, sometimes you have to put up with disrupting influences because you can't stop them. I remember an interview with Manhattan market co-owner, Harold Seybert, for a February 1984, *Good Housekeeping* "New York Metro" article, "Way To Go: Fairway." Seybert answered my questions at the back of the market between calls from wholesalers, while deliverymen hauled crates past and workers carted out replacements of fruits and produce for the store's roughly 30,000 customers weekly. Despite this pandemonium, I maintained a high degree of concentration during the six-hour-long marathon interviews with Seybert, his fellow co-owners, store managers, and department heads. I had come to get certain detailed information, and I was determined that nothing would detract me from my pursuit as I typed interview answers on a loaned portable by the back store's main traffic route.

## PACING AND ENDING THE INTERVIEW

The clock has the final control over your interview time. During the session, keep an eye on your watch and periodically estimate the number of questions and amount of time remaining. Ask the most important ones first to achieve the significant facts necessary for the writing of the article within your time limits. At the end of the interview, check to make sure no major one was omitted. If so, slip it in with an apology. Few will refuse an ardent question at the conclusion of an interview. Then, thank your subject. Let your subject know you'll be in touch by phone about any "pick-up" questions after review of the interview or arrangements for another meeting. And follow up with a call to verify vague answers or fill in missed or confusing facts.

You know from other parts of this book that, were your subject to request to see the finished article, you'd consent only if the piece is to be published as an interview, comprised mainly of your subject's words. When you comply, state you'll accept only changes of fact, because the realm of character motivation or interpretation belongs to the writer. Refuse any request for entire manuscript review by subjects of biographical profiles, a one issue/one interview, or a service article. I always like to call and check the accuracy of quotes in the submitted copy for these forms, but that is my preference.

Upon completion of the article's research, let your editor know whether the original slant still holds, or whether you want to suggest alterations based on surprise information or insurmountable impasses in the interview. State clearly whether you can meet the deadline with the obtained material or need further research. Then do your best to deliver "on deadline."

One more word. In review of any interview, you'll probably discover omissions, material you never dreamed of, and much of what you expected. Interviews rarely turn out completely as you planned. But, like anything in life, if you don't try to do one, you'll get no new facts or saleable insights. Yet if you venture, you won't get everything, but you'll get something. And much of the result will be workable for the article if you did your research and came with a question list focused on the interview's objectives.

# X Introduction:
# Three Forms to Publish
# a Research Interview
# as an Interview

Earlier chapters introduced the basic article forms for reporting an outstanding newsworthy achiever, a brand new product or newly available service, and an emerging issue or timely development. This chapter teaches you three forms in which you can publish a research interview as an interview. In each, the largest part of the printed article consists of your questions and your candidate's matching answer.

## BASIC TYPES OF INTERVIEWS

The first interview form, which I simply call a "Q. & A.," conveys an authority's views on a topic of controversy. In the second form, which has two versions, someone is telling a life story, which the writer later edits for the article's format. In one version, named the "As Told To," the printed interview transmits an extraordinary experience, told in the words of the narrator to the writer. In the other type, which I label "A Day In The Life," the reader vicariously lives the uncommon professional life of someone who has been interviewed about his unusual or outstanding career. The third interview form—the "Celebrity Interview"—is what its name indicates. It is an interview with a famous person about a celebrated life and lifetime of work.

Practice in any or all three elementary interview forms may give you writing techniques, career advantages, and a fee scale no other magazine form may equal.

### Advantage of Interview Forms for Development of Technique

From a technical standpoint, these interview forms will improve your ability to handle quotes in all types of magazine articles. The chapter on the one issue form may have tutored you in the uses of quotes, but from my teaching experience I know many beginners among you are still reluctant to employ them. Work at the interview forms forces you to rely on quotes by necessity. Quotes are the only tool you have in these forms for writing up the discussions about the controversy, the dramatic life story, or the celebrity's life. The interview article format makes you practice using quotes again and again. So the sheer number of quotes that any basic interview article requires will build your confidence in your ability to exploit a subject's spoken words for reportorial advantage in any future profile, service, or one issue article you do.

## Gains for Your Career from Publication of an Interview

Besides developing an essential writing skill, publication of your interview may boost your career. Often editors assign interviews a coverline to ring up the issue's newsstand sales. And with good reason. Interviews do provoke readers' attention. Most of us will borrow or, if necessary, buy a magazine to read a talked-about interview. I remember that notoriety surrounding Jimmy Carter's interview in *Playboy* that appeared during his presidential election campaign.

Interviews attract readers not only because of their controversial contents, but emotional ones too. In an increasingly impersonal, alien society without traditional family ties and work alliances to erase that personal sense of isolation, the best magazine interviews fill a human need for intimacy by recreating a human experience or an indelible insight that prompts readers to recognize something about themselves, their lives, or a life truth and say to themselves inwardly, "I've felt that," or, "That's true." If your interviews can live in their recorded words on the page and from time to time peak with an intellectual or character revelation that evokes sympathetic recognition in the minds or hearts of your readers and, by doing so, frees them for that moment from the pain of aloneness, you will have done something notable. Such moving portrayals of issues or human experience will get your name talked about. As a result, either these noteworthy interviews will bring you more commissions or make it easier for you to sell your next interview query. So interviews can get you coverlines, editorial attention, and help make your name as a writer.

## Financial Advantage of Published Interviews

Finally, in addition to building a basic writing skill and your reputation, interviews pay well—anywhere from $500 to $2500. If you're a good negotiator, you can use the entertainment value of the interview for enlivening an issue and its commercial potential for jacking up newsstand sales to bargain for higher remuneration. If you are willing to haggle over your fee rather than accept scale, you may raise your article income by doing well-compensated interviews.

So interviews can improve your technique, advance your career, and increase your cash flow. Now to instruct you in the three elementary interview forms, so you can add them to your list of forms available to package marketable ideas for magazine assignments.

# XI The "Q. & A.": An Expert's Views of a Controversy or Controversial Viewpoint

When I assign the "Q. & A." in class, students often ask, "How does the "Q. & A." differ from the one issue article?" The two article forms are different in three respects—format, style, and subject.

## PUBLISHED FORM AND CONTENT

### Format
The most obvious difference is format. The one issue article looks like any other magazine article on the page; but the published "Q. & A." has a short beginning and then an interview format. After a roughly 150-240 word introduction to its theme and spokesperson, the "Q. & A." switches to 1500-2000 words of an alternate question and answer sequence.

### Writing Style
Besides a dissimilar page form, the "Q. & A.'s" writing style also distinguishes it. In the one issue article, you, as the writer, with transitions, prefaces to quotes, summaries, and concise paraphrases, share the printed page with the expert. By contrast, the "Q. & A." employs a question and answer format where the authority's voice dominates. This interview form best suits topics where the reader wants only the authority's views, expressed directly in the immediacy of the expert's quoted words. So choose the "Q. & A." form where the expert's voice is needed to explain all of your assigned topic.

### Subject
Third, and most important, the "Q.& A." handles a different type of subject than the one issue article. You'll recall the one issue/one interview article is about a development in an old field of information (such as a new application of an environmental law on a county level), or about a new issue, such as a scientific discovery. The "Q. & A." is not about a change or progress in the world, but about a conflict of current interest.

## DEFINITION

Specifically, the "Q. & A." is defined as an expert's disturbing or controversial opinion on a timely topic of substance, or one expert's view of a present controversy. This definition underscores the reason the expert's voice must dominate the article.

## Types of Topics

You've come across published "Q. & A.'s" almost weekly in *People* in the section, "In His Own Words" (sometimes appropriately retitled "In Her Own Words"), and shorter versions appear from time to time in the Sunday paper's magazine section or the local dailies. In random samples from *People,* interviews have been drawn from politics ("Betty Friedan Is Back On The Barricades With A New Cause: Family," Nov. 16, 1981) or ("Don't Worry That Vidal Is Out Of Oxen To Gore: He Says He's Running For The U.S. Senate," March 30, 1981); sociology ("Beware Of Maggie's Table Switch And Other Ways Ripoff Artists Victimize You," Nov. 19, 1979); psychology ("Many Women Yearn To Be Saved, Just Like Cinderella, Argues Colette Dowling," July 6, 1981); or science ("The Next Ice Age Is 10,000 Years Off, But A Cooling Globe Has Us In Hot Water Now," Nov. 24, 1980). I've also published interviews in this section on contentious topics like diet therapy (health); child abuse (sociology); and moral education.

## Casting: Sources for a Suitable Expert

In searching for a leading expert with pugnacious point of view or perspective on a controversial topic suitable for the "Q. & A." format, turn to the chapter on the one issue/one interview article form for practical casting recommendations for locating the right source for a "Q. & A." Or, scout local bookstores for displays of just-published books on disputed subjects that match your concerns. A glossy new book cover may bear the name of a recognized, articulate expert who will invest available time in a free-lance writer's project on the chance return of free publicity for his or her new book.

## Opportunity for Improving Your Technique

If one issue interviews made you aware of the need for clarity in an expert's answers, the research for the "Q. & A." can sharpen your investigative skills as an interviewer. If you keep in mind the informational needs of the "Q. & A.'s" introduction and format design, you may be able to plow through a subject's cover-ups, rhetoric, or mental blocks for the compelling insights that can make your interview memorable. As an interviewer, you'll have the nerve to persevere despite stubborn reticence, overbearing authority, or plain shyness for the sake of the form's needed material. So prepare for the research interview by mastering the "Q. & A.'s" requirements. Also, don't forget to review the advice in the one issue chapter for avoiding jargon during a research interview prior to yours. The review will insure results in conversational language you can transfer to a publishable "Q. & A." format without further work.

# THE INTRODUCTION: RESEARCH REQUIREMENTS

The introduction to your "Q. & A." states your expert's provocative position, professional credentials supporting his/her authority, humanizing details of personal biography, and concludes with the dominant theme of the interview. Samples of these information requirements published in *People*'s "In His Own Words" section will show you the necessary facts to extract from your expert.

## Expert's Provocative Stand
Examples from the start of published "Q. & A.'s" demonstrate the type of summarized stand you seek.

The interview on ". . . Ways Ripoff Artists Victimize You" begins with its contentious theme phrased this way:

> Scams are the growth industry of the Me Generation. That is the disturbing message in a new book, *Ripoff: How To Spot It, How To Avoid It* (Andrews and Mc-Meel, $5.95), by Chicago Tribune Sunday Magazine senior editor Peter Maiken, 45.

The "In Her Own Words" about "Many Women Yearn To Be . . . Just Like Cinderella. . . ." sounds its theme at the start of the introduction, too:

> Women feel helpless. They yearn for freedom but are afraid to take it. That is the controversial thesis of Colette Dowling's *The Cinderella Complex: Women's Hidden Fear of Independence* (Summit Books, $12.95).

So, mindful that your introduction should contain your authority's stance in its opening lines, remember to query your expert, "Will you concisely give your viewpoint?" Also, ask the expert to stress the timeliness of his views in the answer.

## Expert's Credentials That Certify Authority
Next, the introduction demands your expert's credentials that certify his or her authority for the expressed views. You've already seen one way to demonstrate an expert's credibility in the Maiken opening—by current job, place of work, job title, and age. An authority's present professional status enhances his credibility, but the achievement can be in the past, too, as in the Betty Friedan interview introduction:

Betty Friedan doesn't lack for laurels—or, at the moment, for people who wish she would just rest on them. But instead of quietly rusticating, the 60-year-old founder and first president of the National Organization for Women. . . .

The introduction gives Friedan's most prominent past job to verify her political credibility. In the "In His Own Words" about the ". . . Cooling Globe Has Us In Hot Water Now," the introduction lists climatologist Reid Bryson's current rather than past academic employment for certification of his authority:

> As director of the Institute for Environmental Studies at the University of Wisconsin, Bryson, 60, predicts the future will be colder and drier, with dire consequences for the earth's booming population unless resources are conserved and agricultural methods changed.

Bryson's age, title, institute and university affiliations convince us to take his chilling global weather forecast seriously. So, in preparing your interview questions, include one about current or past professional achievements or employment that can give your expert's opinion clout. Confide to your expert what the answer is for and your authority will know exactly what credit to pull from his/ her resume to give weight to his/her words in your introduction.

After presenting your expert's timely controversial stance, age and professional credentials for his or her credibility, your introduction may highlight other achievements like publication credits to persuade readers to accept your expert's views. Often this type introduction will name the speaker's most famous oeuvre, as in the Friedan introduction:

> [Friedan] . . . is questioning some of the tenets of the movement that she helped start with her 1963 manifesto, *The Feminine Mystique*. In *The Second Stage* (Summit Books, $14.95), Friedan vigorously argues that feminism's antipathy to the values of heart and hearth is causing a popular "backlash" and dooming the Equal Rights Amendment. . . .

Note, when current book titles are listed, so are their publishers and price. Also, a summary of a book's theme elaborates in a natural way the expert's current views. In this case, the summary gives Friedan's present reactionary view of the feminist movement.

Reference to an expert's past and current book titles within the introduction can telescope a huge number of years in a professional resume. The introduction to Gore Vidal's interview deftly uses books by Vidal to condense many professional years into a few lines:

> And Vidal has been at least as provocative in print ever since he wrote a daring homosexual love story titled *The City and the Pillar* in 1948. The West Point-born

son of an aeronautics instructor, he subsequently turned out a succession of best-selling novels (*Myra Breckinridge, Burr, 1876*), and this week, at 55, he publishes his seventeenth novel, *Creation* (Random House, $15.95), an epic set in the fifth century B.C.

Before your research interview, become familiar with your expert's professional resume, so you can ask that he or she clarify the sequence of achievements—which followed which and why. The expert can often pinpoint ones that substantiate his or her stance and also provide links to connect your introductory facts that may be missed on a fast reading of the resume.

Besides statements of thematic position, your expert's age, past or present professional credits, and publications, the introduction may buttress your expert's authority, as in the one to climatologist Reid Bryson's interview, with details of the expert's higher educational degrees, early professional posts, and field travel.

Bryson earned his Ph.D. in meteorology at the University of Chicago in 1948. That same year he founded the meteorology department at the University of Wisconsin and was named director of the institute in 1970 . . . he has traveled as far as the Arctic Ocean to conduct research.

In addition to theme, professional achievements, early educational training, and professional travels, these introductions to controversial interviews—if possible—mention the expert's military service. Perhaps patriotic duty adds to the interviewed expert's respectability, particularly if the topic has any hint of the unsavory. So, the introduction to the "Q. & A." about the book, *Ripoff: How To Spot It, How to Avoid It*, specifies that the author, Peter Maiken, served in the armed forces:

After a four-year hitch in the Navy, he reported for two Illinois newspapers and became the editor of the Chicago Tribune Sunday Magazine before moving to the Washington Star. Now back in Chicago, Maiken . . .

## Expert's Biography
Along with the summary of the interview's controversial theme and brief professional resume of the interviewed expert, the introduction to *People* "Q. & A.'s" humanizes the expert with a skimpy personal biography. The details of these short biographical summaries are so impersonal that no interviewed expert can object to giving these facts. So in your interview, request such details as marital status; numbers of children and their ages; as evident in

Now back in Chicago, Maiken, the divorced father of three sons aged 12-17. . . .

even children's names and their occupations; as in

> Friedan is unfazed by the clamor. Divorced from an ad man since 1970, she describes her relationship with her children, Daniel, 33, a physicist, Jonathan, 28, an engineer, and Emily, 25, a medical student, as "better than ever."

the expert's pastimes; as shown in

> ... Maiken ... is a tennis buff, a self-described "barroom pianist" and a cook who makes his own tomato juice and bakes his own bread.

and place of current residence; as in Maiken's introduction,

> He also raises herbs in the kitchen window of his 19th-floor apartment a block from the Tribune offices.

or, as in the Friedan introduction,

> When she's not on the road lecturing, Friedan divides her time between her house on Long Island and her book-filled 40th floor apartment on Manhattan's West Side where she lives alone.

## Restatement of the Interview's Theme

The introductions for these personable, eminently qualified experts conclude with a cogent restatement of the interview's salient theme; as in the ones with Gore Vidal or Betty Friedan:

> Though Vidal is not yet on the stump, he let fly on politics and personalities to Senior Editor Christopher P. Anderson of *People*.

> There she spoke with Bonnie Johnson of *People* about the current age of women's and men's—liberation.

In summary, the examples of the introductions to the *People*-styled "Q. & A." recommend questions for your expert on personal and professional facts that may have no direct relationship to the views you want to hear. I'll reiterate these information needs for the "Q. & A.'s" introduction: Ask for a cogent statement of the expert's position on the controversy or the expert's primary contention; age at time of the interview's publication date; key professional credits such as current or past employment that support the expert's authority on the subject of the interview; and other facts such as publications, higher educational degrees, and research, that amplify your expert's credibility. After requests for this short professional resume, solicit such impersonal biographical details as birthplace, parents' occupations, marital status, spouse's name, ages, names and occupations of children, pastimes, and area of residence. Then elicit a summary of the interview's intended focus.

## BODY OF THE INTERVIEW: RESEARCH REQUIREMENTS AND STRUCTURE

Now let's examine the research needs of the question and answer interview format by analyzing three types—a "Q. & A." about a sociological trend, an investigative expose, and an all-purpose structural model about the future global climate crisis.

To guide your discussion with an expert steeped in a controversial popular trend, I'll outline the "Q. & A." with Colette Dowling, author of the thesis, *The Cinderella Complex: Women's Hidden Fear of Independence.* Dowling was asked to explain her theory of the Cinderella complex, examples of it, when and why it begins, the first crisis, the consequences, the author's Cinderella crisis, and her advice to women today. Always try to get your expert to personalize his or her theories, as did the interviewer by asking for Dowling's Cinderella crisis. Readers like to know the expert's personal experience with the discussed interview theme.

To structure a "Q. & A." about an expose similar to Maiken's about American ripoffs, consider the points Maiken had to confront—the motives of his informants about consumer cheating, his estimate of the national prevalence of these crooked practices, common examples of ripoffs, his advice to avoid them, his personal experience, the typical victim, and suggested solutions. If you interview an authority on a researched theory, extract national statistics about its incidence and everyday illustrations. Again, ask your expert for personal illustrations which, in this case, was Maiken's regularly inflated parking bill. Statistics, researched anecdotes, or personal examples of the theory add convincing documentation as well as entertainment to the interview.

For an all-purpose structure for "Q. & A." research and the interview's submission, the model format may be the one used for climatologist's Reid Bryson's interview. The interviewer solicits his theory (*"Is the world headed for another ice age?"*); the consequences (*"of a cooling climate?"*); historical research (*"When did this cooling trend come to be recognized?"*); causes (*"What are your predictions based on?"*); solutions (for future populations, public policy, food storage); and personal attitudes (*"Are you discouraged?"*). In a simplification of the format, the "Q. & A." unravels the expert's theory, its effects, historic examples, causes, recommendations, and personal experience with it or personal view. Follow the model for devising your questions and polishing the results for print, and you may achieve a commendable piece.

## GUIDELINES TO EDIT YOUR "Q. & A."

Once you've composed questions for the introduction and main format and done the interview, you'll be ready to edit your research for submission. The succeeding guidelines concentrate on specific methods for editing "Q. & A.'s", the written style for questions, ways to express your viewpoint within the interview, and the quote approval required.

Before proceeding, consult the editing advice in the one issue chapter. Then proceed to read about the methods frequently used with the "Q. & A." format. To insure readability to the "Q. & A.", which rarely is an exact transcription of the interview, you may rearrange the order of answers and rewrite questions for a smooth, logical flow. For instance, if the expert gives a theory early in the discussion and its example later, combine the principle with its illustration for maximum communication and a graceful progression of ideas. Besides changing the order of the interview's information, you may condense several answers into one or divide overly long quotes by questions later written. To clarify direction of the interview, remember, you may eliminate repetition, substitute more vivid words for vague ones, amplify thoughts with added words, or rearrange speech for print. Recall, though you are entitled to change the interview material to intensify or clarify meaning, you never may alter the expert's meaning or invent ideas never expressed.

Don't try to cutesy up the spoken words. Trust their simplicity to be eloquent. Of course, I am advising you to accept a hard lesson I learned from years of overwriting texts that editors later simplified. When I first began as a free-lance writer, I tried to avoid conversational language more often, I suppose, in my profiles, where editors found quotes hard to come by, than in my interviews, where I lavishly used the quotes I received for print. In fact, I was so concerned with the reader reliving exactly what I had heard, I would ask transcribers to include the "Ahhhh" or "Uhhhh," which reminded me of difficult emotional moments in the interview that I would leave in submitted text for the reader's benefit, if the editor permitted. In truth, though, I didn't much care for conversational language. Give my classical Bryn Mawr education in pre-twentieth-century English literature—only one course assigned reading beyond 1900—I believed modern day conversation wasn't "literary." But I've changed my mind since. The more experience I've gained as a journalist, the more I've come to espouse the opposite point of view of what's "literary." If you can edit conversational words to the fewest that express a thought's true meaning, that direct, clear, simple language, put in logical order, will be as eloquent as any line of classical poetry by its sheer force of simplicity. So rather than include all the curlicues of your expert's answers, pare for meaning and trust the simplicity of expression to be eloquent.

## Style for Written Questions

There is a definite style for written questions for submitted manuscript. As you've seen in the questions quoted from the global weather expert's interview, the printed questions lean toward the objective, not the subjective. Rather than "Don't you think that. . . .," the interviewer takes a neutral tack with questions like "Why?", "How?", "What else can be done?" in the published text.

While preserving a neutrality on the topic, the interviewer nonetheless may use a provocative fact as a question. In the 1981 *People* interview with Gore Vidal, the interviewer inquired:

> Meanwhile you sued Truman Capote for writing that you had been thrown out of a White House party in the early '60's. What is the legal status of that case?

By contrast a *Penthouse* interviewer that same year posed a different type of question to confront an Indian activist, Russell Means, because of different latitudes for the interview format.

> *Penthouse:* The Indians are directly controlled by the Bureau of Indian Affairs. In recent years Indians have headed up that bureau. So, some of your enemies must be Indians.

The *Penthouse* interviewer editorializes—expresses a viewpoint—in his question; the *People* interviewer does not. The *People*-styled interview questions in print do not show a slant or viewpoint toward the potential answer of the expert. The *Penthouse* interviewer can and often does expose an attitude in the question. The first example typifies the objective question style, the second, a subjective personal one.

## Ways to Express Your Viewpoint

You can express a viewpoint, but not by the obvious means of biased questions. A writer of a "Q. & A." has several available devices for editorializing. You indicate slant or attitude by choice of material—what is included in the published interview or left out; by the structure of the interview format—what's front-billed, slugged in the middle, savored for the end; by the pacing of answers—their length or reduction.

## Required Quote Approval

A reminder. Where the final form of the article consists mainly of questions and the interviewed expert's words, you have an obligation to show the article to the quoted expert prior to publication. I usually do just before submission. Tell the expert, "You can alter anything for reasons of accuracy, but not for editorial content. That is my province as the writer." Ask the subject to sign or initial each page of the final interview before returning it to you. If the person is out of town, call and read the piece over the phone.

Such courtesy extended to someone whose words comprise the bulk of an entire article may protect you against charges of libel.

The review may also save you from publishing a manuscript with errors of fact that could mar the credibility of your article. As I wrote earlier, I requested this routine manuscript review by Liv Ullmann for the interview published in the November 1976, charter issue of *Working Woman* under the title, "Interview: Face to Face with Liv Ullmann." I said Liv Ullmann corrected nothing in the 3,000-word interview but two misspellings, but I didn't tell you what they were. When I stopped by her suite at Manhattan's Hotel Pierre to retrieve a copy of my interview, which she'd read and initialed on each page, she tactfully informed me I had misspelled her name and that of Bergman. Without any rancour or prima donna airs, she turned and wrote both names on the back of the manila envelope containing the interview. I saw I had missed the "n" in Bergman's first name, Ingmar, and second "n" ending her last name. I apologized and immediately started correcting my spelling errors in the manuscript. There were quite a few.

So don't be afraid to show the subject of any "Q. & A." for publication your text, as long as you draw the lines on the changes you will accept. Rather than censor your work, your expert may be the best authority to rectify factual inaccuracies in the text before submission. So view your expert in this collaboration as your editorial ally rather than your censor. Remember, your expert wants the rewards of publication as much as you.

## SAMPLE "Q. & A."

The past section has given you a definition of the "Q. & A." article form, qualifications for your spokesperson, research requirements for the article's introduction and interview format, possible structural designs, and guidelines for editing your interview with a viewpoint for print. The following section summarizes the circumstances under which I found my first "Q. & A." subject, received the *People* assignment, and the behind-the-scenes events from the text's delivery through its editing for immediate publication.

My first "Q. & A." titled, "The Birth Rate Is Down, But Teenage Pregnancies Are Up, And Janet Hardy Tells Why," appeared March 15, 1976, in *People*. I found the expert and issue for my "Q. & A.", as I have for numbers of my articles, during the research for another assignment. November 1975, I was tracking Eunice Kennedy Shriver, then wife of a hopeful Democratic Party presidential nominee and subject of my *Ladies' Home Journal* commission, to public and private events to research the assigned profile. At Ms. Shriver's invitation, I attended a Senate subcommittee meeting chaired by her brother, Senator Edward M. Kennedy, where Ms. Shriver nervously spoke on behalf of The School-Age and Mother Child Health Act. At the same hearing, I also heard Johns Hopkins pediatrics professor Dr. Janet B. Hardy testify impressively with tersely stated points, moving psychological insight, and humane earthiness—qualities she would also bring to answers for my *People* "Q. & A."

I met Dr. Hardy again during Ms. Shriver's visit to The Johns Hopkins Medical Institutions clinic, administered under The Comprehensive Adolescent Pregnancy Program, which Dr. Hardy co-directed. As the pediatrician and Ms. Shriver questioned the young mothers about their child-care problems, I was struck by how the babies of these teenagers seemed like tiny dolls for their mothers to play with. Also, the girls seemed so young to be saddled with so much parental responsibility. I sensed that they and their doll-size babies represented an abnormal situation that wasn't going to go away, that people should know about. So the idea for the *People* "Q. & A." came from a powerful impression I gained during research for the *Journal* profile.

After I submitted the Shriver profile, subsequently published with a cover line in the *Journal*'s March 1976 issue, I did some phone research on teenage pregnancy. The National Center for Health Statistics, then a section of the federal department of Health, Education and Welfare, gave me some astonishing data. The trend in total births was declining nationally, but in the past two to three years, the births for the group of 15-19-year-old girls was dramatically increasing. Based on the center's figures, the HEW statistician concluded, "The proportion of total teenage mothers in the United States rose from 12 percent of all mothers in 1950 to 20 percent of that total in 1973—the last year for available full statistics."

I brought this data, buttressed by national statistics about teen marriages, teen divorces, children born to teenage mothers, and illegitimate births among teen mothers in ghettos and suburbs, to an editorial conference with assigning *People* Senior Editor Cranston Jones. I went to my meeting at *People*'s mid-Manhattan offices hauling huge brown shopping bags in both hands, like the "bag ladies" I mentioned previously. In my bulging bags were piled all my reportorial goods for future *People* commissions—summaries or the resumes for prospective *People* profiles, supporting items like record album covers, glossy mug photos, newly published books, or just their book jackets. In a display of research for proposed articles during a February 1976 editorial conference at *People*'s offices, I got the assignment for a "Q. & A." on teenage pregnancy.

By the time I arrived to interview Dr. Hardy at her Johns Hopkins office in Baltimore, I had reviewed the entire transcribed testimony of the experts who appeared before the Senate subcommittee considering The School-Age and

Mother Child Health Act. The details of the interview mentioned earlier illustrate the discomforts reporters will endure to get a story. For five hours I perched on hard, thick telephone books to reach a flat nineteen-forties executive desk, to bang out Dr. Hardy's answers on a similar-period "vintage" typewriter. I couldn't waste time copying the interview from an audio tape because final manuscript was due on the desk of my assigning editor two days later.

After I checked the factual accuracy of the final manuscript by a long-distance call to Dr. Hardy, I brought my copy to *People* on deadline and then returned to the Time & Life Building the next day, Friday, to oversee the edit. My interview was going to press that night or, the latest, Monday. I remember I had to wend my way along the building's long, labyrinthian corridors to the office of Richard B. Stolley, listed then on the masthead as Managing Editor (but, in practice, *People*'s Editor-in-Chief), for the recent edit of my "Q. & A." Stolley sat so far from his office doorway that the trek to his desk made a stranger like me quake and beat a hasty retreat to the door, where I stood to review copy.

As I read the print on reams of wide papers bearing consecutively numbered lines, the paper unfolded from my hands like stock market tickertape to the floor. By comparing my submission with the version in hand, line by line, I picked up one minor change. I saw the third interview question had been made up by the editors, and beneath it were the words, "ANSWER TK." And I asked in a matter of fact tone, " 'TK,' what's that mean?"

"To come," Stolley replied.

I had never heard the *Peoplese* for unresearched answers. And I repeated, "To come?", and burst out laughing at the obvious sexual innuendo.

For all his editorial sophistication, Stolley, as the platitude best describes, turned "beet red."

In the next section, the "TK" was gone—replaced by Dr. Hardy's answer, which I had secured in a short phone call.

Later, I remembered Stolley had remarked as I read the edit in his office that it was unusual for the magazine to print any article with so little editorial rewriting. And by careful comparison of the edit and my submission, I proudly realized, as Stolley had pointed out, how little touched by the editor's blue pencil the final version was. The published interview adhered faithfully to my article's structure with only small changes. The editors had lifted a quote from my introduction and used it with a made-up question to start the interview format. Two overly long answers had been broken up with questions inserted later, "And other reasons?", "How?" One question and matching answer had been deleted. But save for those few minimal changes and trimmings at the ends of answers for space, my original questions and answers were printed virtually intact.

When other magazine editors have asked, "How much of your *People* pieces were rewritten?", I'd say, "Truthfully, very little." But from what I knew, the general practice at *People* was to rewrite, even pieces by staff writers. Few editors outside the magazine believed me unless I made a point of submitting copies of my original profile and its published edition in *People* as sample writings with my article proposals. And when I was seeking profile commissions, I sometimes did submit original and published versions.

The "Q. & A." resulting from my Tuesday typing marathon, submitted two days later, that I oversaw for fact check and edit on Friday, went to press the following Monday and came out a week later in the *People* delivered March 8 with a dateline of March 15 to insure a week's sales on the stands. Perhaps the rapid publishing of the "Q. & A." attests to the interviewer's thorough preparation, wisely chosen expert, bold questions, tactful probing for humane examples, supporting statistics, and honest editing of the interview for publication. Or, to the sales value of the expert's view of a timely subject of controversy. Or, to the editorial power and judgment of my assigning editor. You be the judge.

## THE BIRTH RATE IS DOWN BUT TEENAGE PREGNANCIES ARE UP, AND JANET HARDY TELLS WHY

*While the national birth rate has declined in recent years, there has been a dramatic upswing in the number of children born to teenage mothers. This year an estimated 600,000 babies—one in five—will be born to women under 19. One researcher long familiar with the trend is Johns Hopkins pediatrics professor Dr. Janet B. Hardy. As director of the Johns Hopkins Child Development Study, she has followed the progress of 550 teenage mothers and their children since 1958. Recently Dr. Hardy, who is married to Johns Hopkins professor of microbiology Paul H. Hardy Jr. and has two grown children of her own, discussed the plight of the teenage mother with Barbara Kevles for* People.

*Do the children of teenage mothers face any special problems?*
Yes. We found the highest proportion of infant deaths, school failures and social maladjustment among the children of teenage mothers.

*Why do teenagers let themselves become pregnant?*
There are lots of theories, all stemming from the problems of adolescence; the transition from childhood to adulthood. Some girls are in an identity crisis and feel that being loved by a boy helps them find themselves. It's possible that there is a great deal of group pressure to indulge in sex, and girls who don't want to are often made to feel inadequate. Society has changed remarkably in the last decade, and families no longer have as close control over children's activities. My feeling is that very few adolescent pregnancies are planned.

*How many of these teenage mothers are married?*
In all probability, considerably less than half.

*Are parents doing their job of instructing their children in sex?*
Dr. Arthur Richardson, associate professor of sociology at New York University,

and I carried out a study of white and black inner-city women to find out how much they knew about reproduction physiology, contraception and sex education. Between 60 and 70 percent of the women did not know enough about how pregnancy occurs to use contraceptives effectively or to teach their children adequately. Ninety-five percent felt that more effective sex education should be instituted in the schools, perhaps as early as kindergarten. I strongly favor this, but it's important that such a program stress family living rather than just anatomy and sex.

*Is teenage pregnancy primarily a ghetto problem?*
There's no question about its being a ghetto problem, but it's increasing among whites in suburban and rural areas as well. Approximately half of all teenage mothers are white.

*How do suburban teenagers handle their pregnancies compared to those in ghettos?*
Suburban teenagers have more problems. Teenage pregnancy is less of a disgrace among ghetto families. Consequently there is more pressure on suburban teenagers to have pregnancies terminated or to marry. These shotgun marriages tend to break up rapidly once the young couple is faced with being parents.

*How do teenagers view abortion?*
Most women, teenagers or not, have some feeling of loss when they end a pregnancy. However, I think teenagers should realize that while there are alternatives to having and keeping an unwanted child—abortion and adoption—the major alternative is not to get pregnant in the first place.

*What kind of contraception do you recommend for teenagers?*
If a youngster is going to be sexually active, she should go to a family planning clinic to determine the best contraceptive for her. There is an alternative to being sexually active, of course. I don't think we push youngsters enough to indulge in sports and other activities. They are left at loose ends.

*How do teens handle pregnancy?*
Many are still children themselves, and their fears or lack of knowledge of what to expect can act as major obstacles to an easy delivery. Furthermore, many teenage mothers are in need of mothering, and they are very dependent on their families and other adults for emotional support.

*Are teenagers better equipped physically by their youth for pregnancy?*
Within limits. The optimal ages would seem to be from 18 to 30 years. The very young ages, particularly 15 and below, are unfavorable for several reasons. First of all, biological maturity is not reached until about 18. Very young mothers are still growing, and their babies compete with them for nutritional materials for body growth.

*And the other reasons?*
Adolescent mothers are more prone to diseases like anemia and toxemia, whose symptoms are hypertension and loss of protein through the urine. Finally, having a baby is a very real hazard for the adolescent because the bony pelvis hasn't reached its full size. If the baby is large, there may be mechanical difficulties in delivery.

*Do teenagers generally produce healthy babies?*
No. They are more likely to lose their babies or have damaged babies than women 18 to 30.

*How do you define a damaged baby?*
I mean a baby with neurological impairment which actually may be subtle brain damage. This damage can affect a child's learning ability—make it clumsy, hyperactive and a problem in school. Though some poor intellectual performances may be the result of unstable family life, it is clear that teen pregnancy contributes in a major way to producing mentally inferior children. In a normal population, 25 percent have IQ scores of 110 and above, while only 2.5 percent are defective. When the children in our study reached 7 years of age, 5.3 percent fell in the defective category and only 3 percent scored 110 and above.

*Do pregnant teenagers actually have their babies, or do they get abortions?*
About 70 percent give birth. Many teenage mothers come from situations in which there is little love, and their babies are sources of love for them. Unfortunately, when the teenager does not understand the baby's needs and development, she may feel the baby is unresponsive. This is one factor that can lead to child abuse and child neglect, which accounts in part for the higher death rate of babies of teenage mothers. Another reason for wanting to keep her baby may be some sort of status symbol. For a kid who has had few successes in life, producing a baby may represent a major accomplishment.

*What are the social consequences of pregnancy for a teenager?*
For most, pregnancy means dropping out of school and, often, out of the mainstream of society. In Baltimore, 80 percent of the teenagers who leave school with the birth of their babies never obtain further education. Sixty percent of mothers 16 and younger who drop out have a second baby within two or three years at a greater health risk than the first. Some 60 to 70 percent of all teenage mothers nationwide are on welfare within five years after the birth of their children.

*What have you discovered about social maladjustment among the children of teenage mothers?*
We looked at a random group of 100 13-year-olds who lived both in and outside Baltimore's ghetto area. Thirty-five percent of the children failing in school had been born when their mothers were 16 and younger. Another study of children who had set major fires and burned down family residences or caused someone's death showed that 60 percent of their mothers had been teenagers at the time of their birth.

*Do the daughters of teenage mothers perpetuate the cycle?*
I remember in my residency days seeing an attractive young mother with a sick baby, and I said, "Is this your baby?" She said, "No, he's my grandson." She was 28. I think this happens more than we realize.

*How can society cope with the growing problem of teenage pregnancy?*
The most important step society can take is to strengthen the family and to demand that the family take responsibility for teenage behavior. I think teenage rebellion is caused by namby pamby family discipline. I also think the welfare laws tend to work against the family unit, which is basic to the survival of society.

*How?*

Most states will not give aid to mothers and dependent children if the father is in the household, which hampers the development of families by teenagers. Society has to encourage the development of stable family life by radically changing its welfare laws.

*If you had a pregnant teenage daughter, what guidance would you offer?*

I would provide her with the necessary information about adolescent pregnancy. And frankly, if she were under 16, I would strongly emphasize the perils to her health and social well-being to help her make the right choice.

A postscript. There was another text change by my editors. The introduction to the interview you just read profited from editorial help by my *People* editor, Cran Jones. He deleted some original text in the middle of the submitted introduction and used the available space lines for data from my original proposal, combined with an answer in the interview, to give a strong thematic focus at the introduction's start. My final version, as you'll see, did not adhere to the published introduction's national focus throughout its start:

> Dr. Janet B. Hardy, a Professor of Pediatrics, co-directs The Comprehensive Adolescent Pregnancy Program at the Johns Hopkins Medical Institutions. Recently, the program was awarded a third of a million dollar grant from The Joseph P. Kennedy, Jr. Foundation to supplement the hospital's existing care and counseling of pregnant teenagers with greater guidance services up until two years after delivery. Dr. Hardy also directs The Johns Hopkins Child Development Study which, since 1958, has followed 550 mothers and their children. . . .

In my mind, the large grant and prestigious source emphasized the importance of the program my expert co-directed and her professional credentials. In response to the published piece, Eunice Kennedy Shriver wrote me a letter of praise and protest. She praised the credence the Hardy interview had given the program, but protested the omission of mention of her family foundation's support of it. I explained that I had mentioned that fact in the introduction to the "Q. & A.", but Cranston Jones, my editor, had overruled me. Later, he told me he had deleted the foundation's name "because we felt we were being used for promotional purposes." Instead, he had introduced the interview by spotlighting the mammoth national problem of teenage pregnancy rather than a particular program and funding source to solve it. Frankly, from a journalistic viewpoint, I think my editor's focus on the national issue at the beginning of the introduction the wiser choice.

## Analysis

At this point, I want to reexamine particular basics of the form illustrated by the sample "Q. & A." you've just scanned. The discussion will evaluate the suitability of the subject for the form, the informational contents of the introduction, the structure of the interview, the neutrality of its questions, and evidence of my point of view.

Dr. Hardy was not selected, as Gore Vidal was, for her contentious views, but rather, as Betty Friedan was, for her views on a subject of controversy—the dramatically growing national problem of teenage pregnancy.

The introduction stresses Dr. Janet B. Hardy's credible authority by the following facts: her present professional affiliation, medical specialty, current teaching rank, degree, title of her position on a research project, the study's name, number of case studies, and the project's duration.

It also includes such details about her personal life as her marital status, her husband's professional affiliation, professional rank, medical specialty, his name, and the number and ages of her children.

The structure of the interview with Dr. Hardy covers some of the same thematic points suggested by the format for the global weather forecaster—theory, causes, effects, recommendations. This interview touches upon the definition of the problem; causes in terms of peer pressure; family ignorance of reproduction; ghetto versus suburban family attitudes; young women's attitudes toward abortion; personal consequences of youthful pregnancies; societal consequences; solutions and personal advice.

The questions maintain the objective, noneditorializing style suitable for this interview format. A few examples will demonstrate:

*"Are parents doing their job of instructing their children in sex?"*

*"Do teenagers generally produce healthy babies?"*

*"How do you define a damaged baby?"*

Despite the impersonal questions, I did assert a viewpoint about my material. I did it by the editing techniques I've recommended—my choice of material for inclusion or omission; the order of the questions and answers; the length or compression of answers. But I did have a very strong attitude toward the subject of teenage pregnancy. In my covering letter accompanying the submitted interview, I wrote my editor, Cran Jones:

> As for my viewpoint—could you try (and I won't hold you to it) to use Dr. Hardy's advice—if she had a teenage daughter sixteen and pregnant—which is firmly *pro abortion*. I would so appreciate your including this warning against the perils of teenage motherhood.

For whatever reasons, the editors saw fit to include Dr. Hardy's implied advocacy of abortion in the published version in support of my stated slant toward teenage pregnancy. Earlier in this chapter, I advised you to make sure you ask your expert some questions that will apply the discussed controversy or controversial view to the expert's personal life. In these answers, you may find the example that meshes with your point of view toward the subject of your "Q. & A."

## CRITIQUES OF STUDENT "Q. & A.'S"

Students flounder with the "Q. & A." because of a poorly conceived concept. They are apt to do the interview without a current, controversial focus, or with one too broad. Excerpts from "Q. & A.'s" by beginner magazine writers will illustrate these common mistakes by students with this article form.

Debra Severson submitted an interview with a New York tax lawyer about changing life-styles and resulting problems with wills. As you will see from the introduction, there is no timely urgency that presses the material into a strong reason for the reader's attention.

> This country's property laws were predicated on the notion that people marry for life and bear children. By 1973, well-documented evidence showed how this once-favored family form was no longer suitable for many. As one sociologist states, marriage is no more an inevitability or necessarily desirable, and relations need not be heterosexual, exclusive or permanent. Little suggests, however, that laws have changed in accordance with people's changing needs. A woman, for example, who chooses to will her belongings to her roommate, when she dies, cannot take advantage of the same tax breaks her married counterpart can. John Gross, a New York tax lawyer who had drawn up wills for people whose assets range from $500 to $4 million, discusses some of these pitfalls and what to expect from the law.

I won't comment on the introduction's gaps in information except in general terms. The writer needs to prove her claims about changing forms of cohabitation with statistics, and affirm her expert's credibility by professional credits and some personal biography. But the lack of a controversial viewpoint—that compelling reason to care about changing mores and inheritance—is absent. And its absence hinders the effectiveness of the interview that follows. It covers such points as definition of a will, problems of the single woman without one, estate planners' problems with new family forms, estate laws for single women, for unmarried couples, and advice for them. The interview reads more like a draft of a sociology report on changing life-style and inheritance planning than a journalistic interview on a timely controversy. As it stands, the material probably would provide the research for a query for a worthwhile service piece—how to structure your will if unmarried—rather than a "Q. & A."

By contrast, Hy Kozak begins his "Q. & A." about legalization of marijuana with riveting statistics to persuade readers of the subject's timeliness:

There have been about three million marijuana-related arrests in the United States in the past ten years. In 1977 alone, out of 600,000 drug-related arrests in this country, more than 450,000 of them were for marijuana. Of these, "90 percent were for simple possession," says Mark Heutlinger, the recently appointed Deputy Director-Treasurer of NORML, the nation's foremost lobby and citizen's action group representing marijuana users in the United States.

But the interview about marijuna's legalization sprawls over too large a territory to be convincing journalism. In a question apiece, the interview investigates such medical problems as "Does marijuana lead to hard drugs?", "Is marijuana habit-forming?", "Is marijuana a hallucinogen?", "What about recent medical evidence that shows an increased susceptibility among marijuana users to cancer and severe lung damage?" It also touches on possible increased usage and estimated revenues from decriminalization and legalization of marijuana sales. The amount of information to comprehensively answer any of these questions could fill one article for each. Mr. Kozak's interview loses its focus because of an overly ambitious concept.

The examples of student "Q. & A.'s" demonstrate the pitfalls from too weak or too grand a theme for the "Q. & A." The faulty concepts for these interviews stress the importance of your choice of the right limited subject for this article form.

## ADVICE FOR THE "Q. & A." FORM OF INTERVIEW

To achieve success with the "Q. & A," try to keep in mind the following:

1. Select an expert with a controversial viewpoint or view of a controversy to insure a timely, suitable theme.

2. Make sure your expert has either past or present employment, publications, educational training, or published research that verify his or her authority. Mention these relevant credits in your query and introduction.

3. Request the necessary information for the brief biographical section of the introduction before or during the interview.

4. Study the structural models for the body of the "Q. & A." to plan your research and design your interview format for submission.

5. Limit your research theme to one that 1500-2000 words can handle.

6. Probe for examples, anecdotes, and statistics that will illustrate the discussed topic in convincing, concrete terms.

7. When you hear your expert answer in rhetoric, ask for an instant translation into conversational language, lest your submitted text slip to the level of sophomoric propaganda for your expert's cause.

8. Don't forget to ask for an anecdote about practical application of the

theory to your expert's life, if possible.

9. State your theme clearly in your article's introduction and stick to it throughout the interview format.

10. Edit the expert's answers for clarity, smooth pacing, meaning, and space requirements.

11. Rewrite your questions in the preferred neutral, noneditorial style of the form.

12. Get the expert to review the text for accuracy and initial each page. If necessary, read your expert the text by phone for a last fact check.

13. Don't leave out any question or answer that sheds an unfavorable light on your expert's views unless it is irrelevant to your stated theme. You are not a promoter for your expert's cause; you are a journalist.

# XII The "As Told To" Interview: The First-Person Narrative About an Extraordinary Experience or an Outstanding or Unusual Career

# DEFINITION

The "Q. & A.", the first interview form studied, handles a subject of controversy. The "As Told To" interview reports the uncommon slice of life, such as an unusual experience, crisis, or a life at the peak of a profession. This type of interview differs from the "Q. & A." not only by subject, but also by its format. In print, the "As Told To" is narrated by the person who lived the drama or exciting work life. Though the magazine account is told by the "I" who is its source, your by-line on the piece lets readers know its true author.

## Markets for "As Told To" Interviews

The better-known women's magazines publish more first-person narratives about extraordinary experiences than their male counterparts which, more often, focus first-person articles on out-of-the ordinary careers. More often than not, "As Told To" interviews in women's publications cover plots of sex, wrenching traumas, or extreme illness, that titillate, edify, or furnish an escape from humdrum lives. *Cosmopolitan*'s "As Told To" interviews like "I Was A Sleep-Around Girl" or "I Had A Nervous Breakdown" epitomize the form. First-person articles authored by their source, that may or may not be ghosted, also follow this interview style. So I include as examples of the first-person narrative the *Cosmopolitan* autobiographical piece, "I Had an Affair With My Ex-Husband"; or from *Redbook*'s enduring series, "A Young Mother's Story," a mother's account of her newborn's death, "How I Got Over The Feeling That Somehow I Had Failed My Baby"; or from *Ladies' Home Journal*'s series, "A Woman Today," " 'I had my sister's baby.' " Women's magazines, such as *Cosmopolitan,* also feature first-person narratives by women in nontraditional professions, like the article, "I Was a Lady Hard Hat," or by women in very traditional female jobs, like one reporting, "I Was A Nightclub Hostess In Japan," which also appeared in *Cosmopolitan.*

To query a women's magazine for a personal 1000-3000 word first-person story or an interview in the "As Told To" style, you or your candidate must have lived through a catastrophic illness, crisis of birth or death, neurotic sex, uncommon or traditional profession for a woman, and be willing to talk about it for publication.

By contrast, slick men's magazines, as *Esquire* in its former series, "A Day In The Life," favor thousand-word accounts about men of extraordinary achievement or in out of the ordinary careers, rather than dramas of intimate family crises or extraordinary personal lives. First-person narratives in men's publications give readers on the way up the career ladder a taste of professional success or unusual work. Favorites I've saved from old *Esquires* are about, as the series' subtitle states, "Moments to moment with. . . .," the proprietor of the oldest restaurant in Paris, a package designer for famous brand foods and home products, and a detective's work in the underworld at Manhattan's posh Plaza Hotel. If you want to write a first-person interview for a men's publication, try for a fabled name in a chic profession in which the executive office view of clientele, fast-paced work world and personal idiosyncrasies would rivet readers' attention. Or, find someone in a seedy occupation whose behind-closed-doors adventures in sleazy society would attract readers in more conventional lives.

## Chance to Improve Your Technique

At the start of this chapter, I stressed that the three interview styles would force you to employ quotes more generously. The "As Told To" interview consists only of quotes for the entire article. So, during your research interviews, you have to pry from sometimes unwilling candidates their descriptions of their powerful private feelings in any crisis, or telling idiosyncrasies present in any extraordinary work life, to make the narrative work. So work in this form makes you skilled in getting good quotes and, more importantly, using quotes in this and other forms of articles.

## THE BEGINNING OF THE "AS TOLD TO" INTERVIEW: RESEARCH REQUIREMENTS

Once commissioned to do an "As Told To" interview, review the form's beginnings, structural designs, and stylistic devices for the two types—the ones about uncommon professions and the ones about extraordinary personal dramas.

### Introduction to an Interview
### About an Uncommon Professional Life

Unlike the one issue interview article, beginnings of the first person interview about an unusual career don't summarize your own or the subject's outstanding professional credentials, but rather the compelling reasons for the choice of career. Such reasons may be facts of family history, a reminiscence from childhood, or recent circumstances. So at the start of *Cosmopolitan*'s career first-person, "I Was a Lady Hard Hat," by Sarah Bottorff, the construction worker explains the selection of her unusual profession, for a woman, by a childhood memory:

> I'd always been intrigued by construction: when I was a child and couldn't reach the knotholes in the six-foot fence running around a site, I'd go half-mad with curi-

osity. Then when I grew tall enough to be able to see inside, I began to feel left out and a little envious of the closed male society. . . .

a recent job history:

> I had just quit a job typing useless letters-to-the-files, and endlessly shuffling Xerox copies, and I was determined never again to do work that I hated.

and a professional contact made by chance:

> Then I met a young graduate student at a party and found out [what] *he'd* been making . . . as a construction worker.

The explanation for her professional choice concludes with the story of her first job.

First-person interviews with prestigious professionals also use the same type of information to begin. In the *Esquire* "A Day In The Life" interview with Claude Terrail, owner of Paris' oldest restaurant, Terrail's first words give the reasons for his choice of profession. "I AM a child of this world," says Terrail, "this world of haute cuisine." Then he capsules the history of the family business. At the turn of the century, his mother's father ran a celebrated Parisian cafe where his father worked. There his father met and married the boss' daughter. When her father died and the restaurant closed, Terrail's father merged the cafe's wine cellar with that of La Tour d'Argent, founded in 1582.

Besides imperatives of the family business, Terrail cites family pressures as another of his reasons:

> I grew up wanting to be a diplomat or a lawyer or an actor—ah, yes, especially an actor—but my father made it very clear where my responsibilities lay.

Both introductions use the same type of introductory materials—childhood remembrances and alternate professional options. To secure similar beginning materials for this interview form, ask yourself or your subject, "Why do you identify with this profession?", or, "What else could you have been?" The answers may be your beginning.

## Introduction to an Interview
## About an Extraordinary Experience

"As Told To" interviews about intimate personal dramas begin with the cause of the trauma. These personal dramas start with the seed of the crisis and then reach back in time for the initial events that nurtured this seed, and then sweep forward to the crisis. A signed example from *Redbook*'s first-person stories about problems in marriages and family lives of young mothers demonstrates the pattern of such introductions in the interview form, too. At the beginning of "How I Got Over The Feeling That Somehow I Had Failed My Baby," Jeri Fink describes the "gloriously colored" spring of the birth of her sickly second son. From there, she flashes back to her pregnancy, and then forward through the telling events that climax in the doomed newborn's second hospital stay. With an eye for vivid, convincing detail, Ms. Fink begins with the birth and then notes the record cold winter of her difficult pregnancy, her calm labor during a televised David Frost interview with Richard Nixon, her anesthetized delivery, first premonitions about her "quiet, withdrawn" newborn son, the mailing of birth announcements, telling spots on the baby a day before the party for his circumcision, and the siren ride with her baby's face under "a tiny oxygen mask" to the hospital, to the inevitable denouement. If you are interviewing someone who has lived through a trauma, emotionally difficult as it will be for you both, persuade that person to recall as many details or ancecdotes as possible of that traumatic event and those events that preceded and shaped it.

In summary, the beginning of a first-person interview about an unusual career or extraordinary experience answers the question, "Why did this happen?" Whether the specifics describe motives for entering a profession or the events leading up to a climactic trauma, that explanation will give your submission a proper send-off.

## THE BODY OF THE "AS TOLD TO" INTERVIEW: RESEARCH REQUIREMENTS

The body of a first-person career narrative is easier to obtain if you know in advance the materials that suit the form's structure.

### The Body of an Interview About an Unusual Work Life: Research and Structure

Lawrence Frost's feisty first-person narrative about his hotel sleuthing touches in this order on topics that may suggest questions about any occupation: misconceptions about his job:

> The days when the primary job was to make sure unmarried people weren't shacking up together are long gone. What we're concerned with is basic security.

memorable customers:

> We had one woman known as The Spitter who was there constantly. She was terrifying. When we'd try to get her to leave, she'd start cursing and kicking at your balls and spitting in your face.

the biggest tasks:

> The biggest arrest I was ever involved with in the hotel was of a husband-and-wife forgery team. These people had eighteen complete sets of identification on them. . . .

temptations on the job:

> . . . when you'd arrest a hooker and she'd take off a boot and throw $500 at you. This was one night's work for this woman: for us, it was two or three weeks' salary.

reasons for remaining at or leaving the job:

> Finally last year, after three years, I decided to leave the Plaza. I was a little bored— and also fed up. In the house dick business, your face is constantly in the muck.

current work:

> . . . working with a small firm, . . . We do a lot of court work, investigating in behalf of indigent defendants. . . . We make most of our real money on matrimonial work—a euphemism for getting the goods on someone's husband or wife.

job's advantages:

> I really do enjoy this work—it's constantly surprising, and there's no beating the hours. They're incredibly flexible, so I can make it to a hell of a lot of Yankee games. . . .

I want to stress that the required information in these first person narratives generally is expressed as judgments, examples, definitions, summaries. Sound familiar? The work that quotes do in first-person interviews is identical to the work they perform in one issue/one interviews. So abide by the technical standards for good quotes elaborated in that chapter.

Also, make sure the quotes obtained during the research for a career "As Told To" satisfy the structure's informational needs. Probe someone at the height of his field or in an unusual one for myths about that work, interesting or odd clients, the job's difficulties, greatest demands, rewards, its personal meaning or diminished satisfactions, current work challenges. If you guide your questions toward these areas evident in Frost's narrative, you may finish the interview with rich possibilities for the edited version.

## The Body of an Interview About an Extraordinary Experience: Research and Structure

The structure of the first-person about an extraordinary experience is organized more by plot than topic. You may gain the right materials for the body of a narrated crisis if you perceive the main portion as a chain of events that solve the problem introduced at the article's start. For example, *Cosmopolitan*'s "As Told To," "I Had A Nervous Breakdown," starts with the events culminating in a college student's attempted suicide; the rest charts the events and discoveries of therapy that resolve the mental problem and lead the "I" to resumption of normal graduate life at Berkeley.

The problem-solution structure of Kiki Olson's first person, "I Had an Affair With My Ex-Husband," very much resembles the structure of the "As Told To" interview about the breakdown and others about personal traumas. After Ms. Olson introduces her problem—an affair with the "same man I'd divorced over five years before"—and shows how they met, married, lived together, broke up and reunited; in the rest, she resolves her dilemma through scenes of the second affair, illustrations of her personal and professional development since her first nuptials, final rifts, and insights. You can try the pattern to structure similar personal dramas; she starts with a climactic scene of reunion and an explanation of the origins of the problem, then illustrates the disruptive issues in the second affair, and the final therapeutic solution.

A detailed outline of Ms. Olson's plot and the author's progressive change in romantic values provides examples of useable types of events for first-person crisis narratives. Following the bedroom scene from the second affair, Ms. Olson remembers first meeting the artist and bedding down "a half-hour later"; highlights from three "frolicsome" impoverished years of marriage; publication of her first short stories and the start of her writing career; the marriage's break-up ("smashing rocks through every window I could reach"); the quarrels leading to divorce; a friend's chance encounter with her ex-husband "at a gallery opening"; her call; a "steamier" sexual connection "than when we'd been wed"; and post-divorce dates; social embarrassment with an "aging hippie" at her side; the rift; her vacation in Guadeloupe; revived professional ambition; a last quarrel; and her regrets for the "zestful bohemian"; and current sexual attraction for a lover who dresses in three-piece Brooks Brothers' suits" and "reads *The Wall Street Journal*."

An interpretation of each episode will suggest reasons to secure them or similar ones in your first-person crisis interview. Ms. Olson alludes to the thematic clash of values in the first scene.

> We'd been making love under a Pennsylvania Dutch quilt and my new lynx coat. . . .
> "Look," my artist lover said, pointing to the smoky outline the pale mountain of fur that covered us was making, "It's a perfect *sfumato* effect." So like him to hardly register the coat's value—it probably cost more than he'd made in the past two years. . . .

The rest of the events reveals her initial attraction to the "Dutch quilt" life-style and why she abandoned it. In their meeting, the attraction is one of passion. Her years of marriage detail the sacrifices of creature comforts for that attraction to an "earthy he-man;" the writing success introduces the start of her own professional and financial independence; their arguments precipitate the divorce. What follows is the revived amorous connection, its sexual advantages, its disadvantages within the framework of her upwardly mobile personal life-style, her retreat from the second affair with her ex-husband by vacation, a last clash, and new romantic values asserted in her choice of the latest lover. As previously stated, this confessional about a personal life drama mirrors the typical chronological structure of an "As Told To" life crisis—recollections of a recent traumatic problem, past events that triggered it, and subsequent ones that helped solve the problem.

Best to figure out in advance the highlights of a crisis a victim may have endured, such as meetings, growth, quarrels, abandonments, changes, and the like. If you arrive at the interview determined to salvage them or similar episodes with your recording tape for the sake of a sound structural plot, you'll be ready to override protests of invasion of privacy from your subject. Such traumatic confessions usually conclude with confidences about changes in attitudes or the lessons garnered from these traumas. So in the last minutes of the interview, don't forget to ask, "What did you learn from this?," or "How did this change you?" Such questions may prod your subject to reveal the philosophical conclusions that knit events into the resolution required by the form.

## Research Requirements: Stylistic Devices

Since an "As Told To" interview about a personal crisis or uncommon professional life contains only your subject's words, request details during the research that will build, cement, and color the article. If you understand the following techniques and their purpose, and practice the suggested strategies to achieve them in the interview, you will create vivid, smooth, powerful first-person narratives.

### Transitions

Editors of magazines and critics of fiction both talk of "transitions." In this interview form, transitions link one section or series of events to the next. Often, they aid the reader's transit from one block of time to the next; for example, from the past to the future or over huge gaps of years. In *Esquire*'s "A Day In The Life," with famous brand package designer, Charles Biondo, a splendid transition moves the reader from one of the artist's first job interviews with a prominent design firm ("Frank Gianninoto's. I swear to you, when I went/for the interview I thought the place was/owned by two Japanese brothers," Biondo recollects) to the design artist's current work success:

That was more than twenty-five years ago. Today the business is not nearly so obscure;. . . .

In the Biondo first-person, the transition projects the reader from Biondo's past to present. In Jeri Fink's *Redbook* reminiscence about her newborn's death, an equally fine transition carries the reader from the present to the future. After relating how her first son inspected his new brother's "tiny fingers and toes," and noting her own joyful reaction, " 'My God, I've never been/so happy!' " she writes,

Six days later Brian was dead. It began the day before the party.

If you hear the person being interviewed tiptoeing or boldly advancing from one major event to another in a different time zone, ask for a summarizing "transition" to move the reader backward or forward over the days, months, or years separating the two events. By soliciting road signs for a reader en route in the narrative, you insure the edited narrative will have strong bridges from one time sequence to the next. Transitions often can be fashioned from only a line or two.

### The Sketch

In interviews about real life dramas, don't miss any chance to obtain another device for the edited narration—the sketch. A sketch summarizes a daily, weekly, or monthly routine. In the "As Told To" interview article, "I Had A Nervous Breakdown," the sketch by the attempted suicide patient describes a usual hospital day:

A routine was established immediately. I was told when to wake up and when to eat and when to sleep. I was an infant again; someone else took control. Deprived of my own free will, I was also relieved of responsibility. The food I ate for breakfast, the faces of the patients and nurses, the room I slept in at night, the tranquilizers and sleeping pills became familiar and safe. And I was grateful for the sameness of that ordered, structured life.

The best sketches not only summarize routines, but also articulate what they mean to the person interviewed. So the hospitalized college student reports, "And I/was grateful for the sameness of that/ordered, structured life."

Like hospital schedules, work routines also supply good material for sketches. After hotel detective Lawrence Frost, author of an *Esquire* "A Day In The Life," changes jobs and becomes a private investigator, he recounts the usual night on a matrimonial case:

I'll tell you one of the things I like best about being a private investigator: the times when I'm on an all-night surveillance, waiting in my car for some guy who's cheating on his wife to leave his girlfriend's building. There I am, with my radio and a little bit of food and my piss bottle, happy as a clam.

   See, that's what this life is largely all about—solitude and self-motivation.

The confession concluding the hospital routine reveals the patient's mental instability; the one ending the investigator's, his professional satisfaction.

   These interpretations of routines can also begin a sketch. So the proprietor of Paris' oldest restaurant announces his performance standards at the front of a sketch that illustrates to what ends he will go to implement them.

> I am sometimes asked how I see my role in life. Quite simply, I see myself as a performer whose job it is to entertain the five senses. Not only must we offer the world's finest cuisine, but the service, the light, carpeting, the silverware, the table linen, *everything* must be of supreme elegance. There was a time, after the war, when the city of Paris did not illuminate Notre Dame every night, so for a good ten years, I myself paid to have it illuminated for the edification of my customers.

To retrieve similar revelations and examples for your published interview, ask, "Can you describe a routine day or schedule?" Then be sure to inquire, "What did that mean to you?" The query may turn up a value, motive, or dominant state of mind that will richly color the portrait of the narrator of the tale.

### The Single-Time, Climactic Anecdote

Besides transitions to bridge a single event or series of events and sketches of typical, but meaningful routines, another common "As Told To" device is the single-time, climactic anecdote told in great detail. When well-chosen, like the death scene from Jeri Fink's, "A Young Mother's Story," the once-in-a-lifetime event can evoke dramatic emotions:

> Outside the room, my husband waited, unable to watch his son die. I stood next to Brian, holding his tiny hand, watching the EKG go flat and the doctors shake their heads. I had one request: "Let me hold my baby while he's still warm."
>
>    Gently they removed the tubes and wires that had kept him alive for a time. And gently I held Brian in my arms, kissing his face, his head and his neck as his blood stained my shoulder. In the background I heard the nurses crying. But for those few precious moments, somewhere between the end of life and the beginning of death, I held my baby.

This climactic anecdote communicates a highly emotional scene without maudlin excess by its sparse, selective descriptive details. The minute-to-minute narrative of a life crisis envelopes the reader by reported gestures, quoted conversation, actions and reactions. In combination, these described details allow the reader to experience the trauma of the newborn's death remembered by his mother.

The memory of the death is related by external details of the event; but in "I Was a Lady Hard Hat," author Sarah Bottorff describes an emotionally charged moment such as her first job interview on a construction site with more subjective techniques—feelings, expectations, facial expressions, her wardrobe:

> So, one cool September morning I mustered all my courage and walked onto the jobsite. I wasn't *feeling* cool, though. The workers all stopped to stare as I picked my way through the rubbish in my wedgies, and, though I'd expected *some* attention, my face had turned crimson by the time I reached the supervisor's trailer. Inside were *more* huge staring hard hats, and one rather slight red-haired man talking into two phones at once. I guessed he was in charge, and headed toward him.

After Ms. Bottorff made her request for a job as a laborer to the red-haired man, he, in turn, looked for an answer from his supervisor named Don. Ms. Bottorff recalls:

> Don folded his arms and looked at me without expression. "For you?" "Yes," I said quaking. He glanced at the man with the telephones, then back at me, and though he managed to continue looking grim, something odd was happening to his facial muscles . . . the beginnings of a smile, I thought. The rest of the men were taking stock of me: my flower-print office dress, unbiceped arms, blushing face. They were muttering to each other, and I caught phrases: ". . . said *what?* . . . sweet Jesus, looks like m'own dorter . . . got to be kidding. . . ." After just a few minutes, though, the boss shrugged in rather a friendly way and said, "O.K., we'll try you. Get yourself a pair of work boots." As I walked back toward the street, I heard new new coworkers snorting hilariously . . . but I had been *hired*!

Like a climactic event filmed in slow motion, Ms. Bottorff heightened the dramatic effect by remembering detail after detail of that first, never-to-be-repeated interview for a job as a female construction worker. Minute-to-minute narration of an important event will enhance its dramatic power. So when you sense your captive subject of a first-person interview about an unconventional job or personal trauma heading toward an emotionally wrenching event, question that person about every angle of that moment, so you can later convey it like a film director who scripts the camera to glide over detail after detail in a scene, to gain added emotional force in its rendition on the page. By stopping time to elaborate and thereby prolong an account of something that happened in seconds, you amplify your reader's emotional experience to the degree of the number of reported perspectives of its participants or remembered concrete details you can jostle from your subject's memory for a description of that singular event.

To secure these details or points of view describing a climactic moment, gently prod with the following types of questions: "What happened?", "What did you do?", "What did you say?", "What did others say?", "How did they react?", "What did you look like?", "What were you wearing?", "How did you feel?", "What did you expect?", "What did you do next?", and anything else relevant you can think to ask. Your questions should persuade your subject to relive the dramatic edisode or painful denouement with words that will allow you to vividly recall the event in typing the finished interview for submission. If the trauma victim or professional complains about the mundane quality of your questions, remember, that person doesn't fully understand the requirements of the interview form. So explain them. Or, to win cooperation, quote as your defense, as I do sometimes, the advice Pulitzer poet Anne Sexton offered about good writing (later published in *The Paris Review* interview, "Anne Sexton: The Art Of Poetry XV"). During my research interview, the poet told me, "Concrete examples give a verisimilitude." So, drain every concrete detail about the moment from your subject's memory to truthfully relate to your reader the feeling of what it was like to live through that event in all its ramifications. Only that random collection of details describing a momentous emotional episode can tell readers exactly what it felt like to be in that trauma or charged event. So ask as many necessary questions as you need to recreate the succession of moments in that eventful climax with full knowledge you probably won't use all the answers to your questions. Overinterview for an "As Told To" to achieve the best choices of information for your later edited reconstruction of that person's career experience or life crisis. An excess of information from your "As Told To" subject is the only guarantee for success with this interview form.

When you conduct an "As Told To" interview, keep in mind the devices the format allows. When your interview changes time zones, ask for bridging transitions from the past to present or future. Request sketches of routines and their meanings. Elicit motivations and then demand illustrations. When you hear a dramatic moment described, dig for the physical, emotional, filmic detail to convincingly convey it to readers.

## Editorial Guidelines: Methods to Express Your Viewpoint

So far, this section has covered a definition, introductions, structural requirements and technical devices of two types of the "As Told To" interview form. Before proceeding to an example from my published work, I want to discuss how to express your viewpoint in your materials within the constraints of the format. In this type of interview, show your point of view by applying the same techniques used in the "Q. & A." Demonstrate it by such methods as the final choice of materials, space length assigned information, position of material in the article, and by what of the interview you delete from final copy. However, in this form, much of your viewpoint will be expressed first, during the interview, by the persuasive strength you can muster to get your subject to state for publication quotes that express your views, and, afterwards, in your editorial conferences, by how much force you can apply to convince your editor to publish those hard-won confessionals.

Your viewpoint may be in contention during your researches and in later editorial conferences, but also what you editorialize about is different from the first interview form you've studied. Here you're not judging an issue, but your subject's motives or character in a crisis. Your edited renditions of those decisive moments should reveal both your subject and your personal attitudes toward that person. My published example in this genre and its analysis display an illustration of my viewpoint expressed within the restraints of this interview form.

## Editing Guidelines: Required Quote Approval

A reminder. Don't forget to show your final submission to the person you interviewed and obtain initialed approval of its editorial accuracy on each page. Or procure the same fact check by a phone call. You want the material verified as factually accurate before you turn your manuscript in to your assigning editor.

## SAMPLE "AS TOLD TO" INTERVIEW

My published example of an "As Told To" interview, "Notes Of A West Point Woman," appeared in *Cosmopolitan*, December 1978. It was later reprinted for mailing as a brochure to future applicants to the U.S. Military Academy at West Point. Written in an intimate diary style and based on a marathon weekend of interviews, the extensively edited transcription lets one of the first women plebes admitted to the formerly all-male military academy narrate her recollections of freshman training for the challenging job of officer in the U.S. Army. Because of its subject, the piece is defined as a first-person career narrative told by a woman in a profession which is nontraditional for her sex.

Though *Cosmopolitan*'s cleavage-exposed covers idealize women as sex objects, paradoxically, the idea for an "As Told To" interview with a woman training for the highly unusual professional role of an army officer came from *Cosmo*'s editors. Over a year before publication of my "Notes Of A West Point Woman," I visited the magazine's offices for my first editorial conference. The editor I saw was dressed *Cosmo*-cover style like a fifties "sweater girl" with flared skirt and tight sweater amply flaunting a robust bosom under her sagging chin. By that point I had been a Contributing Editor to *Working Woman*, had a dozen profiles and interviews appear in *People*, and had published a critically influential interview in *The Paris Review* that would be anthologized in two books. Yet my forwarded resume of over a decade of published credits in leading national magazines had made no impression on this editor. To her, I was still a first-time writer for *Cosmopolitan*. I was relegated to the $750-$1250 book of assignment ideas, and I was not permitted to make article suggestions of my own.

Dutifully, I thumbed the pages of article suggestions in a large loose-leaf book in search of an assignment I could handle with integrity. Simultaneously, I reeled off my credentials, as instructed, though without much enthusiasm. In a second book of yellow-page-typed article ideas, I flipped over another sheet and discovered the ideal *Cosmo* article for me—the interview with a pioneer West Point woman cadet. The article suggestion wanted the focus on a strong woman successfully competing in a man's world. The idea couldn't have been better timed to match a similar moment in my life. Its focus perfectly mirrored my aspirations as a beginner woman competitor entering the amateur world of long-distance road racing in the early years of the fitness movement.

*Cosmo*'s editors had a clear notion of what the interview should cover, which they spelled out on the assignment sheet. The sheet requested that the first person interview with a woman plebe explain what type of female fights for recognition, position, authority, and importance in a man's world, and whether she has to renounce her femininity to attain her aims. The article was conceived to reflect what was happening to women in the professional world at large at that moment, as a result of the women's liberation movement. The *Cosmo* slant also questioned whether life at West Point was more severe than that of a nunnery because of all the "unnatural restraints" placed on women cadets and because of the permanent temptations of handsome young officers. At my request, the assignment page was removed from the book, photocopied, and the copy given to me for my first commission.

I began my research for an interview by contacting the Public Affairs Office at The U.S. Military Academy at West Point, to request permission to do the interview and to solicit the name of an articulate candidate. In turn, the P.R. officer asked me to mail her some sample writings. I suspect she didn't want to measure my literary talent, but to verify my success as a free-lance writer to write articles that actually reached publication. Once my work and resume were properly screened and my request approved by the authorities, the P.R. lady chose the cadet for the interview. I had qualms about whether the daughter of a career officer could be fair-minded about her life at The U.S. Military Academy, but such apprehension disappeared after our first phone call. Her candor, recall of chilling anecdotes, and lucidly reported detail instantly convinced me of her merits.

Despite protests, I persuaded *Cosmo*'s editor to advance me $200 for the expenses for my research trip to West Point. Customarily, the magazine reimbursed writers who were either more docile or better off than I for their travel expenses. In preparation for the trip, the cadet and I together agreed upon the date of the weekend for the planned marathon interviews, and the P.R. officer reserved her office as the interview site and a room at a nearby hotel for my accommodations.

I remember spending most of my work weekend with the cadet at The U.S. Military Academy's P.R. office sandwiched between oak desks and wood railings reminiscent of a newspaper set out of *The Front Page*. When I left Garrison, New York, Sunday evening on a train heading toward Grand Central, I carried a typed, double-spaced interview transcript that numbered nearly seventy-five pages.

During the editing of the interview for submission, I kept beside my typewriter the photocopied booklet, "Editing (And Writing) Rules for *Cosmopolitan*," given me by my *Cosmo* editor. The booklet's title page said that "Nearly all" the rules were "in *The Elements of Style* by Strunk and White." The rules contained warnings against using the same word or derivative in one sentence or one paragraph, warnings against using cliches or slightly tired words, and the advice to keep "dirty words" to a minimum. I was asked to use "made love" rather than "balled," "screwed," or "fucked," and "climaxed,"—not "came." I diligently kept these stylistic directions in mind as I reviewed and chose the final edited words for my interview with one of the first women admitted to The U.S. Military Academy at West Point.

I did the actual interview sessions the weekend of November 5-7, 1977. I typed the final version in columnar form that replicated in length the character count of columns published in *Cosmopolitan,* checked it in entirety by phone with the cadet, and wrote my cover letter for the manuscript's submission November 29. Two weeks after submission, my editor's assistant returned my manuscript by messenger and advised me to resubmit it, typed with ordinary page margins. I complied immediately and, at the same time, asked for a quick decision on the article and the start of the processing of its payment. Then a day or two before Christmas, another editorial assistant, this one, a male, called me with urgent questions about ten or eleven unclarified points in the manuscript. The editors wanted to know more about why the cadet felt compelled to go to West Point, why her roommates wound up there, and such moot points as "Tell us more about her schedule . . . how many hours to drill . . . who's cadet Fuller . . . how many women were left in her class the first year . . . when and where and how often do cadets date . . . what is her bedtime . . . what exactly are you eating with C-rations? . . . ." I satisfied these queries overnight and wrote yet another cover letter with the request for the start of the payment process.

The interview languished in the magazine's inventory through the next spring, summer, and fall. Finally, twelve months after its submission, it was published in the December 1978 issue. At the time of publication, I remember noting that the editors had tried to cutesy up certain quotes in the first half of the article, but the power of speech in the second half was so great that the editors simply had not blue-penciled it at all.

## NOTES OF A WEST POINT WOMAN
### As Told to Barbara Kevles

Why would any girl who adores soft, silky dresses in pretty pastels settle for a dull gray cadet's uniform? Or give up jewelry, nail polish, and the scent of Ciara to muddy her nose under barbed wire, rappel down dangerous cliffs, or go out on all-night patrols? Well, in my case the answer was fairly simple: I was looking for something meaningful to do with my life, and training to be an officer in the U.S. Army seemed the right answer.

You see, my father was a lieutenant colonel in the marines, and, as his oldest daughter, I felt he hoped I would somehow carry on the military tradition. The day I was born, he sent my mother pink flowers with the message, "The card is still blue—maybe a boy next time." His next two children were girls, though, so I grew up trying to be my father's son. When I was in the fifth grade and he left for Vietnam, he told me to take care of my mother because I was now the man of the house.

Then, too, like my father, I've always been very patriotic, and the feeling was only intensified during the years Dad was stationed abroad. At age fourteen, I heard my first anti-American comments. My family and I had gone to a beach just outside Copenhagen when several people approached me and asked in English whether I was carrying a gun—had I ever killed anybody as people always seemed to be doing in American movies? I was outraged and kept protesting, "Our country's not like that!" Things got even worse once I learned Danish and overheard people referring to "those dumb Americans." Once, in tears, I complained to Dad, who said, "Maybe when you come back some day, you'll be somebody and the Danes will listen to you." Not long after that, in the fall of my senior year, the opportunity to become somebody presented itself: The U.S. Military Academy at West Point, situated in southern New York State, opened its doors to women.

The academy was offering a free college education plus a $365 monthly allowance in exchange for five years as a commissioned officer in the army. To apply, I sent in my Scholastic Aptitude Test scores and took a fitness and medical exam. The fitness test was easy enough; I've always been athletically inclined and had three varsity letters—in track, basketball, and tennis. When a letter arrived in mid-April telling me I'd been accepted, though, I began to have second thoughts. I'm the type who adores dancing and partying; senior year, I was my high-school queen. Could I really enjoy marching? I began to think that perhaps I couldn't.

Throughout this period, my dad was careful not to try to influence me, though I was certainly aware that he *hoped* I would go to West Point. Mother was candid, as usual: If I turned down the academy, she said, I would be making the mistake of my life. We lived near a beach and I began to spend a lot of time there, just sitting and watching the waves ebb and flow. Finally, I decided that I owed it to my parents to give West Point a try.

### The Lady's a Cadet

I'll never forget that hot July day on which I entered the academy. After the welcoming ceremonies had ended, a bus took all the new "plebes," or freshmen— there were over 1,300 of us, including 119 women—to the gym, where the academy issued each of us a pair of black gym shorts, a T-shirt, men's nylon knee socks, and flat, lace-up military shoes. I stared in amazement at my reflection in the mirror and thought, What am I doing here?

Next, an upperclassman with a red waist sash appeared and ordered me to my barracks. As we walked briskly across the campus, he explained that plebes never climb stairs, they *run* them—at 120 steps a minute! By the time I'd arrived breathless at my sixth-floor room, my two new roommates were already there. Thank heavens, *they* at least seemed simpatico. Beckie, like me, was here because her father was in the service, while Joan, a tall brunette, said she'd come to West Point because she liked the idea of the *challenge*. We took a quick look around the stark room—there was a double bunk, a bed, two closets, and a sink (since our floor was entirely "coed," one of the johns down the hall had been designated for women)—and started to giggle. I knew immediately that I was going to like both of them, but there wasn't much time to get to know each other, since basic training would be starting within minutes. We were about to find out why the eight-week period with which West Point initiates its freshmen has always been known as "Beast Barracks."

Downstairs, I reported to the man in the red sash, who took me to join my squad of nine other plebes, four of whom were women. Our first task was to learn to salute, and I, it seemed, was the only one who found that difficult—I kept curving my wrist out of nervousness. Every time the squad leader barked at me, I grew even more inflexible. My father had made it a point never to yell—I'd heard him raise his voice exactly twice—and the shouting unnerved me. Happily, though, I did better with the rest of the day's activities. By five that afternoon, I had learned to march, make my bed, and arrange my possessions in the *army* way. The academy has regulations to cover everything, including the folding of underwear. On the second day of Beast, my squad leader came to our room to check my progress. Everything was fine, he said, except that my underpants weren't folded properly. Women's underpants don't fold like men's, however, so as he fumbled around trying to demonstrate the correct technique, his face grew redder and redder. Finally, he left for advice, then returned to tell me that I should do as well as I could and that in this case, the army would simply have to make allowances.

That was virtually the *only* case in which allowances were made during Beast. By 5:30 A.M., six days a week, we had to be downstairs to perform rifle drills, calisthenics, and runs. Then, after breakfast, it was time for field exercises, including lessons in marksmanship, wilderness skill, marches, and bayonet drills. Sometimes we had to run for several miles while wearing three-pound boots and holding our rifles straight out in front of us, and these runs were the most difficult activity of all for me. Whenever a woman cadet dropped out from one of them—which happened fairly often—you could expect to see her later that day looking *miserably* depressed; all of us were trying so hard. During one run, when I could barely breathe, my squad leader kept shouting, "Get that rifle up. Dress right!"—which means stay in line with the group. I felt like screaming at him that it's impossible to hold a rifle up when you're about to drop from exhaustion, but I contained my frustration—and finished the run. Later, he came to my room and said, "Good job." That bit of praise made my week.

The part of Beast I hated *most* was the bayonet drills. We did them in midafternoon ninety-five-degree heat while wearing heavy metal helmets. The object was to use your rifle to stab at an imaginary target while screaming. "Blood, blood makes the grass grow." or "Gnnnaaa!" I could never seem to make the proper sounds.

Most stressful of all during basic training, though, was the *mental* pressure. Upperclassmen were always ready to "flame on at max"—to haze you as cruelly as possible. One day, when a girl in my squad went to another company's area to pick up the laundry, she heard, "Hey, Ms., halt!"—after which all the doors flew open and someone cried out, "Girl in the hall!" Before she realized what was happening, twelve upperclassmen had converged on her and begun to chide her for the dullness of her boots, her poor posture, etc. Not surprisingly, she started to cry, which made them tease her *more* unmercifully.

Hazing is *traditional* at West Point, of course, but upperclassmen seemed to consider it their duty to "initiate" *female* plebes most strenuously of all. One in particular went out of his way to make *my* life miserable. Whenever I heard his deep voice, I would break into a sweat, wondering, "Are my shoes polished?" "Do I have a good dressoff?" (in other words, is my shirt tucked in?). During the third week, he reprimanded me twice in one day for not having my bootlaces tucked into my combat boots. And since two reprimands for the same offense is considered failure to follow instructions, I was sent before the company commander and given several demerits, which meant a loss of six hours of free time. At least I didn't have to march back and forth with a rifle for hours, a form of punishment about which I'd heard male classmates complain bitterly!

### Boys and Girls Together

One point to be grateful for: Despite the fact that women cadets engage in all the same training activities as the men do, no one at West Point ever forgot that we *were* girls. Once, as I was walking to formation with my squad, another cadet whistled at me. (Alas, I was never sure who he was, since we're required to gaze straight ahead while marching.) And in the plebe dorm, my roommates and I could tell that our presence was, well, *appreciated*. Intimate relationships, however, were frankly discouraged by the administration—and were an impossibility anyway, given the dorm rules. Whenever a male cadet entered our room, the door had to be left ajar, and if both a girl's roommates were away, she was required to bunk in another woman's room. Still, there was an easy camaraderie between the sexes that came of passing each other constantly in the halls. Actually, I think the upperclassmen—who weren't used to having women around—found the coed atmosphere a bit unnerving. One day, I came back to my room to find a junior finishing up room check and complaining to his cohort, "This corps has really gone to hell . . . I just opened the medicine cabinet and found ten gallons of perfume!"

And, yes, I had, optimistically, brought along a lot of perfume. Unfortunately, though, I never seemed to have a moment to use it. It wasn't until the second week of Beast that I had any "privileged time"—free time from Saturday noon till Sunday at six P.M. A dance was scheduled for Saturday night, so I decided to celebrate with some perfume and makeup. I felt as excited as a kid trying on rouge, shadow, and mascara for the first time . . . until, that is, I put on my uniform. Cosmetics or not, I was still wearing regulation trousers, and my image in the mirror was *not* glamorous. At the dance, my classmates were so preoccupied with the civilian girls in their flowing summer dresses, they barely noticed me. I bought myself a hot fudge sundae and, after half an hour, left, feeling totally deflated.

A week or so after that, I did acquire a boyfriend, but even that didn't last for very long. We had met out on the playing field—the one place on campus we weren't required to walk around at attention—and for a while we went to movies together during our privileged time. But our little flirtation died down almost as quickly as it began. We couldn't "display affection" publicly (even in town), since that was a punishable offense. Besides, once classes began in September, neither of us had much time for romance.

## A Plebe's Life

As plebes, our days started at 6:25 A.M. with breakfast, after which we had classes in English, math, geography, a foreign language, phys. ed., plus some subjects you wouldn't be likely to study at any "normal" university: engineering, military science, professional ethics, and terrain analysis. The time from 3:25 to 6:00 was for extracurricular activities, and after dinner, study was compulsory from 8:00 until 11:00 lights-out. Cadets aren't allowed to go home or to attend off-campus parties until their sophomore year, so we had little in the way of serious diversion to distract us.

How did I fill my "extracurricular" hours? Well, just before Beast ended, I became one of fourteen females to make West Point's first women's basketball team. Since the team's average height was small (I'm only five four), the coach decided we should lift weights three times a week to develop our strength—what we lacked in stature, he said, we could make up for in endurance. I complained all the way (weight lifting *hurts*), but his strategy worked. The first time we played, a few male cadets came to see the joke; they didn't *leave* laughing, though. We were in such good condition and were so determined to prove ourselves *worthy* of the academy that we won that game—and nearly every one we played—simply by running the other teams to exhaustion. By the end of the season, we were playing to standing-room crowds, and I was regularly being stopped by upperclassmen who would make sure no one else was in sight before telling me, "Probably no one's said this to you before, Ms., but you have an outstanding basketball team." So my teammates and I felt *doubly* satisfied: Not only had we proved we could play basketball well, we had also done our part in reducing the hostility some of the men at West Point felt toward female cadets.

As I've said, this hostility was by no means universal—even among the upperclassmen. During Beast, romances had sprung up between female cadets and their squad leaders, despite all the rules that prohibit "fraternization" between upperclassmen and plebes (upperclassmen aren't even allowed to call a plebe by his or her first name!). How did such liaisons escape official notice? Well, it's customary for freshmen to bring personal problems to their squad leaders during Beast, so a few girls just kept *on* with the custom after classes had begun. Another strategy was for a plebe to pull on her sweat suit and go "jogging" in a conveniently wooded location where she could meet her upperclassman without worry of punishment for P.D.A.—public display of affection. Occasionally, however, such behavior was discovered, and when it was, the punishments could be severe. One squad leader was relieved of his command for fraternization—he had held hands with a plebe during President Carter's inaugural parade, or so I heard.

Naturally, this place is a veritable rumor factory. And a few cadets who resent having women among their ranks sometimes use the grapevine to stir up trouble for female students. That's what happened to one of my roommates. She and her boyfriend were working at the West Point radio station one night when two upperclassmen dropped by to pick up some dress coats they'd left there earlier in the day. From there, the upperclassmen proceeded to the central guard room, where they notified the officer-in-charge that my roommate's hair was disheveled and her makeup smeared. That wasn't true, as the O.C. who came to investigate quickly determined, but for weeks the rumors flew: My roommate had been topless, so one version ran . . . another had her inviting the upperclassmen to join her and her boy-friend in a foursome. Not a pleasant situation at a school where "reputation" is all-important.

Even the men who *date* female cadets aren't always on our side. A basketball teammate of mine went out with an upperclassman who was constantly yelling at her because her hat brim wasn't dusted or her shirt tucked in tightly enough. Every time a woman plebe left the academy (by the end of the first year, thirty-six of us had dropped out), he gloated openly. Still, by June he had softened a bit—he told my friend he was "proud" of her. And he wasn't the only male cadet whose attitude had undergone a subtle transformation. As the year finished, several men told me they were glad to have had us here—that we had made the academy seem "more human."

We West Point *women* had changed, too. Most of us had more self-confidence than ever before. After all, how many people do you know who can run two miles in combat boots, ride a pulley across a lake, or swim while wearing fatigues and carrying a rifle? On my last day as a freshman, we spent the morning on an obsta-cle course. In one test, we had to walk a long, narrow board fifty feet off the ground; in another, we leaped from a log thirty feet high to catch a hanging rope (no net below, of course). A year before when my class had gone through this course, I'd failed many of the tests, and even now, it took me three minutes to de-cide I would actually attempt that last feat. I did try it, though—and succeeded. I had passed the academy's athletic requirements, and doing so didn't make me feel any less a woman—just the opposite, in fact. Once you learn that your body can do things you'd never imagined possible, you acquire a kind of pride that makes you as attractive as any mascara ever could, and never mind that you happen to be wearing combat boots.

### The West Point Way

In the August after my plebe year, all the members of my class—women and men—were required to report back to the academy for ten days of infantry field training. Among other martial skills, we were taught hand-to-hand combat—how to gouge out eyes and use specific body points to inflict pain, as well as do flips and kicks. Luckily, women had a bit of an advantage here . . . we were never hit or kicked quite as forcefully as the men were. Still, we were expected to dish out pun-ishment with as much vigor as any man. When I didn't kick my male "buddy" hard enough, the instructor demonstrated six times using my buddy's back, so the next time, I kicked harder—much harder. I didn't enjoy those classes—and I still don't like the idea of them. I hate thinking I might, as a soldier, someday have to kill, though I suppose I *would* if it were necessary to defend my country.

In the last phase of field training, I was assigned to lead a patrol of twenty-three men in an attack on two machine-gun bunkers atop a nearby hill. After issuing a warning order, I allowed my men to sleep for four hours while I planned the opera-tion—and the planning paid off: We captured our bunkers, and afterward, several members of my group said I'd done a "super job." None of them seemed to resent having had a woman in command.

That wasn't my only triumph, either. On our final patrol, my "buddy" and I spent two hours in a mosquito-ridden swamp, where he promptly fell asleep from sheer exhaustion. I felt like telling the world, "Look at me—here I am in a misera-ble swamp with a guy who's sleeping, and I'm holding a rifle protecting him!"

Like most of the girls in my company, the first thing I did after coming off that tour was to take a long, long shower. Then I stripped my bed, put on a pretty red dress, and signed out for a four-day leave. When my roommates and I emerged into the corridor, one of our fellow cadets said, "My God! You guys are girls!"

In four more days, classes would be starting again, but this year I knew I'd be able to cope. Actually, I almost hadn't come back to the academy for field training. While living with my parents over the summer, I'd met a good-looking man who was wonderful to me. He didn't say, "Get your neck, plebe," but "You look terrific, really beautiful." After that kind of treatment, it was hard to return to West Point and get into my dirty fatigues. For the first time, I thought of quitting. I'm glad I didn't, though.

I love the feeling that I'm doing something with my life, that I'm accomplishing something *important* here at the academy. I'm in my sophomore year now, and though it's too soon to say whether I'll make it through to the end, the odds seem good that I'll stay. If I had my choice today, it would be to graduate and give the army a chance.

## Analysis

This section demonstrates the ways "Notes Of A West Point Woman" meets the "As Told To's" requirements for casting, a beginning, structure, narrative devices, and editorial viewpoint.

The *Cosmopolitan* interview is a first-person career narrative by a woman breaking new ground for herself and her sex in a highly atraditional occupation for women.

The beginning cites the reasons that make her decision to pioneer the age-old male military profession plausible. The decisive factors include:
the high-mindedness of the goal:

something meaningful to do with my life,

family tradition;

... my father was a lieutenant colonel in the marines, and, as his oldest daughter, I felt he hoped I would somehow carry on the military tradition.

patriotism;

Then, too, like my father, I've always been very patriotic, and the feeling was only intensified during the years Dad was stationed abroad.

practicalities;

The academy was offering a free college education plus a $365 monthly allowance in exchange for five years as a commissioned officer in the army.

family pressures;

> Mother [said] . . . If I turned down the academy, . . . I would be making the mistake of my life.

So this ex-high school queen explains her pioneer choice of an occupation formerly barred to women by deeply felt idealism, powerful family influences, attractive practical advantages, and threat of family ostracism. As in most career narratives, motives for an unusual professional choice derive from a combination of influences. When you interview such professionals, try to secure anecdotes that illustrate the many motivating forces that propelled the choice of career to underscore its believability.

After the opening explanation, "Notes Of A West Point Woman" follows a problem/solution structure. In the assignment sheet, *Cosmopolitan*'s editors defined the dilemma as "What type of female fights for recognition, position, authority, and importance in a man's world, and whether she has to renounce her femininity to attain her aims." The remaining structure explores the problems the plebe surmounts during freshman year at West Point to attain her professional aims and evaluates whether that costs her a loss of femininity. In detail, the structure narrates the plebe's achievements from her first day on the job, through her two-month orientation, and during her first year at The U.S. Military Academy. At the same time, it records the toll of these experiences on her personal expression and identification as a female. In chronological sequence, the interview tracks her from the day of arrival, through the eight-week orientation of "Beast Barracks," and through the academic year where it grades her at social life, sports performance, "fraternization," military athletics, and infantry field training. In the conclusion, the plebe affirms her desire to tough it through West Point in order to do "something with my life" through a career in the Army, despite the conventional temptation of an appreciative suitor back home.

A chronological structure works best when the narrated professional life covers a short time span. Otherwise, choose the structural style evident in past examples of "A Day In The Life" interviews that favor organization by topic rather than by chronology.

This "As Told To" bridges events in one season to another by transitions such as:

> I'll never forget that hot July day on which I entered the academy. After the welcoming ceremonies had ended, a bus took all the new "plebes," or freshmen— there were over 1,300 of us, including 119 women—to the gym. . . .

The transition in the first line telescopes the reader forward from the applicant's indecision in the spring to her decisive entrance to the academy that summer.

The interview includes sketches of daily routines like the following:

> The part of Beast I hated *most* was the bayonet drills. We did them in midafternoon ninety-five-degree heat while wearing heavy metal helmets. The object was to use your rifle to stab at an imaginary target while screaming, "Blood, blood makes the grass grow," or "Gnnnaaa!" I could never seem to make the proper sounds.

The end expresses the plebe's condemnation of violent acts with her personal reaction:

> I could never seem to make the proper sounds.

Finally, the article utilizes well-realized, one-time, powerful events, recalled in multiple detail by their physical setting, feelings, the action, and personal meaning. The web of remembered detail describing the following narrated event helps the reader relive it moment by moment in all its ramifications:

> We West Point *women* had changed, too. Most of us had more self-confidence than ever before. After all, how many people do you know who can run two miles in combat boots, ride a pulley across a lake, or swim while wearing fatigues and carrying a rifle? On my last day as a freshman, we spent the morning on an obstacle course. In one test, we had to walk a long narrow board fifty feet off the ground; in another, we leaped from a log thirty feet high to catch a hanging rope (no net below, of course). A year before when my class had gone through this course, I'd failed many of the tests, and even now, it took me three minutes to decide I would actually attempt that last feat. I did try it, though—and succeeded. I had passed the academy's athletic requirements, and doing so didn't make me feel any less a woman—just the opposite, in fact. Once you learn that your body can do things you'd never imagined possible, you acquire a kind of pride that makes you as attractive as any mascara ever could, and never mind that you happen to be wearing combat boots.

This concluding anecdote resolved the article's theme that *Cosmopolitan*'s editors had asked for on my assignment sheet. Does a woman have to renounce femininity to attain her professional goals in a man's world? By stressing self-pride as the source of personal femininity rather than cosmetics, the narrator explains how she, a former party-loving high school queen, survived freshman year at West Point with femininity intact, despite her success at feats requiring male strength and masculine values.

How did I express my viewpoint in this "As Told To" first-person career narrative? I did so by choice of materials. When the editors of *Cosmopolitan* asked for clarifications and inserts to illustrate them, they had, as mentioned earlier, wanted to "know more about why she felt so compelled to go to West Point." They questioned, "Were there open family arguments or was the pressure just understood?" So I revised my subject's account of her decisive choice of college to incorporate her mother's comment.

> Throughout this period, my dad was careful not to try to influence me, though I was certainly aware that he *hoped* I would go to West Point. Mother was candid, as usual: If I turned down the academy, she said, I would be making the mistake of my life.

By the added notation about parental pressure, I expressed a point of view about my subject's motives for family approval and the decisive role of her family in her professional choice. In retrospect, I was glad that *Cosmopolitan*'s editors had requested that I clarify this pivotal moment. The described event made the girl's later sacrifices of feminine expressions—the abandonment of pretty clothes, perfume, reduced chance for romance at a first dance—more understandable.

If you sense a moment in your narration is pivotal because it summarizes what formed your subject and impels subsequent actions, dig for all the motivational analysis your subject wishes to reveal in anecdotes and detail. In the reconstruction of this decisive, telescopic moment in your subject's life, you may find the most significant explanation of your subject's character and your personal viewpoint.

## CRITIQUES OF STUDENT "AS TOLD TO" INTERVIEWS

Beginners at the "As Told To" interview form often produce weak narratives because of problems with technique or neglect to give a curious reader desired information. For example, an interview with a social worker—"Down At The Home," by Jules Trachten, mishandles the sketch. There aren't enough illustrative anecdotes to support the analysis. The caseworker lectures the reader on the disillusioning effects of city social work, but she doesn't provide enough substantiating evidence to validate her claim. Here are the excerpts; see if you agree:

> Sometimes the courts sabotage us, and even each other. One boy was convicted in Manhattan and Queens for separate crimes, and was given conflicting probation—therapy plans by the two judges. I tried to coordinate the two plans, but neither judge would recognize the authority of the other. I think the impasse was finally broken when one court lost the papers.
> Do I sound bitter? Certainly disillusioned. Good social work is important. It's not a question of power; the power should be in the relationships. It's hard to take when you work with someone for years and the person simply disappears one day. Sure, the burn-out from some of my experiences has eroded my enthusiasm. I

wouldn't recommend social work to young people; I would probably warn them against it.

The caseworker's excessive analysis of her professional disillusionment should be balanced by more examples of her discouraging work with serious juvenile offenders for stronger narrative impact.

By contrast, some beginners at this form overly rely on illustrating anecdotes. As a result, their interviews lack the depth of analytic insight. The next excerpts from an "As Told To" with a storage company bookkeeper by R. A. Perri is an example of this shortcoming.

> However, a good deal of the excitement is not in the work itself—payroll, customer accounts, access fees. It's in the things that crop up daily. It's the never knowing that makes the job exciting. For one thing, you never know who will be on the phone.
>
> • • •
>
> For example, Barbara Streisand called recently. She was in a rage because she feared that we lost an antique bathtub in transit from New York to California. Instead, it had never left the vault.
>
> . . . Then there was Kate Smith, who was always very pleasant and always ended her conversations with, "God bless you." I just always felt she would burst into "God Bless America!"
>
> • • •
>
> Another strange one was the woman who for several years spent about $300 a month for three rooms. When she closed the account, we found that she stored old newspapers. She spent thousands on these worthless papers.
>
> There was also the Nazi!

If an interview subject simply rattles off incidents about famous customers, kooks, or bizarre ones, readers won't gain much understanding of the person's compulsions for the career. Is this storage company accountant motivated in his job by his excitement as "stage door Johnny," or is he simply a detail-obsessed compulsive who has found his analogue to ledgers in the accounts of other people's stored wares? In the excerpts, the "stand-up" comic sketches don't really unlock his custodian's drive or give a keyhole view of an offbeat service industry. The sketches don't move from the surface level of personal memorabilia to portray a reason for his professional choice, or particular life on the job in a specific professional world.

A few beginners achieve dramatically illuminating narratives by a balance of anecdote and analytical insights in "As Told To" career interviews. An outstanding student example—"Christine Cornell: Court Artist" by photographer Anne Marie Cornell—deftly blends illustration and interpretation as the succeeding excerpts demonstrate. They cover the court artist's attitudes toward free-lancing, routines for a "job call," and the demands of drawing court scenes for TV evening news shows:

> Although I've had to deal with the uncertainty of working, I can go for months ... for literally months without working. Get to feel like I've lost my identity as a courtroom artist. I bought myself a suit ... so they'd stop seeing me as the kid they pull in off the beach ... who is brushing the sand out of her navel. I'm twenty-four years old. I ought to be more of a fixture than just a flighty element they import.

> When I work for any of the networks or Channel 13, WNEW, WPIX, or the Post, I get paid about $100 a day, sometimes more. A couple of years ago, I made a killing. I know they love me. They still forget about me. Who can fathom their brains?

> What happens is that I get a phone call that usually wakes me up and they ask if I can work for them today. And they'll tell me that, for example, there is an arraignment in Queens Criminal Court. It doesn't matter if I get called early, like 6:30 a.m. That I love, because that usually gives me a little bit of time. I have a routine in the morning. Certain things I have to do. I take a shower. Have a cup of coffee.

> You have to get there pretty much as fast as you can. I can be practically anywhere in about an hour, if I leave with my hair wet.

> NBC once sent me in a helicopter. They were in a terrific rush. We took a cab to the Wall St. Heliport and then we got in the helicopter and we swung around the tip of Manhattan like a pigeon taking off. We were over Manhattan in two seconds. So it's exhilarating, you know, to speed out my door. It's like I'm on a mission ...

> As a matter of fact, I really want to get in there. Get my version in too. I make a point of telling everybody my impressions. Like, "Oh, my God, and then she pulled out her handkerchief. And she burst into tears and I started to cry, too." Whenever anybody cries, I start to cry, and I feel bad for them. When they leave I sort of want to follow them out. I have to keep professional.

> I don't like to be a vulture. . . . They look up to you as being part of the press, but they also get kind of creeped out by you. I prefer not having to draw the family of a defendant, though actually, I'll do it gleefully. Because when somebody's there hurting, that's more the story than anything. It's the grief the family feels. You're purposely walking in there with big feet to see what kind of story you can make of it.

These excerpts interweave sketches and their meaning together in an engaging display of the form's stylistic device. But on the whole, this "As Told To" does not give all the form's required information, such as how or why the court artist obtained her foothold on this hard-to-reach cornice of the art industry, nor the toll on her psyche of repeated contact with social disorders. Exposure of the downside of her occupation would give an extra human dimension to her tough professional posture. That omission, and the story of her professional beginnings, would satisfy the form's informational demands for the interested reader.

## ADVICE FOR THE "AS TOLD TO" INTERVIEW FORM

Keep the following prescriptives in mind for publishable results in "As Told To" interviews:

**1.** Choose the right professional at the top or one in an unusual field for a career narrative, or select the survivor of an extraordinary life crisis for a first-person life trauma.

**2.** Study previous examples of the form published in the assigning magazine to make sure your interview questions touch upon areas of repeated interest to readers.

**3.** Interview a professional for the reasons for the choice of a career; a survivor, for the cause of the trauma.

**4.** For a life-crisis interview, try to get anecdotes about a search for solutions and resolution of the crisis. For a professional narrative, review topics like ones in the structure of the hotel detective's first-person narrative.

**5.** Make sure you ask the survivor for the meaning or lesson of the trauma; and the professional, for the sustaining challenge of that type of occupation.

**6.** Don't omit revealing quotes from the final version of the interview.

**7.** Request bridging transitions, sketches of repeated routines and personal attitudes toward them, and as much detail as possible, particularly for once-in-a-lifetime episodes of climactic significance, to help readers relive them moment-to-moment.

**8.** Verify the factual accuracy of the entire interview with its source. Fight hard against any censorship.

# XIII The "Celebrity Interview": A Famous Person on a Celebrated Life and Famous Work

The first interview form, the "Q. & A.," best reports an authority's view on a controversy or an expert's controversial viewpoint. The second interview form, the "As Told To," is a first-person narrative about an extraordinary experience or an outstanding or unusual career. The "Celebrity Interview"—the third and last type covered in this book—differs from the other two interview forms in two ways: the fame of the person interviewed and the dual focus on the celebrity's personal and professional life.

# DEFINITION

The "Celebrity Interview" is a timely, minimum 3,000-word interview with a famous-name celebrity like Charlton Heston, Michael Douglas, or the late Henry Fonda. The interview doesn't center only on a controversy, life crisis, or the profession alone; it deals with the combination throughout a lifetime. For example, the interview may probe for first-hand reminiscences of childhood, telling influences on personality or career, drives, the celebrity's side of famous professional conflicts or a divorce, historic moments in a career, life philosophies. The "Celebrity Interview" of the kind that appears in *Penthouse* and *Playboy* is almost a full-scale biography told by the writer's introduction and in the words of the celebrity interviewed.

## Format
The format resembles the "Q. & A." I employed this style format—introduction followed by questions and answers—when a Contributing Editor to *Working Woman,* for interviews with such luminaries as actress Liv Ullmann, television comedy writer/novelist Gail Parent, Oscar-winning costume designer, the late Edith Head, and actress/director, Jeanne Moreau.

## Advantage of Form for Your Career
Because of its famous subject, complex focus, and occasional newsworthy revelations, the "Celebrity Interview" can help your career by boosting your reputation and income. Such articles command high fees because of their commercial value for the assigning magazine. Interviews with famous people often produce cover lines or cover photos to pitch the newsstand issue. They'll build your journalistic reputation because editors take note of writers with entree to celebrities whose photos may spruce up a competitor's cover. I remember once I felt elated that a *Harper's Bazaar* Features Editor, at our first editorial conference, referred to my recent *Working Woman* coverline "Celebrity Interviews."

# CASTING YOUR SUBJECT: REQUIREMENTS

A suitable candidate for a "Celebrity Interview" should be, first and foremost, a household name. Then, your subject needs a timely peg. Lastly, the "name" should represent something meaningful to you and should live or temporarily reside nearby.

## Famous Name

Your query for a "Celebrity Interview" will possess more sales appeal to the magazine if you're proposing to interview a recognizable name like that of Robert Redford. However, it's not true that your proposal for an interview in this genre, targeted for publications like *Playboy* or *Penthouse,* has to be a screen star. Past *Penthouse* interviews have featured sports figures like body builder and actor Arnold Schwarzenegger, World Boxing Council heavyweight boxing champion Larry Holmes, and controversial political figures like Russell Means, cofounder of the American Indian Movement. They also have included people in the news headlines, like a New York City civil-court judge known for his no-bail or low-bail advocacy, nicknamed "Turn 'Em Loose Bruce" Wright. In effect, suitable "name" candidates can have celebrity status because of their famous achievements, involvement in a national conflict, or controversial views on a significant issue.

## Timely Peg

Regardless of whether your candidate is a famous figure in the entertainment world or has name value because of current newspaper headlines, your subject has to have timely relevancy. For instance, when the *Playboy* interview with the late Henry Fonda was published, the actor not only fit the slot of "famous name" screen star, but the interview possessed timeliness because it appeared just before the release of the critically acclaimed film, "On Golden Pond," in which Fonda costarred, and just after publication of the seventy-six-year-old actor's authorized New American Library biography, *Fonda: My Life.*

Sometimes though, you will not know to what timely event to peg your interview till you actually plunge into the research. When, at the request of *Working Woman's* editors, I secured the promise of an interview with eight-time Oscar winner, costume designer Edith Head, the interview had no relevant focus. I found one after arrival in L.A., as I said earlier. Following many unreturned calls to Head's cottage office at Universal to pin down an appointment, I was finally told that she was still fitting the stars for *Airport 77,* due to start filming the following Monday. I realized the film credit would be my "peg." Though I was more keen to do the interview because of this discovery, I had to threaten to leave town without it to secure time with the costume designer the first day of filming.

Then I used that scene, as I waited for the lunch break on the set just beyond the lighted plane interior, to introduce the interview with an anecdote that called attention to this legendary costume designer's credit on a future movie release. I started the interview, "Edith Head: A Talk with a Hollywood Legend" (*Working Woman,* January 1977):

> I wait on the set of Universal's multimillion-dollar production, *Airport 77,* to interview eight-time Oscar winner, costume designer Edith Head, who is checking Brenda Vaccaro and Olivia de Havilland for their first appearances on the set. She wears a beige pants suit which, combined with her bangs, bun, and horn-rimmed glasses, gives her 5'1" imposing authority.
>
> She apologizes for not getting "really dressed up. I'm working on the set of an airplane, and I have to climb stairs, so I wore pants and flat shoes," she says, as if sensible attire needs explanation when it's worn by someone who, for nearly forty years, has made a living glamorizing the glamorous with the best costume tricks in town.

Sometimes when you deal with an enduring professional, the timely focus for the interview will emerge only as you do your research. In such instances, good nerves, faith, and patience are your only resources for "waiting out" the period till the appearance of the required peg for your story.

Besides the release of a future work, a current political issue can provide a timely hook. For instance, the complex court battle for American Indian rights gives the *Penthouse* interview with well-known American Indian rights activist, Russell Means, currency. Similarly, the law and order issue that catapulted Judge Bruce Wright into international prominence also supplies the timely focus for *Penthouse*'s interview with this pro-defendant advocate of low- or no-bail verdicts.

## Personal Identification

To guarantee the sale of your "Celebrity Interview" to the assigning magazine, choose a candidate not only with a recognizable name and timeliness, but a person whose life, work, or point of view has meaning to you. For instance, when I left the movie theater where I'd seen *Lumière,* the first film directed by actress Jeanne Moreau, who also played its lead, I knew I wanted to interview Moreau for *Working Woman.* I explained why in the published piece, "Jeanne Moreau: An Uncompromised Life," which appeared in the March 1977 issue of the magazine. *Lumière* had been the first film I'd ever seen that assessed the life of a professional woman. I wrote that Moreau "concentrates on the liabilities and satisfactions of the professional woman whose identity is not only in a man or love, but in her friendships with other women and in her work. On the strength of my gut identification with Moreau, I persuaded *Working Woman's* editors to commission the interview. I added the argument that Moreau was a timely subject for American audiences because of her cameo appearance in the current Paramount release, *The Last Tycoon,* starring Robert De Niro.

## Accessibility

Lastly, try to find a celebrated subject who is accessible. It's unlikely that a magazine will assign a first-time interviewer a subject that demands a large expense advance for a trip to Hollywood. So limit your choice by practical considerations. Try to find a celebrated subject who lives nearby or will temporarily be in your vicinity.

In summary, when you're about to select your candidate for a "Celebrity Interview," think of a famous name with a timely project or newsworthy involvement with whom you personally identify—who is accessible.

### Special Research Guidelines

Once you've secured a commission and the promised cooperation of your celebrity, scrutinize published pieces in past issues of the assigning magazine—particularly if the "Celebrity Interview," the publication, or both the form and outlet are new to you. I often make lists of categories of subjects within the published introductions and interviews of the assigning magazine before I devise my research questions. If you know in advance the editorial territory your interview must cover, you can avoid the return of your "Celebrity Interview" with editor's queries for additional material and the delay of payment till you've complied.

## THE INTRODUCTION: RESEARCH REQUIREMENTS

The following section helps you recognize appropriate topics for introductions to "Celebrity Interviews" by listing and then explaining repeated ones that appear in many published examples of the form.

Just as introductions to "Q. & A.'s" give credentials for the expert's authority, so introductions to "Celebrity Interviews" offer explanations for the subject's fame. They present reasons for the fame of the name, kudos from his or her career which created or confirmed that fame, often a biographical profile, current life-style, conditions of the interview, the interviewer's attitude toward the celebrity and, finally, themes within the interview or a myth punctured at the start.

None of the above topics is a must for every introduction to a "Celebrity Interview." The succeeding analysis of these areas may guide you in deciding which facts to request for yours. Keep in mind that your introduction should build a framework of information to enable the reader to scale the interview.

## Requirements: Explanation of Fame

Once, when I stressed that such introductions should explain the famous reputation, one of my students shot back, "Why? If the interview subject is a famous name, aren't you stating the obvious by saying why that person is famous?" You can assume your readers will recognize your subject's name, but you cannot expect each reader to dredge up the precise facts for why that "name" is well known. So, help your readers. At the introduction's start, give the reasons for your celebrity's fame to rivet readers' attention.

What are plausible reasons for fame? In the *Playboy* introduction to an interview with Henry Fonda, the actor is billed as famous for a film role—Tom Joad in *The Grapes of Wrath*—which epitomized an era in American history. *Penthouse's* interview with Judge Bruce Wright introduces the New York City civil-court judge as famous for a minority position on a political issue of majority concern. *Penthouse* subject, Charlton Heston, has "starred in more epic films and played more legendary characters than any other actor in motion picture history." Heavyweight boxing champion Larry Holmes is the current top competitor in his sport. In other words, an outstanding or distinctive type of achievement qualifies as a suitable reason for a candidate's fame.

Convey these claims to fame with facts and illustrating anecdotes. For example, the *Penthouse* interview with Judge Bruce Wright begins with a representative anecdote of his popular professional appeal: his swearing-in ceremony for a ten-year term as a civil-court judge before cheering hundreds of "blacks, whites, Hispanics, young, old, male, female. . . ." The subsequent examination of Wright's bench record concludes in his world-headlined verdict to release without bail an employed black man accused of knifing a decoy cop. The opening anecdote, Wright's judicial record, and most famous case offer evidence for his fame as a low- or no-bail advocate.

*Playboy's* Fonda interview introduces this legendary actor by a list of the artifacts in his Bel-Air home. They symbolize the actor's aging, illness, many career credits, and one in particular that brought him lasting fame. Like a camera panning close-ups of the set with the actor's first entrance, the lead begins:

> . . . There is a full-time male nurse with him as he slowly moves with the aid of a walker from one room to another. A hospital bed has been installed in a small room off the kitchen. Large cylindrical tanks of oxygen are delivered and stored in a corner of a bedroom. In another room, a new painting of a rumpled denim jacket hanging over a chair awaits his finishing touches.
>
> And then there is this: a drawing of a book opened to page 312. Resting on the top half of this page is a magnifying glass that highlights the last paragraph of chapter 21. . . .
> It is a page from John Steinbeck's *The Grapes of Wrath,* and the artist is the man who brought Tom Joad to life in the 1940 film.
>
> It was the 21st motion picture of Henry Fonda's career, a career that has spanned six decades, including more than 80 films, dozens of plays, two TV series—and two children who have followed his path to acting, fame and fortune. Of all the plays and films he has made, it is *Grapes of Wrath* for which he is most remembered. . . . In his portrayal of Joad, Fonda left his stamp upon a character and a time.

## Requirements: Professional Credits Responsible for Fame

After conveying the distinction most responsible for the famous name, the introduction often proceeds to synthesize past and recent professional credits that contributed to making the subject more famous. For instance, the *Penthouse* professional resume of heavyweight boxer, Larry Holmes, confirms the fighter's championship stature by his record of wins in the ring, mat style, and spectacular financial rewards. The Holmes' resume in support of his fame starts:

> Undefeated in 37 pro bouts Holmes is a superb stylist who's equally adept at offense and defense. The 31-year-old resident of Easton, Pa., possesses the most damaging left hand in boxing today, and he uses it like a battering ram. He is perhaps the only fighter in the world who can deck an opponent with a single left jab. Still, Holmes generally isn't regarded as a devastating puncher, even though the Ali fight was his eighth straight title defense to end in a knockout. . . . The Ali bout was Holmes' biggest fistic payday, but the so-called Easton Assassin has been hauling in seven-figure purses since winning the title in '78. Holmes received 1.5 million for defeating lightly regarded Ossie Ocasio in his second title defense, and his bout with Earnie Shavers in '79 brought him $2.5 million. For a young man who was so poor that he could not afford shoes at the start of the seventies, Larry Holmes has clearly come a long, long way.

The introduction then launches into a personal biography of the World Boxing Council heavyweight boxing champion with enlivening quotes.

## Requirements: Personal Biography Leading to Fame

Not all "Celebrity Interviews" contain biographical profiles. When editorial space permits, however, these short biographies reveal the celebrity's alienation or identification with his era; early talents; stumbling blocks to the right career choice; professional mentors; formal or on-the-job training; the first lucky break; instructive defeats and successes.

For example, in the following excerpted portrait from *Penthouse*'s Robert Redford interview, notice how the undistinguished biographical facts— Redford's early rootlessness, poverty, sporadic jobs, and slow rise to stardom— humanize the "name" subject for the ordinary reader.

> He was born in Santa Monica on August 18, 1937, . . . . He found the fifties a spiritual wasteland. Too late for the dramas of the depression era and World War II, the children of the fifties, says Redford, had no way to identify.
> "We did not project anything of our own, unlike the sixties generation. It was maddening, and I wanted out." Though he was good in athletics, winning a baseball scholarship to the University of Colorado, he soon dropped out and headed for Europe, where he spent several months trying to become a painter, while flirting with starvation.
> He returned to California in 1958, depressed about himself. There he met and married Lola von Wagenen. With her encouragement they moved to New York,

where his interests shifted from painting to set designing. Then, on the advice of his instructor, he enrolled in the American Academy of Dramatic Arts. Discovering acting was, he says "like an explosion." An agent spotted him, and in 1960 he had a walk-on part in *Tall Story,* a Broadway play about a basketball player. There followed other parts in *The Highest Tree* and *Little Moon of Alban* and starring roles in *Sunday in New York* and *Barefoot in the Park.*

He went back to Hollywood to make his first film in 1962, a low-budget melodrama called *War Hunt.* No one noticed. Then came *This Property Is Condemned* and *Inside Daisy Clover,* both with his friend Natalie Wood, and *The Chase,* . . . . But it wasn't until 1979, when he and Paul Newman struck sparks as *Butch Cassidy and the Sundance Kid,* that Redford became famous.

## Requirements: Rewards of Fame

After detailing the potholed, maverick route to fame, the introduction invariably registers some of the perks of the celebrity's fame for the readers' vicarious entertainment. For Michael Douglas, the commercial success of "One Flew Over The Cuckoo's Nest" brought the producer "acclaim beyond his wildest dreams, including an invitation to the White House to attend Jimmy Carter's inaugural parties." For Redford, fame has meant not social invitations, but social influence as a board member of influential environmental organizations such as the National Resources Defense Council and the Environmental Defense Fund.

## Requirements: Celebrity Life-style and Conditions of the Interview

After profiling the celebrity's rise from lackluster anonymity to fame-generating achievements and the perks, these introductions usually describe the celebrity's current life-style—hobbies, daily routines, personal luxuries, marital status, residence. At the same time, they portray the conditions under which the interview is conducted. For instance, *Penthouse* sent reporter Lawrence Linderman to meet Charlton Heston at his Beverly Hills home. Linderman's summary of Heston's daily work schedule led into a summary of the interview conditions.

> Linderman reports: "At 56, Charlton Heston is still a great-looking man who keeps himself in superb shape. A regular on the celebrity tennis scene for many years now, Heston is usually up and exercising by six o'clock every morning. After that, he reads or fiddles around in his study until the rest of Hollywood begins functioning, which is why I recently found myself beginning our interviews at the unusual hour of 7:00 A.M."

Linderman then painted the home of Heston and his wife as

> "a huge comfortably furnished home at the very top of Coldwater Canyon, and as long as the L.A. rains don't wash it away, the couple will continue to enjoy the most spectacular view in town."

With the Robert Redford interview, the chronicled life-style and interview conditions concentrated less on evaluating the actor's appearance and posh address and more on Redford's strategies for dealing with the demands of fame. *Penthouse*'s editors wrote in the concluding section of the introduction:

> In line with his preference for privacy, Redford has rarely granted interviews in recent years. He does, however, occasionally make appearances at colleges. . . .

So two *Penthouse* contributors—Jeffrey Wells and Dan Yakir—joined a student audience during a Redford speaking engagement at Yale and shot their interview questions at the celebrity along with those of the students. This unusual set-up for the interview led to this amusing statement at the introduction's end:

> Although the questions were posed by several persons, for ready reference in the dialogue below, all of the questioners are identified as "Penthouse." All of the answers were, in fact, given by Mr. Redford.

Whereas *Penthouse*'s interviewers had Redford in the proverbial "sitting duck" situation, Larry Holmes' interviewer had a much more difficult, time-consuming task. Here, as in Redford's case, the anecdotes about the conditions for the interview illuminate another celebrity's reaction to the insatiable demands of fame. Again, the reporter is Lawrence Linderman.

> "Larry Holmes is currently one of the sporting world's hottest commodities, and getting him to sit down for an interview isn't easy. Since defeating Ali, Holmes has been constantly on the road to attend various sports and charity functions, and although we began our interview in Easton, we ended it in New York, just before Larry was about to board a plane for New Orleans."

With body-builder champion Arnold Schwarzenegger, the conditions for the *Penthouse* interview revealed something about the physical abilities contributing to the new film actor's former professional success:

> Interviewer James Delson met with "The Austrian Oak" while [the movie] *Conan* was being filmed in Spain. Talking over a two-week period there and again last summer in Santa Monica, Calif., where Schwarzenegger resides, Delson was impressed by the athlete-actor's style, openness, and willingness to give of himself despite physical injury (a strained knee ligament in Spain) and exhaustion (the final conversations were crammed into a marathon thirty-hour session, with only a six-hour sleep break at the halfway mark).

In summaries of interview conditions, interviewers often record the celebrity's reaction to the interview to forewarn readers how much candor to expect in succeeding answers. With "The Austrian Oak," Delson recorded Schwarzenegger's "openness, and willingness to give of himself"; in the Heston interview, reporter Lawrence Linderman noted the famous actor's celebrated "stuffed shirt" reputation among the press and Heston's rare contradiction of it during the *Penthouse* interview. Linderman wrote:

> "Over the years, Heston has gotten a reputation among journalists for being something of a stuffed shirt, and I hoped that wouldn't turn out to be the case. It didn't. Although it's true that Heston is formal to the point of stiffness, he's also friendly and more than capable of needling his own egocentric excesses. Having listened to more than my share of film idols, I must say that the hours I spent with Heston were as instructive and enjoyable as any that could be spent interviewing an actor."

If, during an interview with a celebrity reputedly known for reserve, you overcome his Maginot Line of defense, note the battle won in your introduction, as did Linderman. You want to broadcast the probable presence of some never-before-expressed material to pique reader curiosity about the interview ahead.

## Requirements: Themes of Interview
Finally, the interviewer may list the themes of the interview to give readers a taste of the conversation to follow. Delson writes of Schwarzenegger's interview:

> In the interview that follows, the ex-body builder waxes philosophical on politics (he is conservative), personal freedom (he would limit it for the good of the country), religion (he is Catholic), gun control (he is opposed), freedom of the press (he thinks it's dangerous), the fifty-five mile speed limit (he is violently opposed), his acting (he wants to be the next Burt Reynolds), heroes (from FDR to Reagan) and a number of unusual aspects of body-building (homosexuality, groupies, psychological warfare during competition, women's involvements, and money's ruinous influence).

## Requirements: Statement of Essential Famous Talent or Achievement
The introduction usually leads into the interview with some reference to the celebrity's famous talent or achievement and a newsworthy point, as in the Arnold Schwarzenegger interview:

> For a man who has pushed his body to its physical limits, the use of steroids in sports seemed a natural starting-point for the conversation.

or a past media event, as in the Larry Holmes interview:

> "Although Holmes has begun preparations for his June title defense against Leon
> Spinks, the Ali fight was still on his mind, and it provided the opening subject for
> our interview."

or the celebrity's mystique from a certain type of film role, as in the Heston interview:

> "Although Heston has in fact played a wide variety of film roles, he's best known as
> the commanding presence that has dominated some of the most gloriously enter-
> taining films Hollywood has ever produced. That led to the opening question of
> our interview."

At your introduction's end, you can express your opinion about the essence of
your subject's fame admired most by the public.

In summary, introductions to "Celebrity Interviews" may touch on the distinguishing reason for fame, professional achievements that have heightened that
fame, may profile the rise to stardom, its perks, the celebrity's life-style, the conditions for the interview, the interviewer's reaction to the famous person, themes
covered by the interview, quintessence of the celebrity's fame. Don't let the list of
recommended subjects for the introduction intimidate you. These topics are only suggestions. After you launch the research, you'll find out which are the right
topics for your "Celebrity Interview."

## THE BODY OF THE INTERVIEW:
## RESEARCH REQUIREMENTS

A review of the type of information presented in published "Celebrity Interviews" may act as a guide for your research and editing. Conversations with celebrities usually explore formulative childhood conflicts, influential mentors,
pivotal professional decisions, important or controversial work projects, famous collaborators, relevant political, religious, or professional views, and
fame's problems and rewards. Try, as in an "As Told To," to persuade a celebrity
to remember details and anecdotes that communicate concretely what it was like
to be in that quarrel, momentous decisions, or the like.

Whatever insight prompted your choice of a celebrity, or whatever meaning a
celebrity's life or achievement has personally for you should dictate your choice
of what to ask or pursue in the verbal portrait. "If a celebrity has been interviewed 50,000 times, don't you have to have some obscure research to devise
questions and get answers no one ever thought of before?" asked a former student. Though I believe you have to familiarize yourself with the life and career of
any subject you interview, I don't think you have to do extensive detective work
into a famous person's past to secure the best questions and most illuminating

replies. You need to be confident of your gut reaction, though, to the celebrity. You should choose a famous person as your subject because that person represents something you are trying to work out or confirm in your life or career. It's from that self-knowledge about what that celebrity represents for you, that you should fashion the themes of your questions and arrange the resulting taped answers. Your guts are the best guide to the right choices for the submitted text. You'll do the best interview and find the best printable materials not on the basis of research, but on instinct.

## THE BODY OF THE INTERVIEW: STRUCTURE

You can organize "Celebrity Interviews" by two methods. You can start with a recent celebrated credit and move backward in time to significant influences in childhood, or you can use the reverse pattern—anonymity to stardom. You've already met the *start-to-present* pattern in the "As Told To" form. In this structure, the interview begins with the celebrity's entry to a profession and moves chronologically forward with small digressions, as in my *Cosmopolitan* interview, "Notes Of A West Point Woman."

If your featured celebrity hasn't worked at a well-reported project in the months preceding your conversations, consider organizing the material by the *first job to fame* chronology. Just the exciting story of your celebrity's rise from a nobody to a famous person will interest readers who may enjoy following a famous person's stepping stones to success.

*Penthouse's* interview with Arnold Schwarzenegger flirts briefly with his views on a controversial sports issue—steroids—before loosely tracing the former Mr. Olympia's orbit from the dark, freezing gymnasiums of his youth to his first prize winnings in international competitions. This organizational structure serves the Schwarzenegger interview best because of its timing in Schwarzenegger's career. The former body-builder was just launching his acting career with a starring role in Dino De Laurentiis' film, *Conan*. The film's release wasn't scheduled until well after the interview's publication. Since Schwarzenegger's career was in transition, and he had no recent news-making major achievement on which to stake the interview, the chronological structure was the best choice.

If your celebrated subject recently garnered wide press coverage for a kleiglight event, your subject's first-hand account of this event may provide an excellent start for the interview. Your subject's memories of that zenith career point will give a dramatic beginning because readers are fascinated by eyewitness views of a famous project or happening. For instance, *Penthouse* interviewed producer-actor Michael Douglas after he produced *The China Syndrome,* a film about the dangers of nuclear power. So the printed interview begins by exploring the reasons for Douglas' connection with this commercially successful, controversial project, and then retraces the professional backward through past credits to revelations about formulative childhood influences that make Douglas what he is today. Decide which organizational pattern applies after you've done the interview.

## SAMPLE "CELEBRITY INTERVIEW"

Interviews with celebrities are often hard to get. You're competing with many journalists for a celebrity's limited free time. Then, after you win consent for the interview for your assigning publication, you have to labor to get an appointment in the celebrity's jammed calendar in time to meet your deadline.

I've told the story of my successful pursuit of internationally acclaimed actress and film director, Jeanne Moreau, for a *Working Woman* interview earlier in this book. I'll repeat it briefly to stress some instructive points. The scheduled day of the interview, Jeanne Moreau's New York representative was waiting for me at the tiny registration desk at Manhattan's posh Hotel Pierre. I came lugging an attache case full of photocopied clips from the French Film Office's files. The swath documented Moreau's career from its inception. Moreau's New York representative informed me of Moreau's cancellation. She had taken ill. When well, she would leave for L.A. immediately. The representative apologized for not contacting me sooner. He pointed out that my home number is unlisted. I stood at the registration desk with my typed questions in one hand, heavy attache case and tape recorder in the other, trying to absorb the message. I had to get that commissioned interview.

The following day I phoned the publicity department of Paramount Pictures, which had recently released a film in which Moreau played a minor role. I informed my connection of the commissioned interview for *Working Woman*. My contact requested the magazine verify the assignment in writing, which the editors did by messengered letter. A few days later I had secured Paramount's backing, flight tickets, and the name and number of the publicity agent for Moreau in L.A.

Though Paramount bankrolled the trip west for an authorized interview with a star in a company picture, once I arrived at the film capital my humiliations were not over. I still had to wait for Moreau to set the time and day for the interview. So each day, I'd call the representative and each day he'd assure me Moreau knew I was in town and it was just a matter of time till she agreed to see me Finally, I got telephone confirmation that Moreau was available at eleven the morning of the following day.

A chauffeured limousine transported me to the home of Hollywood film director William Friedkin where Moreau was staying. She greeted me at the door in an unpretentious ecru smock with no makeup. Once inside, I felt at ease because Friedkin's dark Victorian furnishings reminded me of the decor of many suburban Philadelphia homes I'd frequented during my years at Bryn Mawr College.

Moreau guided me to a couch and coffee table at the back of the living room, lighted by daylight cascading through the rear terrace doors. As I plugged in my tape recorder before a gleaming Oscar that presided over the fireplace mantle, as I said earlier, the 5 foot film director asked why I had followed her 3,000 miles for an interview.

I replied that all the creative women I had known or admired had committed suicide. In the same way the Bible lists family generations connected by the word, "begat . . . begat . . . begat," I reeled off the names of women artists who had killed themselves—"Anne Sexton, Sylvia Plath, Diane Arbus." I told Mo reau her movie, *Lumière*, in which she had starred and had directed, had moved me tremendously because it dealt with the satisfactions and disadvantages of a single professional woman who endured. So I tracked her 3,000 miles, I said, to find out what gave her life purpose. Since she lacked the conventional ones like husband and children, what kept her alive?

Perhaps because of my utter candor, she began the taped interview with an autobiographical reminiscence. She said.

> Did you know . . . I was meant to be a boy. My name was to be Pierre. And when I was born, my father got so depressed because I was a girl, that he got drunk and had to be taken to the town hall to register my birth by some friends. Really, I was in great danger because I was meant to be called Pierret. And the registrar that day was sane enough to protest: "What a terrible name. Why should you treat that baby that way? Why not call her Jeanne?" And my father said, "Do whatever you want." And that's why I have only one first name. My name is Jeanne Moreau, that's all.

It had never occurred to me to ask whether she was supposed to be born a boy or girl. I hadn't known the family story or others that Jeanne Moreau proceeded to tell from the autobiography she was then writing. Her childhood memories revealed so much of what formed her, I took them gladly because her remembrances fitted in with the interview's planned themes, though they preceded the time frame the editors—in review of my submitted questions—had agreed on prior to my departure. When relevant, I also asked prepared questions or spontaneous ones directly related to the preconceived themes for the interview.

We stopped for a French country-styled lunch of hard-boiled eggs and fruit. Moreau served it in the kitchen atop a tall room-long butcher's table which we of similar height reached by climbing atop high stools. At the table, she told me the Orson Welles story included in the piece. I did not fathom the meaning of this apocryphal tale then, nor even when I edited it into my manuscript for submission—only months later. But during that first hearing, I knew the tale held an important revelation not only about Moreau, but the nature of life. Instinctively, I felt the story's symbolic truth transcended that moment or the specific sociological themes of the interview.

Moreau cut the interview short after lunch. She had to prepare to leave for a taping with Johnny Carson.

I never saw Moreau again. Nor could I check the factual accuracy of my interview by phone with my subject. Moreau left for Paris before our next appointment to be with Malraux's daughter upon the death of that great statesman. The following interview, "Jeanne Moreau: An Uncompromised Life," published in March 1977, is based on two and a half hours of taped conversation from that single session.

### JEANNE MOREAU: AN UNCOMPROMISED LIFE
#### by Barbara Kevles

The large iron gates swing open and the limousine swerves up a steep incline to the Beverly Hills mansion where internationally acclaimed actress Jeanne Moreau is staying during the last lap of a promotion tour for her film *Lumière,* the first Moreau ever wrote and directed. Over the phone, she said she intends to limit her L.A. interviews, "because," she explained, "one needs time to refill. Otherwise, one repeats."

Moreau has been besieged by the press, not only because of *Lumière*'s artistic success (it was described by *New York Times* critic Vincent Canby as "close to . . . perfect"), but because of her new personal level of achievement. As a young girl, Moreau studied acting privately over her father's objections, and then successfully auditioned at eighteen for the Conservatoire National d'Art Dramatique. This was followed by a meteoric debut with the Comédie Française a year later. Moreau admits her drive to act came of a desire to lead "life my way. Not to be somebody else."

In 1958, after ten years of unexceptional films, Moreau established herself as the prima actress of the New Wave with Louis Malle's film, *Les Amants;* Antonioni's *La Notte,* (1960); Truffaut's *Jules et Jim,* (1961); Buñuel's *Le Journal d'une Femme de Chambre,* (1964); and Malle's *Viva Maria!,* (1965). Since then, however, despite successive films, Moreau's reputation seemed on the decline, until she progressed from acting only to directing as well, from simply reflecting men's visions of women to expressing her own. Moreau has said, "The women I played . . . were trying to find themselves (as) part of a man's life." In *Lumière,* she concentrates on the liabilities and satisfactions of the professional woman whose identity is not only in a man or love, but in her friendships with other women, and in her work.

Inside the mansion, the gleaming Oscar on the living room mantle identifies the paneled walls, tasteful antiques, and deep velvet couches as the property of the thirty-seven-year-old director of *The French Connection,* William Friedkin, whom, a month later, Moreau will announce her intention to marry. Moreau enters, dressed simply in a shapeless ecru smock. Like Sarah, whom she plays in *Lumière,* she wears heavy pieces of jewelry—two large rings and a watch on a band studded with turquoises. But the face of the forty-eight-year-old Moreau bears none of the deep wrinkles of the aging actress she portrayed in *The Last Tycoon*. On the contrary, she is youthful and petite, with freckles and incredibly wide sensual lips that at times form the childish pout for which she is famous.

She brings glasses of white wine, settles comfortably into a chair, and begins to trace the causes of her inability to submit to the conventional female destiny, a rebellion born of the repressive, male-oriented culture of her birthplace; a stern, authoritarian father, a local hotel owner in Vichy, France, and the frustrations of her British-born mother, a former chorus girl, with her wifely lot in the narrow-minded French provinces.

Hours later we adjourn to the kitchen for a lunch of fruit and hard-boiled eggs. Moreau is exhausted from "wishing to speak truly of things I felt." For as she retold her childhood, she lived it—with rage, tears, laughter, and cleansing compassion.

Is Jeanne Moreau your real name?

Yes. When my mother got pregnant in 1927, I was meant to be a boy. My name was to be Pierre. And when I was born, my father got so depressed because I was a girl, that he got drunk and had to be taken to the town hall to register my birth, by some friends. Really, I was in great danger because I was meant to be called Pierret, the woman's diminutive for Pierre. And the registrar that day was sane enough to protest: "What a terrible name. Why should you treat that baby that way? Why not call her Jeanne?" And my father said, "Do whatever you want." And that's why I have only one first name. My name is Jeanne Moreau, that's all.

Did your parents encourage you to be creative?

Not exactly. First of all, there were no books or records in my parents' house. There was nothing related to imagination. I discovered that through my mother's fantasy.

What do you mean?

I was about four and I was a tyrant. I didn't like to eat. So my mother and I would lock ourselves in a room, and I would say, "I'm going to eat if you dance." She had been a chorus girl and danced at the Folies-Bergère, and that's how she met my father. So after she danced, I would promise to eat something else, "if you will sing."

So the fantasy you shared with your mother was that she was a successful performer on the stage?

Yes. Though she was a wife and mother, she never fitted her role. And maybe I didn't help because I was always bringing out her desire to perform. She told me sometimes she could have been a great dancer, except she got pregnant with me when she was twenty. I mean, it's quite a blow when you're a child and you discover around eight years old that you were not wanted.

How did you react?

I robbed some household money and flew from the house on my bicycle. I got caught about six or seven hours later.

Were you always considered something of a rebel?

Yes, but I don't think I was. It's just that I wouldn't submit. And I suppose I acted differently because in the provinces, among my father's family and the peasants, my mother was treated as a foreigner. And because of the link between us, I felt exactly the same.

Did your being a girl make a difference in how your father treated you?

No. He loved me as long as I was a child, because I was very bright, I read early, and I was different. He adored me until I became an adolescent and began to discover the truth about adult relationships.

When I was about fourteen and a half, I discovered things as they are—unhappiness, sex, violence . . . I found out my parents married out of convention when my mother became pregnant. And when their marriage seemed to them to be a failure, my mother got pregnant again. My father surely decided that. And knowing that, my attitude changed completely. I became more secretive, and my father couldn't reach me anymore. And in fact, I profoundly disliked him. So then he started adoring my younger sister, which showed me his weakness.

You mean he could only love a child who wouldn't challenge him?

Quite. Someone who wouldn't judge. My father's been dead now eighteen months, and I'm concerned that he was unhappy. But if he hadn't been my father, I wouldn't have shown any curiosity or interest in him if ever we had chanced to meet.

When did you leave Vichy?

When my sister was born, my father went to Paris to work. And my mother, sister, and I eventually went to England to stay with my grandparents in the south of England. In Sussex. We were still there when the war was declared. I have the impression that my parents were very close to a divorce, and if it hadn't been for the war, we never would have gone back to France.

On the basis of your parents' relationship, how do you see marriage?

As something stable, but destructive, because it is based on an enormous lie. Truffaut said that in women's novels, there's always the moment when the heroine looks at herself naked in the mirror. But men don't have to look at themselves in mirrors because they go through life with mirrors all around them—the women who are listening to them, looking at them, and expressing their interests. And relationships based on that are, I think, an enormous lie. Because they don't allow for equality. If besides passion and attraction there is not esteem, respect, tenderness, friendship, it's bound to end disastrously.

What were the war years like in Paris?

The war was a very happy time for children because all the ruling fathers were in the army. We cared about them, but because they were not in the house all the time, we could be open to the world. We could speak up. We could say what we liked or what we disliked in terms of society. For example, my high school, which was all girls, was located in Paris near three other high schools for boys. And when the sirens went on, it meant a German raid. We all had to rush into the subways—and it was *fun*. Suddenly, we all gathered, boys and girls, and we were flirting and talking about records and music and books. I mean the war was an excitement, an adventure.

During that period didn't you live above a brothel?

No, it wasn't a brothel. In the hotel where we lived, there were no apartments. There were rooms where prostitutes would take their clients for two or three hours. It was what we call in French, a Maison de Passe. And we lived in two rooms on the fifth floor.

What was it like being a teenager in that environment?

I must have had a very deep instinct for refusing, so I would be able to stay in a state of innocence. In winter when the Germans occupied the country, I remember going to school when it was dark, and the men were lining the staircases waiting for the prostitutes. Some were half undressed with (and she pats her arm) their trousers on their right arm. When the liberation came in 1945, I was already seventeen, and to make a little money, I would translate the correspondence these girls had with their soldiers, clients, whatever you can call them. So, in fact, the first love letters I ever wrote were for other women to men I didn't know.

And yet you remained a virgin?

Well, I was quite flabbergasted at times by some of the expressions they used, sometimes referring to something very romantic and sometimes to a very precise physical performance. But I had and still have a very solid, strong and indestructible reliance on myself. I am not easily influenced.

What impelled you to go see your first play?

First of all, that it was forbidden. Secondly, my friends were allowed to go, and they were ecstatic about the theater, so I really wanted to see it. Lastly, I was fascinated by literature, poetry, passions which were expressed in written words all around me. I wanted to *hear* the language of beauty and passion, spoken, so I went to a play by Anouilh, *Antigone*. The protagonist was dressed in white and she stood in the middle of the lighted stage; she and the other performers looked at by a crowd of anonymous people. And I felt myself so deeply attracted that I felt that world in which the players moved was my world.

In what way?

In terms of purity, of total dedication to one's absolute idealism. The world of the people on stage was the world I wanted to live in. I wanted to be careless about myself. I was surrounded by people who cared very much about themselves, about what their neighbors would say, how things had to be done. On stage, I could abandon the rules of the game, disregard them.

Did the lure of the stage also lie in a desire to play other people?

I didn't want to be somebody else. I wanted to live life *my way*. I was beginning to be a person, and I wanted to be totally responsible for myself.

Can you illustrate that part of your life with some anecdote?

There are no scenes. I mean life is like a river, so anecdotes weaken the impact. You cannot drop names or tell little tales unless you find some tale as powerful as a riddle or a fork in the river. For example, Orson Welles tells one in a film called *Mr. Arkadin*. Anyway, the story is that there is an enormous flood and a frog wants to cross the river, only the bridge is destroyed. And when the stream is less strong, the frog readies to swim. And a scorpion begs to go with him. But the frog refuses, saying, "What happens if you sting me?" And the scorpion argues, "But I'll drown." So the frog reconsiders and agrees. But in the middle of the river, the scorpion gives him a sting. And the frog says, "You see, I was right." And the scorpion says, "I know, I'm going to die, too. But that's my character." The story means that one cannot escape one's character. I like stories like that because they tell so much more than the living incident.

Did your parents approve of your auditioning for the theater?

My mother did. My father knew nothing about it. And when I succeeded, he resented the idea of my becoming an actress. For him, a woman wanting to be an actress was associated with extraordinary, sexually-tinted aspirations. He had the classical attitude that all actresses were prostitutes.

What was the value of your classical stage training?

For me, it was essential. It taught me a discipline and made me reflect on the nature of discipline. I mean if discipline is just an expression of power by somebody else, then I resent it. But if discipline is related, you say in French, to an *exigence*. . . . Meaning, if you want to be faithful to the purity of the work and the neatness of its expression that you have to maintain in order to communicate it to others, then discipline is absolutely essential.

Does discipline prevent the actress' personality from overwhelming the work?

No. It prevents the personality from exploding in all directions and losing its force. Discipline helps to build a skeleton, a morality. That's why I'm against the conventional rules of the game. On stage, you discover a world of your own and build your own moral structure. Not the usual morality related to good and bad. But a set of fluid principles that you can live with according to your conscience, according to how you think life ought to be.

What do you consider the uniqueness of your acting talent?

I think my unique characteristic is that I'm always moving . . . and moving with the world and the times. And the need for truth, however destructive it can be.

During your early acting career, you married to make your son legitimate. In some sense, weren't you repeating the pattern of your mother?

Yes and no. I got married because I was pregnant. But I didn't take it the way she did. My son was born the 28th of September. I got married on the 27th, and I went back to work October 5th, and eventually other women looked after my son. So the birth didn't stop me from working. I enjoyed giving birth. I thought it quite an experience. And when it was done, it was over. But then people expected me to act like a traditional mother and I couldn't. I felt responsible for my husband and son, but I knew that I could really live without them. Not only that, but I sometimes didn't feel married. I just went on living the way I wished. That was not regarded as normal for a wife and mother.

Some American women feel European men handle independent women better than Americans. Is that true?

Maybe they say that because they're Americans. As a Frenchwoman, I don't find it that easy with European men especially if they come from the South—like Italy, Spain. Then they have that fatal image of the woman as being either the sacred Virgin Mary—the wife and mother—or the whore. She's not considered as somebody active, constructive or equal. But that's the result of their education, and also of the way women have accepted their role. Sometimes, I discover that the strongest enemies of women are women.

Can you explain?

Some women will not accept in others the idea of independence. I have plenty of examples. Women come up and speak to me in restaurants and places where I make films. And they ask me questions about my life, not in order to know me, but to compare our lives. And if they see their life does not match mine, I see them change immediately. They resent my independence, and my joy of living, and, for example, my attitudes toward aging.

Why?

Because the majority of women feel that after a certain age, life is over for them, and its just because of their conditioning. A woman usually feels she has to get married or sex is terrible. So she marries on false pretenses. Let's say sexual attraction lasts a certain time. Then there is adultery, then frustration. Then the children. Then the child-rearing. Then the children are grown. Then the husband doesn't need his wife anymore. Then her life ends around forty-five. That's a life? Five years of happiness and blooming, then, suddenly (claps) cut off? Better shoot yourself.

But if the traditional woman's life ends when she is no longer needed by others, what sustains the professional woman in later years?

Her work, her activity. Participating. Having ideas and acting on them. The use of what is in *her*. For me, first, there are the things that have been given to me, and then I have my experiences. The choices I made, the energy, the depressions, I mean all of that is constructive. All that leads somewhere. When you have the impression you're facing a wall, what's really reassuring is the notion that nothing lasts in life. Not even despair. Not even happiness. It'll be changed into something else, and that too will change again. This cigarette I smoke, when it ends, I will use it to light another. So that's renewing. It's little death by little death—meaning resurrection. So why should women out of tradition accept an ultimate ending of life at forty-five? It's impossible to accept. A woman doesn't have to seek identity or the meaning of life if she's involved in an action. What's important is the action. My life will end with death. But it won't stop growing until then.

## Analysis

As a "Celebrity Interview," the Moreau interview satisfies the requirements the form demands. At the time of the research, Moreau, a famous-name French film actress who was debuting as a director, had two timely film credits gracing American marquees. The subject's personal meaning to the interviewer has been one of the book's oft-told tales, as has been the reporter's maneuvers to regain lost access by nothing more than a 3,000 mile trip bankrolled by independent financing. So the Moreau interview meets the form's casting demands for a recognizable name, currency, and personal identification by an interviewer with entree.

The interview's introduction covers all the topics mentioned in this chapter's previous examples of the "Celebrity" form. The introduction touches on the reason for Moreau's reputation, her new professional achievement in film, her attitudes toward fame's demands, her professional biography—its beginnings in unexceptional and then star vehicles, her drives, the interviewer's approach, conditions for the interview, Moreau's life-style, the interview's themes, and its subject's candor and exhaustion from "wishing to speak truly of things I felt."

In specifics, the Moreau introduction realizes these topics in the following manner. At its start, physical details like the setting—"large iron gates," "steep incline," and remoteness of the "mansion"—physically paint the interviewer's difficult access to this famous person known as an "internationally acclaimed actress." Moreau's quoted apology for delay of the meeting reveals both the timely peg for the interview and the film director's reaction to fame's exhaustive demands.

Then the introduction focuses on her new cinematic achievement, its critical success, entree to the profession, motivation for the choice, famous film credits, and drive for professional change.

After introducing readers to the reason for Moreau's current fame and route to it, the beginning offers close-ups of its subject and her understated, elegant life-style—tasteful decor, simple attire, sparse ornamentation, youthful lack of makeup, no-frills lunch menu.

The introduction concludes by alerting readers to the interview's dominant theme—Moreau's rebellious drive against the "repressive, male-oriented culture of her birthplace"—before it ends with arguments for the reader's trust of the following interview because of its subject's uncensored candor.

The interview uses clusters of events from birth to present, to explain Moreau's unconventional life and career.

It begins by unwinding the net of formulative influences on Moreau from birth through teen years—her father's hope for a son; the fantastical, theatrical aspects of her mother's childrearing, her rebellious flight, and stubborn innocence during the war years in Paris.

Next, it explores her attraction to the theater—its oral beauty, permanent offer of freedom from constrictive bourgeois dictates, its license to be herself, her vocation as another rebellion against her father's puritanism. Her remake of her mother's shotgun marriage sets off a widening web of comments about her refusal to submit to the conventional wife/mother role, reactions to a woman's independence by both sexes, the comparison of women riveted in biological identities with ones sustained by their talents and work.

The structure progresses chronologically forward—from Moreau's birth, to her upbringing, girlhood disillusionments, war years, choice of a profession, unconventional marriage and motherhood, views of women's traditional and changing identities and goals.

Thematically, the interview captures the portrait of a woman's life lived against the female norms. That was this interviewer's approach. Based on *Lumière*, I sensed Moreau could tell me what lay at the end of the feminist tunnel, at the lit station, ahead for the aging professional woman without family of her own. I wanted to know what sustained such career women. Moreau replied, "A woman doesn't have to seek identity or the meaning of life if she's involved in an action." By these words, she meant, as she stated at the answer's start, "Her work, her activity."

This was the reply to the pulsating urge that prompted me to do the interview with Jeanne Moreau. I said previously the "Celebrity Interview" gives you professional benefits of heightened reputation among discerning editors. On a personal level, they always have offered me something more—a revelation that answers some deeply felt question that, without my totally comprehending it, dictates the choice of that subject at that point in my career. And the resultant message awaiting me within the interview material sometimes strikes such a fathomless chord that I understand its meaning only months later. These revelatory inscriptions that I ponder or take with me for later unmasking are the unexpected personal benefits of doing the difficult-to-obtain "Celebrity Interview." And sometimes these unheralded messages drawn from probing conversations with a particular celebrity are so instructive that they become spiritual sustenence to sustain me for an entire professional period, till the next level of personal growth nurtures another question, search, and interview pursuit.

## CRITIQUES OF STUDENT "CELEBRITY INTERVIEWS"

When I evaluate student "Celebrity Interviews," what I seek is not the right information in the introduction and interview, or even a logical structure—those things can be gotten or fixed; I look for a viewpoint. If a writer chooses to interview a timely, accessible "famous name," the talent of the writer can be measured by the degree to which an overall viewpoint pervades the finished "Celebrity Interview." The degree to which a writer investigates beneath surface facts for a celebrity's motivations reveals the presence or absence of that informing point of view. The degree to which an interviewer reflects some unfathomed personal concern in probing questions is the measure of that interviewer's ability to utilize his or her individual slant to produce a distinctive portrait with depth.

Lack of a point of view produces glaring superficiality, as the following excerpted interview demonstrates. In the introduction, the interviewer, Stephen Cohen, writes, "Philip Burke, 22, is one of the newest caricaturists on the New York scene, with drawings appearing in *The Village Voice, The New York Times Book Review, New York* Magazine, and many other publications." The writer has selected a fit subject—an "up and coming" name who draws timely, famous personalities for major publications. However, as the excerpts about the artist's goals, work methods, and reaction to the public prove, Mr. Cohen never probed beneath the surface of the artist's replies. Hence, the interview never registers the driving pulse of this new talent from the interviewer's perspective.

Q. *What about people who say that caricature is just making people look ridiculous?*
A. What about them? . . . When I do a caricature, all I am doing is taking what I see as the strong elements of essential character of something and just exaggerating that. Caricature is not just trying to make someone look ridiculous. It's not necessarily ridicule at all.

Q. *How do you do a caricature?*
A. What I like to do is look at the photos for awhile, and do some straight drawings that aren't really exaggerated, to learn the face. And then, um, start the caricature, but I've been away from it. I like to say overnight, but the face has been in my mind all night. I don't know, it's almost like I do the caricature when I'm away from the photo, because when I come back it's stronger. What I like to do also is put the photos up on the wall so that I'm looking at the face all the time, even

though I don't consciously look at it. So that by the time I sit down to draw, I know the face very well.

Q. *What is there to know about a face?*
A. I see certain thrusts in the face. I see things like this (Points to a drawing of Nabokov). I try to play on the thrust. And actually what I do is I exaggerate each feature. I don't pick one or two features, but draw on all of them.

Q. *Do you always draw from photographs?*
A. The best way is if I can see the face in movement, like on T.V. . . . Photos can be so restrictive. In motion you can see certain mannerisms.

Q. *How long does it take you to do a caricature?*
A. To do a good caricature, I find it necessary . . . to draw it many, many, many times. I mean when I did this drawing of Koch, and you can see how simple it is, I had to draw him fifty times.

Q. *How do most people react to seeing caricatures of themselves?*
A. Most people love it. Some people get offended, but they don't take it seriously.

While Mr. Cohen has caught Philip Burke's speech rhythms in good answers to the questions posed, Mr. Cohen's questions do not go far enough. They don't scrape away Burke's defensive concern with craft to expose what motivates him to do caricatures, what kicks he derives from drawing distorted faces of famous people, what power over the famous through the art of distortion Burke enjoys, and what that power reveals about the artist personally. These omissions of a probing viewpoint deplete the interview of potential for success.

Another student, who interviewed a subject without the prerequisite saleable "name" or "timeliness," nonetheless displayed a solid personal stance in the questions. The following excerpts demonstrate how a curious interviewer can push a subject unwittingly to self-exposure. In the selections, a little-known bandleader comments on his band and his stylistic intent:

Q. *The band transcends a certain musical style. How could you describe it?*
A. Like I said, we have an equal musical rapport, which shows in our performance. When we play, we try to get as mellow a sound as possible . . .

Q. *I've seen you grow from passive, subdued vocalist who just sat, played the piano, and sang without any gimmick or side antics.*
A. (He interrupts suddenly) Yeh, Now I often jazz up the act some more by playing more sophisticated chords with my elbows (and get bruised). I hold out high notes longer. Anything to emphasize my inner emotions. It's all part of the show. . . .

Q. *Do you play for the audience, or is it what the band likes?*
A. It's a combination.

By asking, "Do you play for the audience. . . .?", the interviewer questions whether the band leader has jazzed up his act and sold out his musical integrity for audience approval and more bookings. Whether the reader believes the musicians play both "for the audience" and "what the band likes" in "combination," the interviewer has cast doubt about the motives behind the band leader's new style simply by the question. It's probes like these, which inspect a possible "sell-out" to commercialism, that mark the talented writer as separate from the mediocre one.

The following student excerpts exhibit the work of a talented writer with a viewpoint and saleable subject. A student of the visual arts and former Londoner, the interviewer chose as subject the celebrated proprietor of New York City's famous haunt, "Elaine's." As the following samples demonstrate, the Elaine of "Elaine's" became the doppelganger for the student's British working-class background, fashion interests, and keen expatriate curiosities.

Q. *What prompted you to open a restaurant?*
A. I wanted a business that could be shared by my friends. Who were mainly writers, actors and designers. Each one needing another form of support other than their own profession.

Q. *How did you start off in the beginning?*
A. Very slowly, I've been here for 18 years, I still have the same people that I started with, many came from England. It was in the days when the world was discovering London as the design world for clothes and everything else. The people who became involved were Jean Muir, Mary Quant, Joe Macen, Vidal Sassoon, Leonard, Ozzie Davids, and many more each bringing along his own friends. I remember an old friend once sent me a young French film director who brought me his crew. It was a joint effort: they knew me, I knew them and we all liked each other.

. . .

Q. *Do you come from a family of restaurateurs?*
A. No, but at one time they were involved with foods, a lot of my family came from Russia and were in the dry food business.

. . .

Q. *Do you offer a specific menu?*
A. We mainly serve Italian food. It became a second nature to me from living among the Italians in the Village.

. . .

Q. *Did you have a college education behind you?*
A. No, just high school; I had only practical experience. That I learnt from the Italian people.

Basically, the writer, who would like to be successful in the fashion world, employs her special vantage to draw from an established compatriot the lessons from her success in business. The interview, which probes how Elaine, as a foreigner, established her well-known restaurant in America, retrieves fresh copy and new insights from an often-interviewed "name."

Invariably, if you are venturesome enough to put your instinctual reasons for doing the interview on the tenterhooks of your questions, you, too, will make your interview worthy of publication and attention of other magazine editors.

## ADVICE FOR THE "CELEBRITY INTERVIEW" FORM

These guidelines will help you perform a professional job with your "Celebrity Interview":

**1.** Choose a famous person whose timely achievement is now, not years ago.

**2.** If you can't get to your assigned "Celebrity," inform your editor and, at the same time, offer an alternate "name" with currency.

**3.** Review topics in published "Celebrity Interviews," particularly those in past issues of the assigning publication, and decide which ones could produce fertile questions for your introduction and interview.

**4.** Obtain copies of already published profiles and interviews with the celebrity and become familiar with your subject's career and personal history prior to the interview.

**5.** If necessary, type up a chronology of the subject's most famous achievements and their dates for ready reference during the interview.

**6.** After a review of your tapes from the interview, decide on a structure.

**7.** If the celebrity has disclosed some newsworthy fact or revealing information, include it in the published interview. Be loyal to yourself as a journalist and aim to report what is truthful. Don't withhold incriminating materials from print. Agents are hired to protect celebrities; you're hired as a journalist to report what is truthful.

**8.** Don't forget to have the celebrity review the submission for factual accuracy and initial each page, if possible. Otherwise, do your fact check by a reading by phone.

# XIV Writing Discipline: How to Get Through a Writer's Block & How to Outline an Article

## HOW TO MAINTAIN WRITING DISCIPLINE: HOW TO DEAL WITH A WRITER'S BLOCK

Once you discover a saleable article idea, scout a likely market, draft an effective query, negotiate the best possible commission, do the essential spadework, persuade subjects to be interviewed, barrel through their defense for the information—still something may impede you from finishing the article: a writer's block. Mine are chronic. I procrastinate the actual writing of almost every assignment. My blocks represent my worst terrors and self-doubts about my writing. Though I can identify their source and, by doing so, lessen the fear enough so I can work, I can't make these painful doubts go away forever. So this section will explain the mechanisms of common blocks that get in the way of writing, their reasons, and ways to resolve them. The advice may help combat the paralysis of will that stops you from writing or, over time, get you through a block and to your work desk sooner, but it will not rid them. Your struggle will be unending.

You delay writing an article because you're afraid to. When readying to write, one student confessed, "I get an inexplicable urge to clean the kitchen." Another admitted, "I read the Sunday papers, look at football on TV. Pretty soon it's Sunday evening, and I haven't done anything about the article."

My escape valve is running. Once, I had to do my workout before I could settle in before my typewriter. But I've changed my mind about that. The whole summer of '84, I trained to race the 200m at the New York State games where, with a personal best of 30:06, I had a chance for the "gold" in my age group. But the Monday following the state competition at Albany, I had a deadline for two articles for *American Health*'s November 1984 issue. So, I made the wrenching decision not to attend the games upstate. There would always be another race, but there would be only one November issue of the magazine.

If you want to be a magazine writer, then that's the arena where you want to perform. If writing and publishing articles is a life priority, then get to your desk to achieve it.

Another student shared her method for ending her procrastination. She termed it, "the radio announcer technique. I pretend I'm on radio and the interviewer says, 'Can you tell me in one minute what your piece is about?' and that compels me to do it." She added, "If you don't tell the announcer the answer, you've missed your chance."

If you don't write the piece and make your deadline, you may miss the chance of publication. When I trained for the New York City Marathon in '79, I had two *Glamour* feature articles assigned. After the marathon, when I was ready to write up my research, I called *Glamour.* My editor was gone and the new one didn't want them. If you have a deadline, make an appointment with yourself. Begin the assignment on a day when you have uninterrupted time to stay in and write. If you've drafted a query, gotten a commission, and done the research, you won't respect yourself unless you write the article.

You may avoid sitting down to write because you fear being alone. One student said, "I feel guilty about staying in Friday night." Sometimes I restrain an acute desire for social life by remembering my professional commitment to my editor. I imagine my assigning editor pacing his office thinking, 'Where is it?' At such times, I turn on the answering machine and attempt to reschedule my running later in the day, believing, 'I have to come through for him. I have to deliver the piece to make him look good for his superiors.' The weekend I cancelled my trip to Albany, I kept thinking, 'I made a promise, and I have to keep it.' Or, I'd tell myself, 'I don't want to let him down.'

Besides remembered editorial obligations, imagined benefits for the article's readers may keep you company and help you endure the solitude of writing. Such hopes gave me the stamina to write four different versions of an *Esquire,* April 1984 *Sports Clinic:* "The Chiropractor: The long-misunderstood profession is making a comeback." To start each separate draft about the chiropractic approach to sports medicine, which provides a radically different one from that of the A.M.A., I often told myself, 'This will help somebody.' That belief in the article's worth to someone else can dull that ache of loneliness while writing. And, in truth, some actually do benefit readers. One source of an article published in *American Health* April 1985, about new treatment methods for common yeast infections, received twenty-five new patients in the issue's first weeks on the newsstand.

The needs of others will not motivate you to write if you fear you have nothing to say. On some level, this is a fear that the article will show you're unworthy. Once, a talented student explained this marvelous solution to the writer's fear of being found inferior. He said, "I sit down to write and I think, 'You are the most insignificant thing. You are the most obscure voice in the world. You have no chance to be noticed.' " At such times, he said, "I try to cultivate the feeling that something wants to be said." In effect, though he judged himself to be mediocre, he believed what he had to say was worth writing. The distinction he made between his perception of himself and the article's information is an important one to keep in mind. A belief in the significance of the material can power you past a disbelief in your own self-worth or writing talents. If you review your proposal for the original reason you wanted to do the article, you may say, as I sometimes do, 'This is important. I have to get the message out.' So the desire to communicate valued material may force you back to the typing keys.

When I face writing an article, I don't fear loneliness, nor do I fear that the writing will expose my inferiority. I fear failure. That fear propels me out of the house at any excuse to be away from my work desk. The source of my fear is a repeated childhood experience as the daughter of a high school mathematics teacher. When I was growing up, what passed for dinner conversation often were simply math problems. My father would pose complex algebraic equations and ask my older brother and me to solve them. I always failed to perform well with this advanced coursework for which I was totally unprepared. I always succeeded in getting the wrong answer. As a result, the performance of those habitual algebraic exercises that boosted my father's ego at the expense of mine inculcated a belief there is only one right answer. When I contemplate beginning an assignment, my fear of writing an inaccurate answer forces me away from my desk or, once there, paralyzes me from writing.

When I unearthed the source of my writing block several years ago, I told myself, 'Well, I can always rewrite if I get it wrong. After all, writing is really rewriting.' With that approach, I could calm my fear of making a mistake and get through the first draft of one paragraph (when the fear is great, that's how much it affects my production); or a whole page, or, at times, two or three. I took courage from the knowledge I could correct my imperfect answers by rewriting. If I haven't written for awhile, I am blocked and have to relearn this lesson.

At times I use another device to leap the barriers of self-doubt created by the rigid orientation of my past. I acknowledge I'm scared to begin writing for fear of failing to find the right answer, so I tell myself, 'There are many ways to write this. There is no one right answer.' Nowadays, when I feel that familiar crippling fear, I say, 'I don't know, but I'll figure it out.' As a result of my probing, this is as far as I've come. From the helpless child who believed, because of countless failures in an area of expertise that was not her forte, 'I'll never get the right answer,' I console myself, 'I'll find out.' And the assertion is the difference between the helpless child I once was and the assertive professional I became. The road from that child's terror of the wrong answer has led to the mature professional's awareness that ultimately the writer has all the right answers because the writer has created the examination.

## MAINTAIN DISCIPLINE: OUTLINE THE ARTICLE

An outline of your article helps surmount some of the blocks just mentioned. For the writer who fears having nothing to say, an outline is convincing argument to the contrary. For writers like me who fear getting the facts wrong, it familiarizes you once again with your research and all the possible right answers. The review also reinforces your desire to discover what the article is going to say. And for those whose unrealistic timetables for the article's completion impede their writing, an outline helps to truly assess the duration of that journey.

In summary, an outline can help estimate the article's production time, build confidence in the merits of its message and instruct you in its contents during its design.

To construct a good outline, follow these steps! Read your proposal. Isolate your article's theme, then review your interview questions for basic points that expand it. Next, study your interviews in the sequence you did them. You may have to spend two or three sittings carefully considering penned 5"x8" cards or typed pages. Next, reread related periodical research—newspaper clippings, magazine articles, pamphlets. Then lay everything aside.

In a clear desk area, lay a blank paper folded down the middle. I like plain, white paper used for photocopying. Jot down some important thematic points in any order. Then number them. Open the paper, and on the adjoining side, copy the now numbered points in numerical order. Add more notations anywhere, in one or two word phrases, on the second side. Number them, and transfer this hodgepodge in numerical order to another side of a new sheet. Repeat this process methodically.

In these moments, I feel I'm being carried by a wave of thought that I'm helping create. I begin to comprehend facts in new ways and make connections between formerly unlinked ideas. As I recognize these new ties, I make more insertions and reorder my jottings. When you have repeated the jottings, linking, insertions, numbering, recopying, to the point you have a workable outline, type it. Then review quickly all your research—query, questions, interviews, periodicals—and add salient bits of relevant information to the typed structure. In phrases. Never whole sentences. Then reorganize the structure for logic, and retype. The result is your final outline.

An outline is the best shortcut to the well-written article, so never leave it out—no matter how short the article's assigned word length. The successive versions are analogous to many drafts of an article. An outline allows you to play with sequences of ideas without attention to language, spellings or clarity. By rearranging or deleting elliptical symbols, like paragraphs, to eliminate redundancies or disorganization; I improve the outline's structure draft to draft. Consequently, I do less structural revision with the actually written piece. An outline is the essential scaffold on which successful articles are built.

But once I've done an outline, I rarely refer to it after writing the article's introduction and perhaps the first section. Then, I just like knowing it's there. It gives me confidence the piece has a beginning, a middle, and end. When I finish a section or the entire article, I'll consult it to see if I've omitted any well-stated phrase or important idea. Also, when I reach an outlined idea, I may find I've already said it earlier in the article another way and can move on to the next. I don't follow outlines word for word, but as I've stressed, they are essential to good article writing. They shepherd you through common writing blocks by reacquainting you with your research materials, their intrinsic merits, and expected production time. They give the article structure and well-paced writing. And they offer writers a guide for reference from beginning to the end of the writing of the article. Never write an article without one.

## Maintain Discipline: Avoid Interruptions

Once you've begun to write, avoid the normal interruptions that can break your momentum. Telephones are major menaces to your discipline. If you've set aside certain hours to write, you cannot take calls during those hours. Turn on your answering machine or alert your service. Or if you take a call, tell callers, "I'm writing. When can I reach you?" Knee-deep in projects, I may mumble to friends, "Listen, I'm in my head, can I call you back?" Try not to waste energy or lose a train of thought to a sudden call. Hold fast to your work privacy. Sometimes, I don't answer. I sit and count rings. Sometimes, by the number, I can tell who's calling. Once, I heard the phone ring for five minutes and still did not answer. If you must call out, schedule those outgoing calls at the start or end of a workday to preserve that uninterrupted dialogue with your materials on the typed page. When on the street heading for a newsstand, I may not say hello to neighbors. I try very hard to protect this private dialogue.

Sacrifice social life and obligations, if necessary, to preserve your momentum at the typewriter. When you withdraw from normal social exchanges and routine get-togethers to write, you find out whether friends want your friendship as a reflection or reinforcement of their values, or sincerely value you for yourself. At the start of a long work project, I informed my running partners I wouldn't be available for weekly training sessions. I gave up consistently running for five or six days weekly for about a month. At the end of this time, when I called my running mates, some had filled our times, and others, if they had, willingly scheduled another.

Andre Gregory, celebrated avant garde theater director, once told me, "When you come back, most people are where you left them."

Besides phone calls and social routines, errands can also distract you from assigned writing. Take care not to leave your material at the wrong time of day or for too long a period. If you remain away too long from your desk, you may forget what you memorized during the outline process and have to relearn your material once more to conquer your fears of writing. So don't let errands become an excuse to avoid writing. Different writers work at different hours, so the best time for errands differs. First thing in the morning may be an ill-advised time. Best to wait till lunch or, better, the end of your workday. After all, cleaners, shoemakers, hardware stores, banks, and groceries are open for their customers' convenience. If you must make an extended bus ride or use public transportation for a length of time, take your "buddy," as a student called her two-year doctoral thesis, with you. Think about an introduction to the next section or its structure hanging from a subway strap or between the bleach and rinse cycle at the Laundromat. But don't leave for errands till your workday is over. If you do not take yourself seriously as a writer and keep the appointed hours required for any business to turn a profit, you may never type the final page of that commission or article on spec that entitles you to call yourself a professional writer. New York lawyer Gerald Dickler alludes to the necessary discipline of the successful free-lance writer in his cogent definition, "A writer is one who stays in and writes."

## Maintain Discipline: Keep a Work Log—
## Day by Day, Week by Week

Decide the amount, kinds, and timing of work disruptions or relaxations you can sustain during peak production by monitoring them through a daily desk dairy. In mine, I mark down the hours I give my work and what else I do—incoming and outgoing calls, sprint training, shopping, social life, and housework. At the end of each week, I summarize these daily entries for accomplishments of the week, as well as primary work distractions, in a special notebook. I also itemize and analyze the preceding week day by day. By these dual outlines, I figure out in what categories I've wasted the most writing time. I note them at my report's end and resolve to reduce their consumption the following week. For instance, if I've accidentally wasted eight hours experimenting with a new soup recipe, as I did recently with one for black bean, or spent too much time on the phone socializing, or hyped future articles to editors when I should have been at work on current ones, or worked out when I should have been writing—I try to resist those avoidance strategies the next week. To be disciplined about your work, you have to know how you apportion your time and attempt to minimize, defer, or eliminate those unnecessary distractions when possible.

Some days you have more work discipline than others. If you clock your activities, you'll discover and utilize more of your best hours for concentration to write. If you work at your writing discipline, you'll get better at maintaining it free of disruptive distractions. When I begin a long writing project, it takes two or three weeks to pare down my day's activities to be disciplined. Gradually, I disengage from strong interests in morning training runs, shopping for fashion, or other superficial activities that give me self-pride. When I finally secure my hold on my identity as a writer, I become fascinated with my own mind and its insights. Then I begin to resent any interruption.

For adults employed in 9-5 jobs, you have a harder time establishing and sustaining a writing discipline as a free-lance writer. Calls for interviews have to be wedged into coffee breaks and lunch hours and your research has to be scheduled after work or weekends. Explaining how she finished a multiple-interview expository article, one student, who works as a hospital superintendent, said, "You get up earlier and go to bed later." For the part-time free-lance writer, resign yourself to doing as much as possible—even if it's only a sentence—within the constraints of your time limits. If you assign yourself increments of work and are pleased if a paragraph, a page, or a rewritten page is all you can accomplish during a self-designated appointment, your pride in the small accomplishments of your writing will eventually be rewarded with the old newspaper symbol - 30 -, which means you've come to the conclusion of your article.

This section has exposed the ordinary escapes from common writing blocks and their sources and proposed attitudes and methods such as an outline and a desk diary to gain and retain the momentum of disciplined writing. But remember, at the very start of this book, I said, "You only fear failing at the things you care about deeply." So if you have a block work through it, because not to will cost far more.

# XV The Expository Article Form: How to Capture an Emerging Conflict or Complex Development from Many Viewpoints

# DEFINITION

The expository article reports a new conflict or complex development from multiple viewpoints.

## Markets and Topics for Expository Articles

Popular with small local weeklies, big city dailies, and national monthlies, this versatile form handles areas any other issue-oriented article can. It can adapt to nuts and bolts law and order topics (". . . Plan to Improve Security in Park," *The New York Times,* Monday, April 16, 1984); sociology ("Paternity Leave: A New Role For Fathers," ibid., Monday, December 7, 1981); or a high-tech revolution in medicine, like a *Vogue,* 1983, piece on the new computerized X-ray device, the CAT scanner. Subjects for this adaptable form sound almost identical to ones for other forms previously covered, but they're not.

## Subject Requirement: Necessity for Multiple Interviews

Select the expository form over the one issue article or the "Q. & A.," when one expert opinion simply won't suffice. The multiple interview form best serves to portray in depth a new complex development like the world's first in-hospital program for home care units ("A Touch Of Home In Hospital Care," *The New York Times Magazine,* Nov. 27, 1983) which demands evaluation from multiple points of view. It's also the preferred form to report a serious, multisided conflict, as for example, one about injurious or fatal disciplinary punishment in high school or collegiate sports ("Athletes Testing Issue of Discipline," *The New York Times,* Dec. 6, 1981) which requires fair presentation of all sides. The organized, well-paced expository article commands research from multiple perspectives to achieve objective depth of reporting.

### Explanation of "Different Perspectives"

What is meant by different perspectives? In an expository article on a complex educational development, the simplest examples of these differing viewpoints would be those of a teacher, principal, and parent. First-rate examples of differing points of view are in the piece, "Sex Abuse: The Child's Word Isn't Enough," (*The New York Times,* Monday, July 11, 1983). It deftly weaves together diverse testimonies about a complex legal development—a proposed modification for prosecuting nonforcible sexual abuse of young children. The piece about New York State legislature bills to repeal the corroboration requirement for a prosecution, based on the word of the sexually abused youngster, effectively employs points of view by prosecutors, legislators, and members of the American Bar Association to explain the current statute and proposed changes in the state legal code. The article draws on such varied experts as a chief of the Domestic Violence Prosecution Unit of a suburban county D.A.'s office who lost a grand jury case against a sodomist of a youngster under the corroboration requirement; a Brooklyn District Attorney who favors modification of the requirement; a New York State Assembly sponsor of a repeal bill to substitute a judge's examination of the abused child; critics of the Assembly bill from the Bronx D.A.'s office and the American Bar Association's National Legal Resource Center; support of the Assemby bill in the voices of the chairman and counsel of the lower house's Codes Committee; and a final mitigating word on the different Senate and Assembly versions of the repeal bill from the District Attorney of Manhattan. Each interview adds a special interpretation to the discussion, based on the expert's vantage point. Together, these perspectives give the article objectivity and depth. What's more, this comprehensively researched article on pending modifications in state law covers only five newspaper columns, five paragraphs in length apiece.

So a worthy topic must require in-depth reporting from many points of view for best use of the form. Secondly, a multi-sided topic for the form must have saleable news value.

## Subject Requirement: Saleable News

To win an assignment, the topic must promise newly discovered information or news of a social change. A splendid example of an expository article with timely theme, "The Battle Of Wounded Knees," *The New York Times Magazine,* Sunday, December 7, 1983), reports new controversial treatments such as arthroscopic surgery as remedies for the surge of knee injuries resulting from the sudden participation of millions in the fitness movement. The same weekend edition of *The Times* carried another article in the expository form, with the requisite news currency, which documented a change in perspective toward the nearly hundred-year-old profession, "The Literary Agent."

## Career Advantage and Financial Disadvantage of Form

A timely, well-researched expository article about a newsworthy phenomenon is a big challenge. Consider carefully before you undertake this journalistic commitment its demands on your time for multiple research interviews. Some of you will be able to parlay the time-consuming prerequisite into larger compensations during negotiations, if the assigning publication's pay scale permits. I confess I was mortified to learn my "top" fee for a 1500-word expository, "Dispute on Wheelchair Athletes Stirs New York City Marathon" (published in the *Sports*

Section of *The New York Times,* Sunday, October 7, 1979), would be $150. An acquaintance, who, with partners, commands over 200 Con Ed accounts in New York City, told me "I would gladly pay to be in *The New York Times.*" Another friend who heard my complaint about such a tiny fee for so much work said, "The more prestigious the publication, usually the smaller the fee." So you should decide, I suppose, before you query about an expository, whether a byline in a prestigious place and the revenues for your reputation are worth no matter what the research costs you in unpaid work time. A well-researched piece, well-placed, though, can give you more of a name with which to gain entree to new markets or bargain with present ones for higher fees.

## RESEARCH GUIDELINES: LIST VIEWPOINTS TO INTERVIEW

Once an editor has assigned you anywhere from a few hundred to a couple of thousand words for an article on a timely, multidimensional development, follow these research guidelines to create the special list of interviews essential for this multiple viewpoint form. Before a single research call, note all the different types of perspectives that will help provide thorough coverage of the complex development or controversy. Then decide who best represents each vantage point. If, at the start of your research, you organize an interview list with multiple perspectives, the final draft of your expository article will possess objective, in-depth coverage that marks quality reporting in this journalistic form.

### Casting Your Interviews: Value of Consultants

If you can't identify all the factions or vantage points, consult someone who can. For the article published in the New York Road Runners Club publication, *New York Running News,* "Should Wheelchair Racers Run?" in April 1979 (which that fall, with more developments and research, became a *Times* Sunday "Views of Sport" article on the same topic), I turned to NYRRC President, Fred Lebow, for a list of whom to contact about the dispute on wheelchair entrants and the New York City Marathon. I always asked Lebow's advice in casting my early articles about the national running scene, because I trusted his political sense about which people held which positions. At the time, the New York Road Runners Club and its president, Fred Lebow, were in litigation under the state's human rights law for discriminatory practices against the disabled in a place of public accomodation, because the 1978 New York City Marathon Committee had rejected the race applications of two wheelchair racers. Lebow suggested a raft of names for my research interviews, and for each he summarized the views of the person recommended. People under political attack usually know who their opponents are, and the opposition's arguments as well as the opposition. In fact, you usually get some of the best background information from the opposite side. Lebow's summaries proved accurate representations of the wheelchair athletes and their supporters. His recommended interview list enabled me to report fully and objectively this multifaceted conflict. Be sure, though, before you follow through on a recommended contact, to check the credentials of the proposed expert against the preferred qualifications listed in Chapter VIII. You don't want to call someone who lacks a creditable vantage point as a result of a consultant's nepotism.

## Casting Your Interviews: Types of Credentials

Besides experts qualified by professions, affiliations, or educational degrees, don't forget the credible ones qualified by experience, like someone with the right personal history or eyewitness view of events. These sources offer vivid impressions or pungent insights that you can quote, like experts, to give things you have no authority or right to say. For example, when I devised my interview list for the *Harper's Bazaar* coverline story, "How To Finish A Marathon," (May 1982), I made sure to contact top women runners who had recently ranked in each of the article's ten reported road races. I specifically wanted to know from each ranking finisher her first-hand difficulties with that race, annually held at that time of the year on that famous course in that day's weather. So, for example, 1981 Boston Marathon Women's Division winner, Allison Roe, said of the intense heat of one July 4 10K Peachtree Race she ran, "It was like being in an oven." Luckily, some Atlanta residents were spraying runners with garden hoses from the curb. As a result, Roe recalled at the race's end, "I wound up looking as if I'd just stepped out of a swimming pool." But she was the first woman to cross the finish line, and her time—32:38—set a new women's course record. Roe's report of this summer heat race and methods for overcoming the high temperatures were responses I could not have imagined. The top finisher's first-hand comments about the hot day she set a course record in the country's largest 10K added credibility to my race report. So evaluate any preliminary list of multiple source interviews, devised by you and through consultation, for its thorough coverage of essential vantage points, qualifications of its experts, and inclusion of relevant names with the right experience.

## Preparation for Interviews: Print Research: Sources and Uses

Comprehensive background research is a must for this type of assignment. At the cost of repeating some of the advice given in the section on how to prepare for an interview—which, of course, you should review—I want to stress some key points for your preparation for expository interviews. Before your meetings, do the necessary library and bookstore research for better interviews. Call the public library's readers' service for titles, authors, publishers, and publication dates of recent books on your topic. Ask publishers' public relations or publicity departments for review copies, on the premise that you may quote from the book (as indeed you might), in your article. Visit a neighborhood library and check the "Readers' Guide To Periodical Literature," which indexes articles in magazines. Follow your leads to the stacks where photocopy machines are handy for take-home copies. These books and magazines will focus your mind on primary or critical issues of the assigned topic so you can construct more sharply focused questions. Familiarity with recent clippings or related books prior to your appointments will arm you with an informed critical perspective, so you can quickly understand answers to your queries and, if necessary, probe for more honest ones. Your background research makes you a less gullible, tougher interviewer less ready to accept answers at face value. Don't neglect it, particularly in preparation for expository interviews.

No matter what information you learn from books, articles, or other sources, approach your interviews with an open mind and without a predetermined verdict. Existing articles, hardcover books, or quality trade paperbacks are references for facts, a general chronology in which to place the interview questions, or suggested areas of controversy to pursue during your interview. But don't accept the research in print as truth written in concrete. Direct quotes or facts from published materials should always be checked with their source or attributed spokesperson. Never, ever, use a direct quote from a published source without checking, because you can never be sure its connotative meaning is what was intended. Use only your own original research interviews for directly attributable quotations. Question authorities or eyewitness participants fairly. The form requires you portray each side even-handedly to achieve a balanced objectivity.

## Journalistic Devices for Difficult Interviews About Controversy or Other Serious Matters

For interviews about an inflamed controversy or grave development, be ready to rescue reluctant subjects fearful of public exposure with pledges of "N." and "A." ("Not be Attributed"), and promises of camouflaging devices like "a member of the staff" or "a source who asked not to be identified." Or, use your journalistic devices like masking case histories or identities with pseudonyms in exchange for the desired interview material. And never go back on your promise. Also, before an assault with a tough question, prepare your subjects. Ask their support of you in your difficult moment of asking it, or their support for their cause by answering it. Or support them with an equally vulnerable experience out of your life as the exchange for one of theirs.

During my researches for the piece about wheelchair racers and the New York Road Runners Club for *New York Running News* and, later, for *The Times,* I was so scared of unknowable repercussions from arguing for disqualification of the disabled in footraces by definition of the sport, that I had an elaborate preface for my "toughies." I actually would say I believed well-pitted competitive arguments made for the best of Shakespeare's greatest dramatic moments. So I was going to repeat the worst possible criticism of their views so they could give their strongest rebuttal. Then, almost holding my breath as my pulse rapidly quickened, I'd say something devastating and wait for their furious defense. That is the technique by which I gained the strongest arguments for each side that were so convincing in both versions of the article, so that each thought their side came out the winner.

After you've completed the necessary background research and done the interviews with representatives of opposing sides of the reported controversy, or different vantage points on the multisided development, review your entire research. Then reread your proposal to find out what you thought you wanted to write about before you discovered so much more than you initially knew. Decide whether you agree with your original position or whether, after your researches, you've changed your stance. Whichever is the case, that view of the complex development or timely conflict at the core of your focus belongs at the start of your expository article.

## THE BEGINNING: REQUIRED INFORMATION: STATEMENT OF TIMELY THEME

Beginnings of articles in this form summarize or telescope what's in the article ahead. They answer the reader's rightful questions, "Why should I read this?", "What's in it for me?".

The expository form permits a number of ways to tell readers the article's theme. *The New York Times* article on proposed modifications of prosecution statutes for sexual abuse of children rivets readers with a poignant introductory anecdote about an uncle of a five-year-old who used Sunday babysitting to sodomize the child. When the child ultimately disclosed the wrongdoing, the prosecution failed to win a grand jury verdict because of the statutory requirement of corroboration by a guilty plea, witness, or medical proof. By dramatizing the facts of a real case with fictitious names, the anecdotal beginning gives the problem within the current criminal justice code, the resolution of which the article explores.

Complex developments in regions of criminal justice, health, education, or even fashion emerge in response to specific problems. So, almost always, as a rule of thumb, you can start with an illustration of the predicament you're reporting. Besides an example of a reason for the development, a variety of strategies can introduce your expository article—well-selected statistics, a short profile of a person representing the troublesome condition, or a bold direct summary of the problem itself.

The piece, "Adolescents, Parents and Birth Control" (*The New York Times*, Monday, March 8, 1982), summarizes its conflicted theme for readers with a series of deviling questions:

> Do parents have the right to know that contraceptive drugs or devices have been prescribed for their adolescent children? Or do teenagers have the right to obtain birth control without the knowledge—and possible disapproval—of their parents? Do they have the same rights as adults to confidentiality in sex-related matters?

Snagged by these questions, readers learn that "The Department of Health and Human Services has proposed a regulation that would require that parents be notified when minors treated in federally financed facilities receive prescriptive contraceptives." Besides answering the reader's question, "What's in it for me?", your expository beginnings have to fulfill another requirement, as this one immediately does. Beginnings have to stress the second defining feature of a saleable expository article emphasized by the question, "Why is this timely?" Both the theme and its urgent news value are essential components for openings of this article form.

All of them—succinctly focused theme and timely feature—are present in a favorite example, *The New York Times Magazine* piece, "The Battle Of Wounded Knees." Its first paragraphs herald the theme with description of a scene—San Vincente Boulevard, where, among its "elegant houses, its exotic coral trees ... joggers. From early morning to last light ... trot, lope, waddle ... along the five miles of the safety island that runs down the middle of the broad avenue." Accordingly, "Orthopedists in the area have wryly dubbed San Vincente, 'The Street of the Wounded Knee.' " Then the article links the street's resulting injuries to the larger context of the fitness bandwagon that "middle-aged, middle-class Americans all over the country have hopped on. . . . " Resoundingly, the article sounds its timely motif: "the single biggest casualty of all that running, jumping, twisting, and pounding may be the genus of joint known as the knee." And the article then spins on at a decent clip about "The Battle Of Wounded Knees." In effect, with wry wit, the initial paragraphs deftly use description of a place to symbolize a contemporary problem.

It doesn't matter what device caps your timely theme at the start—dramatized example, literary symbol, a cascade of questions. What you should keep uppermost in mind is this: Try to answer the questions of a friend who asks, "What's your article about?", "Why are you writing it now?"

During the class assignment of this article form, a student once asked, "How can I write an exciting beginning?" I suspected she meant exciting because of some lofty, multisyllabic phrases. To disabuse her of this false requirement for the beginning of the expository, I said, "Because of required course reading, college students often prize the language of literature as the only literary one. But for what purpose? Literary language or lyrical descriptions belong to the realm of fiction or poetry, not nonfiction. You're not trying to be a poet or novelist in your expository. You're trying to write for magazines."

I was arguing that the standards for creative writing can't be applied to the medium of nonfiction. If you synthesize your theme and its timeliness for your article's start with quotes and framing exposition, anecdotes, concise description, or a summary of the problem, and write that beginning in simple, well-ordered, logical prose, your beginning will be eloquent. Simplicity of language, clarity of ideas, logical structure will guarantee an exciting start. If, when you are writing up your reporting, you reach for a word that describes what you are thinking rather than parrot textbook language or your expert's rhetoric; if, when you sit at your writing pad, typewriter, or word processer, you choose the word to accurately mirror the concrete fact, your language will ring with veracity and vividness because it means what it says. That kind of eloquence will guarantee your beginning good writing. Florid phrases will not!!

## THE BODY: GUIDELINES FOR ORGANIZATION

The structure of the expository article differs from other article forms you've studied. Unlike the profile, service, one issue/one interview article and "Q. & A.," there is no formulized construction suitable for all complex subjects or controversies. The expository article handles too many diverse areas for one structure to fit all. Rather, the successful structure of an article in this format rests on good pacing.

### Pacing: Logical Movement of Ideas
*Pacing* means two things in this context. First, expository articles about a timely phenomenon or conflict are well-paced when each paragraph or section thematically progresses from one to the next in logical fashion. Not only do sentences within paragraphs flow one to the next, but also paragraphs follow one another in logical sequence. So first, good pacing rests on the construction of the logical movement of ideas throughout the expository article.

### Pacing: Progressive Flow of Information
The second important element for good pacing is this: Each paragraph must contain a significant idea about your theme. These ideas must add, contrast, contradict, or in some manner develop the article. In effect, each paragraph should supplement the information in the preceding one. Whatever technique you employ—anecdote, quote, or exposition, your paragraph must move your theme forward not only in logical sequence, but with fresh material about the theme to sustain the pace.

Once you understand that good pacing means a logically sequential flow of ideas, and apply that concept to your writing, the quality of your written articles will improve by a giant step.

*The New York Times Book Review* essay, "The Literary Agent," illustrates the logical sequence and flow of ideas in well-paced writing. At the start, a successful agent observes that publishers have changed their attitudes toward his profession in the last half century from disdain to grateful dependency. Then the piece surveys the calling by its dubious types—"tough-talking potentates who might . . . demand an awe-inspiring sum for a . . . postwar history of the toothpick."; by its requirements (" '. . . it helps if you can read, but it's by no means a must. . . . a cat burglar could become an agent.' "); by the traits of the "Good agents . . . the perspicacity to know which editor has an unslakeable appetite for books on arson. . . .' "; the agent's functions ("dabble in editing. Contracts . . . all sorts of permutations. . . ."); editors' views of agents (" 'I think they back us up to the wall quite a lot.' "); authors' use of agents in their fiction (as in the "uproarious Mark Harris novel, *Wake Up, Stupid*."); the advantages of the large agency with intercontinental offices and specialists for the book with multiple-market possibilities. And so on.

In this nine-paragraph introduction, each paragraph's topic supplements the piece's theme with new information. Their sequence—the change in the profession's status, its types, professional qualifications, impressions agents make on editors, on writers, various size offices—logically proceeds to profile the article's subject. The pace is maintained by a steady, organized progression of new material. The rest of the article keeps the pace. The remaining paragraphs touch on the agent's advantage to an author; some agents' goals; their styles or reputations—the tough guy, the extraordinarily honest one, the wheeler dealer; and finally the profession's future capsuled in an example of an up and coming one-woman operation.

## Pacing: Guaranteed by Well-Designed Research and an Article Outline

Good pacing in an expository article can be guaranteed by a well-conceived list of research interviews and a well-designed outline. If you include opposing, supplementing, or extreme perspectives in your research, the new information reported from these diverse vantage points will push the pace of ideas forward. For instance, if in organizing the research for a timely political theme, you plan to contact experts from opposing sides or different segments of society—i.e., government, the law, partisan activist groups—their representatives' interviews can make your piece progress at a lively rate from paragraph to paragraph or section to section as you track one group's viewpoint to the next.

Paragraphs in this form may differ one from the next not only by contrasted information, but by new thematic points, as in "The Literary Agent." In this case, you extract from your interview only the quote relevant to the theme at that juncture in the piece. But if you don't plan your research interviews from multiple perspectives, you'll only have one or two views on which to string your developing points. So better to flesh out the research at the start with a comprehensive list for richly reported thematic points.

So remember, at the start, answer the reader who asks, "What's it about?", "Why now?" Then organize your multiple views of the complex development or timely conflict into a sequential flow of information for objective, comprehensive reporting and polished, well-paced writing.

## SAMPLE EXPOSITORY ARTICLE

I found the timely subject of my controversial expository article, "The Chiropractor: The long-misunderstood profession is making a comeback," published in *Esquire* in April 1984, by personal experience. During the spring and summer of 1982, I was out of competitive running due to a leg injury—achilles tendonitis. Finally, out of desperation, I saw a chiropractor who started me on a comeback. At the time, athletes didn't publicly admit their use of chiropractors, but, little by little, I began hearing about famous athletes who did. I sensed a trend was emerging in sports medicine.

When I approached *Esquire* with the proposed article in the fall of 1982, I had just had my first piece published in the magazine's August 1982, issue with the coverline, "Where to marathon." The Service Features Editor recommended me to the editor in charge of the *Sports Clinic,* who commissioned the piece about the growing use of chiropractors by amateur athletes.

My interview list of over fifty sources included such diverse perspectives as the Associate General Counsel for the A.M.A., the arch rivals of chiropractors; a past president of the American Chiropractic Association; the U.S. Olympic Committee Sports Medicine Division Director; nationally known sports chiropractors in the east, west, and midwest; famous athletes; state licensing bureaus; and many more, as well as pamphlets, books, journal extracts, records of ongoing litigation, and any printed matter persons interviewed willingly sent me. The trend was so new that, at the time, few references on my topic existed in mainstream publications that I could refer to as models for authoritative reporting.

In January 1983, when I turned in my first version, tailored to my editor's directions, the same editor sprung requests for additional research that went beyond the perimeters of the prior-approved original proposal. The editor wanted stronger opposing criticism and a comparison of A.M.A. and chiropractic diagnostic and treatment procedures. When I had completed the new research and submitted the second version, the section had a new editor. That editor's requests were the opposite of those of the previous editor—compression of the historic A.M.A. rivalry, expansion of the treatment by the chiropractor, clarifications, added evidence of chiropractic's worth from the viewpoint of the amateur athlete, and a more authoritative, assertive tone. My third version, submitted early in July, was accompanied by a cover letter listing the changes requested by both editors, with which I had complied in each of the three drafts, and a request to call it a day and see an agreement letter. Two weeks later one arrived, and a check for $1250 quickly thereafter.

In August, I saw a truncated version hastily edited for a cancelled November publication which demanded a concentrated review to correct over three dozen new errors from the editing, and a long editorial conference to get my revisions approved. This fourth version was rescheduled for publication. In October, I saw a second edit with some of the requested changes incorporated in such a way they created more errors than in the previous truncated version. After another long conference, I mailed in the supplied photostated copy of the piece with the agreed corrections and a letter urging:

> When the piece is circulated among your colleagues, can you ask they not change any part related to scientific medical information? I am dubious that anyone without knowledge of the practice and theory of chiropractic sports medicine can improve those parts that directly report it. I remind you . . . we have been through . . . a reconstitution of the rushed truncated version for cancelled November publication and then, today, through the clarifications of the edits we made before the December issue took . . . your time and delayed review of those edits. I remind you of these two in-depth editing sessions and of the current version enclosed with about thirty changes for scientific fact to impress you with the complexity of the reported information within the piece and to urge you to—if possible—ask your fellow editors to be wary of changes of information reported in which they are not steeped. . . .
>
> I applaud your patience and commitment to the truth of medical accuracy. When this controversial piece is published in ESQUIRE, at least the medical facts will not be up for dispute—thanks to all we have done.

Soon after, the word came from my editor that the managing editor had read our last version and it didn't make sense. So, I read it, and it didn't make sense to me either, and I had written it. I said I'd do another rewrite. I didn't want the effort of all that research and all those drafts to be for nothing.

I had more information that strengthened my resolve. As an amateur runner, I had learned firsthand the value of chiropractic treatment from injuries sustained in '83 from being hit by a carriage horse in a NYRRC race, a bus during a run on a main Manhattan thoroughfare, and a dog during an interval workout. I had also heard that pole-vaulter Billy Olson, former holder of the indoor world record, used chiropractors. And I knew Geoff Smith, who'd set a world record for a debut marathon in the 1983 New York City Marathon, had received chiropractic treatment months prior and at the finish line of his maiden record race. So I did more interviews. Before I submitted the sixth version, I called and checked the new quotes with all the famous athletes, and the medical material, as in every past draft, with Dr. Mac Goldstein, the official chiropractor for the Millrose Games and the TAC Nationals (the USA/Mobil Indoor Track and Field Championships). Since this Brooklyn chiropractor starts office hours at eight in the morning. I rose about 6:30 a.m. and tried to sound "with it" reading my article through to Brooklyn before dawn. My sixth version, turned in just after Thanksgiving in '83, was the basis of the one that went to press. The researcher turned up a couple of errors. Billy Olson had remembered his first national record indoors incorrectly and something else.

But my editorial conferences were not over. Just before the Christmas holidays, I received another edit and called in with more than two dozen changes for accuracy of fact. The day before Christmas vacation, the editor was under seige and wanted me to write my changes down and mail them in a letter, but I refused. Unless the editor approved them, I knew they'd never get into the piece. So, I held my ground. A sample change from an equal number of my corrections in the edit I saw mid-January, '84, demonstrates the lack of editorial knowledge of sports medicine I was combatting draft to draft. In the January discussion, I pointed out such things as Geoff Smith could not have "felt pain in his thigh" during a speed session and "The next day, the leg was too sore to stand on." The text had to read as originally written, "sit on," since a pulled hamstring muscle (the muscle under the thigh) can't be felt standing upright, only seated. On one hand, I bitterly resented the exploitation of my unpaid time by laborious text reviews and conferences to correct errors of fact created by editorial changes in previously factually correct material. But, on the other hand, I was extremely grateful for the chance the conferences afforded to correct these errors that otherwise would have been published under my by-line. And I always got a fair hearing and won an inordinate number of my suggested compromises. I saw three more repros and made changes for accuracy in each. Only one error remained unchanged in the published version.

The piece was reprinted by the country's two major chiropractic professional journals—by the International Chiropractic Association in their magazine, *Today's Chiropractic,* and by the American Chiropractic Association's *Journal Of Chiropractic.* It received several letters of criticism from members of the A.M.A., ones of praise from chiropractors, and a request from a public relations firm claiming to represent osteopaths for a piece on that long-misunderstood medical profession.

Not long ago, I decided my race distance was the sprints. Just before my first quarter-miler, I said to my coach, who for years had been sending athletes to

"Doc" Goldstein, "I don't have any form. I don't have any speed. I don't have any wind. What do I have?"

He replied, "You never give up."

## THE CHIROPRACTOR
### *The long-misunderstood profession is making a comeback*
### By Barbara Kevles

When pole-vaulter Billy Olson, former holder of the indoor world record, hurt so bad he wanted to drop out of the '82 Vitalis/U.S. Olympic Invitational, meet director director Ray Lumpp personally escorted him to the chiropractor for help. Olson's back and legs were in such bad shape, the chiropractor's twisting and cranking so rough, Olson thought he'd never move again. Yet on his next jump he cleared the bar and went back to the chiropractor for more. Then on his next attempt he set his first national record, with the height of eighteen feet six and one-half inches.

Nowadays, top-ranking athletes and amateurs alike see chiropractors for the gamut of injuries from the sprains and strains common to any sport to the more serious overuse injury. In 1978 track star Mary Decker developed sciatica, an acute injury of the major leg nerve, and had to stay out of competition for six months because neither cortisone shots, physiotherapy, nor any other traditional cure gave her relief from the excruciating pain. "As a last resort," says Decker, she started seeing a chiropractor. After treatment almost every other day for nearly two months, she began a slow comeback to racing.

During a tough speed session in the summer of 1982, runner Geoff Smith—ranked number two in the world in the ten-kilometer the year before—felt pain in his thigh, but carried on. The next day, the thigh was too sore to sit on; the diagnosis was a pulled hamstring. In succeeding months, neither ultrasound, ice, wet heat, nor sessions with a podiatrist or orthopedic surgeon could alleviate his pain. After being out the entire fall season, Smith went to a chiropractor.

"It made the difference," says Smith of his three postseason visits. The next time he saw his chiropractor was in the medical tent at the finish line of the 1983 New York City Marathon, just after Smith had come in second in his first marathon.

Though no scientific studies prove it, there is an increasing body of empirical evidence that indicates that chiropractors get results: such as Smith's recovery that culminated with his finishing time of 2:09:08—the world record for a debut marathon—and the fact that the first chiropractor used at the U.S. Olympic Committee's 1982 National Sports Festival treated nearly three hundred of the hopefuls there.

Although chiropractors use methods unlike those of any other medical professional, theirs is a licensed profession. Chiropractors are state-regulated practitioners who have completed specified undergraduate science requirements, graduated from a four-year chiropractic college, and passed national or state professional examinations.

Their philosophy is unique as well. For example, chiropractors believe that a ramming blow, a fall, or weak back muscles may throw the spine out of its normal S-curve. The displaced vertebrae, they believe, will press on nerves that exit between them and as a result deprive a part of the body of its normal energy flow. So chiropractors will often blame a leg injury on misaligned vertebrae. By contrast, a medical doctor would view a leg sprain as a problem of only the limb. But a chiropractor would trace an inflamed tendon in the calf to nerves in the spine that can't fire properly because of interference by displaced vertebrae.

Whether you're suffering from a blow to your back or a leg injury from overused muscles in a sport, a traditional chiropractor may treat you with two methods neither an osteopath nor M.D. is specifically licensed to use. He will first balance your back by separating the displaced vertebrae (traction) and then return those displaced bones to their correct position in the spinal column to assure free flow of nerve impulses throughout your body (manipulation).

Since the dawning of the fitness craze, which spawned increased numbers of sports injuries, chiropractors who've specialized in treating injured athletes have developed a new twist to old doctrine. Now not only do they say that spinal distortions precipitate injuries, but they also believe that overuse problems in your limbs such as muscle pulls, spasms, and sprains are the primary cause of misalignment in the back. You can throw your back out with a leg injury because you compensate by favoring your well leg over the injured one. And you can also develop spinal compression because of the way your body adapts to pain, like the pitcher who unconsciously tilts his neck to one side because his opposite elbow aches from too many curveballs. So a sports chiropractor will first treat the specific limb problem with electrical stimulation, ice, heat, whirlpool, or massage to reduce inflammation and relieve tightness, and then manipulate. Finally, unlike an orthopedist's prescription of rest, drugs, and physical therapy, a chiropractor will prescribe daily exercises to strengthen the injured area, increase circulation, and reduce swelling to help the body heal itself so the athlete can continue to train and compete as part of the treatment.

Twenty years ago, according to AMA associate general counsel Betty J. Anderson, chiropractors believed in one cure—spinal manipulation—for all human ailments. So in 1966 the AMA mounted a national crusade to eliminate all chiropractic medicine by threatening to ban any AMA member who gave chiropractors business by referrals.

Chiropractors defended their profession by launching a national political campaign for recognition of their legitimate medical status. In 1972 Congress amended the Medicare Act to include benefits for limited chiropractic services, which in one year alone amounted to $30 million. In 1974 the U.S. Department of Education acknowledged the Council on Chiropractic Education as the national accrediting authority for chiropractic colleges and as monitor of their educational standards. In 1978 the AMA House of Delegates rescinded its blanket indictment of their methods as devoid of therapeutic value and voted to lift its ban against referrals by physicians to licensed chiropractors.

Not long ago Mark, a ranking masters road runner, was referred by his coach to Dr. Mac Goldstein, the official chiropractor for the Millrose Games and the TAC Nationals (the USA/Mobil Indoor Track and Field Championships). Mark had increased his training from forty to fifty miles in one week and complained of pain in his lower right leg.

When Mark came to his office, Dr. Goldstein noticed the spinal distortion by Mark's posture. His head was cocked to the right side, his shoulder and hip were higher above the injured leg. When Mark lay on the chiropractor's table his right leg measured one quarter of an inch shorter than the left.

Certain standard orthopedic checks of Mark's leg movement eliminated possible neurological causes for this. But specific tests for limits of motion and tenderness of joints identified the problem. When Dr. Goldstein flexed Mark's right foot back and forth, he reported pain behind his ankle where the Achilles attaches. When the doctor tried to jiggle the tendon, like a rusty hinge it hardly moved. The diagnosis was Achilles tendonitis.

Dr. Goldstein explained. Mark's increased mileage and training on hills had stressed his rear leg muscles and inflamed the Achilles. Because of the pain, Mark had compensated by hitting the ground toe first instead of heel first on his injured leg to reduce the pull on the irritated tendon. The strain had thrown his back out of balance.

Dr. Goldstein's treatment, as well as his diagnosis, concentrated on both of Mark's problems—his injured foot and his distorted back. First, Dr. Goldstein manually stretched the right tendon and connecting rear leg muscles. Then he attached wired pads linked to a machine to Mark's right knee and ankle to electrically stimulate muscle contractions. After three consecutive twenty-minute sessions, Mark's Achilles was more flexible because increased blood circulation in the area had reduced the swelling and tightness.

With Mark lying facedown, Dr. Goldstein adjusted the spine between his shoulders. The chiropractor pressed down with both hands. Like a pianist playing familiar chords, he descended the backbones from Mark's neck to his ribs to open the seventh and eighth dorsal vertebrae and free spinal nerves linked to Mark's legs. Then Dr. Goldstein separated and realigned vertebrae in Mark's neck and lower back. At the end of treatment, Mark's right leg was only slightly shorter than his left.

Dr. Goldstein's homework for Mark was action-oriented—slow two-mile runs on flat roads daily and also toe raises on a board to stretch the tendon, rebuild weakened muscles, and help hold his spine in place. Six weeks later Mark was doing hard workouts and was back in competition.

In a book entitled *Health Quackery,* compiled by editors of Consumer Reports Books in 1980, it was doubted whether a chiropractor's spinal realignment and removal of nerves interference is effective.

In his rebuttal, Dr. Lee R. Selby, then-president of the American Chiropractic Association, said, "The medical profession condemns us for not having creditable research to substantiate our health care, and, on the other hand, denies us access to hospitals, their equipment and personnel that could provide it."

Though chiropractors are prohibited from practicing in most U.S. hospitals, many athletes nonetheless can't do without their treatments. During track season, Decker says, "I can't go without seeing a chiropractor once a week." So until science catches up with the realities of athletic life, the controversy will have to rest on the results of chiropractic care for both amateur and professional athletes.

After the 1983 New York City Marathon, with help from three medics, second-place finisher Geoff Smith hobbled into the medical tent where Dr. Goldstein was helping out. "Doc," Smith cried in relief at the sight of his own chiropractor. He pointed to his right leg where he'd felt shooting spasms for the race's last six miles. Dr. Goldstein took care of the leg spasm and then adjusted Smith's back. In two minutes Smith, though sore and hurting, was up and walking to the press tent for questions on his new world record.

## Analysis

The expository article, "The Chiropractor: The long-misunderstood profession is making a comeback," meets the requirements of the form.

It possesses a timely controversial theme, which is announced in the second paragraph:

> Nowadays, top-ranking athletes and amateurs alike see chiropractors for the gamut of injuries from the sprains and strains common to any sport to the more serious overuse injury.

The piece qualifies as an expository because it heralds a controversial phenomenon in sports medicine—the new use of an atraditional group of medical practitioners for the care of sports injuries.

This emerging trend demands exploration and evaluation through multiple perspectives for reportorial objectivity. The published article refers to the experience, opinions, or facts from a number of sources representing only the tip of a stack of interviews. The cited ones include world-famous track and field athletes, ordinary amateurs, administrators of the U.S. Olympic Committee and its National Sports Festival, state licensing experts, the A.M.A. Associate General Counsel, employees of the Council on Chiropractic Education, Dr. Mac Goldstein, editors at Consumer Reports Books, a past president of the American Chiropractic Association.

The beginning anecdote testifies to the value of chiropractic treatment. The anecdotal endorsement draws authority from its narrator's identification as a "former holder of the indoor world record" and successful results. The illustrative anecdote and thematic statement that follow tell readers right away, "What's in it for me?"

The flow of information proceeds in a logical sequence throughout and reveals many thematic points in rapid succession. An outline demonstrates the organizational logic and quick pace of information. The start of the piece testifies, as mentioned, to chiropractic's effective treatment of sports injuries with three endorsements by famous athletes—Olson, Decker, and Smith—buttressed by the U.S.O.C. Sports Festival statistics. The next section specifies state licensing qualifications for chiropractors and, in particular, their educational requirements.

Then the article explains traditional chiropractic theory and treatment of athletic injuries. Next, it announces the new theoretical interpretation and treatment methods by the new specialist within the profession, the sports chiropractor.

After the testimonials, licensing regulations, and explanation of medical theory and methods, the article summarizes the profession's uphill history—the A.M.A.'s crusade and arguments against chiropractors, the profession's legal success to insure survival, improvement of educational standards, and the A.M.A.'s cancellation of its financial boycott.

What follows is a case history. It illustrates the chiropractor's diagnostic technique, hands-on treatment, follow-up procedures, and results with a common athletic injury.

The article finishes with criticism of the chiropractic, a rebuttal, and empirical evidence of the benefits of chiropractic care.

To assure objectivity, the article balances the greater preponderance of information in favor of chiropractic care of sports injuries with notation of the lack of scientific proof and "creditable research to substantiate" its worthwhile results, as well as the A.M.A.'s criticism of this rival profession.

So "The Chiropractor" fits the expository article form because of its timely, multidimensional theme; multiple viewpoints; succinct illustrative start; logical, well-paced progression of information; and objective reporting.

## CRITIQUES OF STUDENT EXPOSITORY ARTICLES

Students who've attempted expository articles have had trouble selecting suitable themes for the form, condensing their focus into concise beginnings, and avoiding disorganization in the construction of the article.

The following excerpts from "Your Dog's Health" by Esther Paige show a problem in theme selection. The subject divides into two:

> A conscientious veterinarian is eager to have every animal in good health. The first rule in taking care of your dog is: When your dog is sick, take him to a veterinarian. Heed with caution the advice of friends or people who are supposed to be "old, experienced dog breeders." Only a veterinarian is qualified to diagnose trouble and prescribe treatment.

> Most veterinarians agree that dogs should be vaccinated against distemper, hepatitis, leptospirosis and rabies. Booster shots should be given as suggested by your veterinarian periodically during the dog's life.

> In 1971, a new disease called Canine Parvovirus was discovered. Research workers at the Walter Reed Army Institute of Research reported isolation of a coronavirus from outbreaks of diarrhea among military dogs stationed in Germany. Initially, the disease appeared to be an unusual phenomenon.

> The first encounter in this country with Canine Parvovirus was in 1977.

The rest of the article gives preventive care, incidence, symptoms, and treatment of this disease. Then the writer abandons this theme and delves into diets for healthy dogs, older dogs, and, in particular, vitamin supplements for puppies, pregnant bitches, or very old dogs. Then the piece ends with general emergency medical care available for pets. This informative article breaks into two themes. The outbreak of a new disease among American dogs, which has a newsworthy focus, can be explored by multiple viewpoints in the expository form; the trailing one about proper canine diets better fits the service format.

The beginning of Morris Kamelgarn's expository article presents another frequently unresolved difficulty.

> What is a bank? A big imposing building, with glass or marble facing? A row of smiling tellers eager to serve us? These buildings and tellers still exist, but today, when we think of a bank, we are more apt to think of a computer terminal in which we stick a small plastic card, and which can tell us how much money we have, and even give us some of it if we know the correct word. Now many of us know, however, that this electronified Groucho Marx is but the tip of the iceberg when it comes to changes in banking in recent years. Today, more and more of the things that were previously done by people are being done by machines. But how do we know whether these changes are benefitting us, the customers, or only the banks and their stockholders? More than one of us, on receiving a monthly statement charging us with checks that we have never written, has probably asked himself that question.

Mr. Kamelgarn should get to his opening theme sooner. It is

> Today, more and more of the things that were previously done by people are being done by machines. But how do we know whether these changes are benefitting us the customer, or only the banks and their stockholders?

Without a quickly stated focus, the article risks losing readers.

"Women Entering Law," by Susan Pechman, exhibits a strong thematic focus at its start. Then its paragraphs stride forward in logical progression marred by only one unnecessary digression, which breaks the article's flow. First, though, a sample of the successful start:

> When Nancy Finley graduates from the top fifteen percent of New York University Law School in May, she will go to work for a large, Manhattan general corporate practice at a salary of $38,000. Nancy is one of the more lucky lawyers-to-be. For most, finding a law job—for full time or the summer—is not a cinch. Joan Price, a second-year student at Fordham University School of Law, who is in the top thirty percent, has sent out seventy-five resumes to New York City firms and forty-five to firms in Philadelphia. So far she has nothing definite lined up for the summer. The law job market is tight for both men and women graduates and although women have come far in the profession, some feel there are lingering antiquated attitudes among firms which make their job search even more trying—and sometimes more difficult.

Ms. Pechman introduces her theme of the difficulties of the job search for female lawyers with an effective paradox—one subject's successful search contrasted with the unpromising job hunt by another female law student. The bulk of the article touches on the impediments to the women law school graduates' quest for entry-level employment—the personal interview with hidden agenda, restrictions by firm size, preferences of firm clients, prohibitions against women lawyers in certain areas of the law, alternatives to private practice, and a summary. Ms. Pechman's expository article moves at an exemplary pace with a logical, seamless flow of information, except in one instance. After the article raises the question of voiced or hidden interview agenda about a woman's job priority versus marital or childbearing obligations, it includes testimony by a former employee of a commercial litigation firm about dud female attorneys. One had "fallen in love and moved . . . to Vermont where her boyfriend lived and the other they just felt was incompetent." The allusion seems irrelevant. The piece's theme is the difficulties faced by female law school graduates in their employment search, not the poor employment experience of law firms with unstable or incompetent women attorneys. The switched viewpoint interrupts the article's progression.

## ADVICE FOR THE EXPOSITORY ARTICLE FORM

The expository form is not an easy one to master. These suggestions may help:

1. A suitable theme demands multiple points of view to explore the complex development or conflict. Does yours?

2. Devise an interview list and then consult with each subject for further suggestions of experts or eyewitnesses.

3. Do the necessary background research and bring a list of questions to any interview.

4. Review the last interview and revise your questions before the next.

5. Construct an outline before you write the article, not after.

6. Express the theme at the start with the least detail.

7. Don't interrupt the flow of the article's information with unrelated material or repetition of points.

8. Strive for balanced reporting. Include opposing viewpoints and criticism in your submission.

9. Don't omit quotes, which will document your facts and enliven the writing. Your research has not qualified you as the authority.

# XVI Standards and Guidelines for Professional Magazine Writing

My students often ask for my standards for professional magazine writing. In general, these standards are based on my original concepts of the forms of magazine articles and implicit principles within them for good writing. If you choose the right subject for the article form, construct an introduction which immediately gives the article's focus, research and report the information required for the body of the article, devise a logical, thematically progressive structure, and convey the facts in conversational language, you'll be writing in good form.

Violation of good form leads to weaknesses in magazine writing. The choice of the wrong form for the subject, lack of an introduction, failure to report the form's required information, a disorganized or repetitious structure, and use of rhetoric or imaginary facts contribute to bad form and poor journalistic writing.

To practice professional magazine journalism, use the following guidelines;

Send out concise, researched, well-focused queries stating the uniqueness and timeliness of your theme, your slant, and your qualifications to write the proposed article.

Don't give up trying to find a receptive market for article ideas you believe merit publication.

During negotiations for a commission, ask for the fee your track record, research, and theme deserve.

Sell First North American serial rights only for first publication.

Plan your list of interviews carefully and never go to one without adequate preparation.

Construct from your research a logical outline of the article.

Write to form, to the assigning magazine's style, and to the assigned word limit. Rewrite for incisive beginnings, illuminating quotes, clarity, precision of language, the pace of logically flowing ideas.

Check all facts and quotes before submission.

Request galleys to ascertain that the editing inadvertently has not caused inaccuracies in the text.

Never compromise your honesty. Cultivate a reputation for integrity as a professional free-lance writer.

Keep going. You won't get everything you reach for. But if you try, you'll get something.

# Index

# A

"Adolescents, Parents and Birth Control," 243
*American Health,* 36, 39-40, 61, 63, 102, 103, 107, 108, 111, 112, 114, 229, 230
*The American Journal of Medicine,* 102, 103
Anecdote: in "Celebrity Interview," 207
in expository article, 252
single-time, climactic, 183-85
Article ideas: firsthand resources for, 35-39
friend as sounding board for, 37-38
preserving title to, 12
secondhand resources for, 39-42
"As Told To" Interview: author's advice for, 200
excerpts from, 176-77, 178-79, 180, 182-83, 184, 197-98, 199
introduction to, 176-78
markets for, 175-76
researching, 176-85
sample of, 189-94
structure of, 179-81
*See also* Transitions; Quotes; Sketch; Anecdote
*The Atlantic,* 5, 91
"Ay, There's the Rub," 67, 71

# B

"The Battle of Wounded Knees," 243
"The Birth Rate Is Down, But Teenage Pregnancies Are Up, And Janet Hardy Tells Why," 162, 165-68
analysis of, 168-70
"The Bottom Line: The Doomsday Man," 114
"Breast cancer: less surgery is in," 99
*Broadway Bill of Fare,* 40
*The Brooklyn Paper,* 37
" 'Burn Before Reading,' " 112

# C

*Cahiers du Cinema,* 50
Camouflaging devices for fearful sources, 241
"Carry-Out Cuisine," 79-80
"Celebrity Interview": author's advice for, 227
body of 212-14
career gains from having published, 203, 223
choosing a subject for, 204-06, 212-13
defined, 203

# Other Books of Interest

**General Writing Books**
    Beginning Writer's Answer Book, edited by Polking and Bloss $14.95
    Getting the Words Right: How to Revise, Edit and Rewrite, by Theodore A. Rees Cheney $13.95
    How to Become a Bestselling Author, by Stan Corwin $14.95
    How to Get Started in Writing, by Peggy Teeters (paper) $8.95
    How to Write a Book Proposal, by Michael Larsen $9.95
    How to Write While You Sleep, by Elizabeth Ross $12.95
    If I Can Write, You Can Write, by Charlie Shedd $12.95
    International Writers' & Artists' Yearbook (paper) $12.95
    Law & the Writer, edited by Polking & Meranus (paper) $10.95
    Knowing Where to Look: The Ultimate Guide to Research, by Lois Horowitz $16.95
    Make Every Word Count, by Gary Provost (paper) $7.95
    Pinckert's Practical Grammar, by Robert C. Pinckert $12.95
    Teach Yourself to Write, by Evelyn Stenbock (paper) $9.95
    The 29 Most Common Writing Mistakes & How to Avoid Them, by Judy Delton $9.95
    Writer's Block & How to Use It, by Victoria Nelson $12.95
    Writer's Guide to Research, by Lois Horowitz $9.95
    Writer's Market, edited by Becky Williams $21.95
    Writer's Resource Guide, edited by Bernadine Clark $16.95
    Writing for the Joy of It, by Leonard Knott $11.95
    Writing From the Inside Out, by Charlotte Edwards (paper) $9.95
**Magazine/News Writing**
    Basic Magazine Writing, by Barbara Kevles $ 6 95
    How to Sell Every Magazine Article You Write, by Lisa Collier Cool $14.95
    How to Write & Sell the 8 Easiest Article Types, by Helene Schellenberg Barnhart $14.95
    Writing Nonfiction that Sells, by Samm Sinclair Baker $14.95
**Fiction Writing**
    Creating Short Fiction, by Damon Knight (paper) $8.95
    Fiction Writer's Help Book, by Maxine Rock $12.95
    Fiction Writer's Market, edited by Jean Fredette $18.95
    Handbook of Short Story Writing, by Dickson and Smythe (paper) $8.95
    How to Write & Sell Your First Novel, by Oscar Collier with Frances Spatz Leighton $14.95
    How to Write Short Stories that Sell, by Louise Boggess (paper) $7.95
    One Way to Write Your Novel, by Dick Perry (paper) $6.95
    Storycrafting, by Paul Darcy Boles $14.95
    Writing Romance Fiction—For Love And Money, by Helene Schellenberg Barnhart $14.95
    Writing the Novel: From Plot to Print, by Lawrence Block (paper) $8.95
**Special Interest Writing Books**
    Complete Book of Scriptwriting, by J. Michael Straczynski $14.95
    The Complete Guide to Writing Software User Manuals, by Brad M. McGehee (paper) $14.95
    The Craft of Comedy Writing, by Sol Saks $14.95
    The Craft of Lyric Writing, by Sheila Davis $18.95
    Guide to Greeting Card Writing, edited by Larry Sandman (paper) $8.95
    How to Make Money Writing About Fitness & Health, by Celia & Thomas Scully $16.95
    How to Make Money Writing Fillers, by Connie Emerson (paper) $8.95
    How to Write a Cookbook and Get It Published, by Sara Pitzer $15.95
    How to Write a Play, by Raymond Hull $13.95
    How to Write and Sell Your Personal Experiences, by Lois Duncan (paper) $9.95

How to Write and Sell (Your Sense of) Humor, by Gene Perret (paper) $9.95
How to Write "How-To" Books and Articles, by Raymond Hull (paper) $8.95
How to Write the Story of Your Life, by Frank P. Thomas $12.95
How You Can Make $50,000 a Year as a Nature Photojournalist, by Bill Thomas (paper) $17.95
Mystery Writer's Handbook, by The Mystery Writers of America (paper) $8.95
Nonfiction for Children: How to Write It, How to Sell It, by Ellen E.M. Roberts $16.95
On Being a Poet, by Judson Jerome $14.95
The Poet's Handbook, by Judson Jerome (paper) $8.95
Poet's Market, by Judson Jerome $16.95
Sell Copy, by Webster Kuswa $11.95
Successful Outdoor Writing, by Jack Samson $11.95
Travel Writer's Handbook, by Louise Zobel (paper) $9.95
TV Scriptwriter's Handbook, by Alfred Brenner (paper) $9.95
Writing After 50, by Leonard L. Knott $12.95
Writing and Selling Science Fiction, by Science Fiction Writers of America (paper) $7.95
Writing for Children & Teenagers, by Lee Wyndham (paper) $9.95
Writing for the Soaps, by Jean Rouverol $14.95
Writing the Modern Mystery, by Barbara Norville $15.95
Writing to Inspire, by Gentz, Roddy, et al $14.95

## The Writing Business
Complete Guide to Self-Publishing, by Tom & Marilyn Ross $19.95
Complete Handbook for Freelance Writers, by Kay Cassill $14.95
Editing for Print, by Geoffrey Rogers $14.95
Freelance Jobs for Writers, edited by Kirk Polking (paper) $8.95
How to Bulletproof Your Manuscript, by Bruce Henderson $9.95
How to Get Your Book Published, by Herbert W. Bell $15.95
How to Understand and Negotiate a Book Contract or Magazine Agreement, by Richard Balkin $11.95
How You Can Make $20,000 a Year Writing, by Nancy Hanson (paper) $6.95
Literary Agents: How to Get & Work with the Right One for You, by Michael Larsen $9.95
Professional Etiquett for Writers, by William Brohaugh $9.95

To order directly from the publisher, include $2.00 postage and handling for 1 book and 50¢ for each additional book. Allow 30 days for delivery.

Writer's Digest Books, Department B
9933 Alliance Road, Cincinnati OH 45242
Prices subject to change without notice.